DON'T CALL ME UGLY

ALICIA DOUVALL

Don't Call Me Ugly

AUSTIN MACAULEY
PUBLISHERS LTD.

A CIP catalogue record for this title is available from the British Library.

ISBN 978-1-78612-349-7

www.austinmacauley.com

First Published (2015)
Austin Macauley Publishers Ltd.
25 Canada Square
Canary Wharf
London
E14 5LQ

Printed and bound in Great Britain by Bell and Bain Ltd, Glasgow

CONTENTS

I would like to dedicate this book to my children
Georgia and Papaya

ACKNOWLEDGEMENTS

I would like to thank Simon, my mother and Austin Macauley for believing in me, and all the characters (named and unnamed!) that have made the book what it is and me what I am.

I would also like to thank Joseph Sinclair for his amazing cover photo and Ryan Essex for giving permission to include some of his many photographs of me.

CHAPTER ONE

Born Ordinary

I HAVEN'T ALWAYS BEEN Alicia Douvall the glamour model. I started life as Sarah Howes, an ordinary, shy girl with two older half-sisters and a strict Catholic upbringing in the Sussex countryside.

My parents made us go to church on Sundays and on any holy occasion. We joined the Brownies and Girl Guides. On the outside we were a picture-perfect family.

I never really got the religion that was rammed down my throat. I looked forward to the pat on the head and the piece of food. The sing-songs were always fun too, but the lectures meant nothing and seemed so far-fetched I honestly would be confused. Okay, so Jack and Jill didn't really go up a hill to fetch a pail of water but God and Jesus were real and they created everything and set some pretty strict rules that we all had to live by or we go to Hell? So that's my first admission of confusion. Religion, I didn't buy it, especially as I had an older sister who was very quiet but was a secret atheist. She told me we started off as fish and grew from there, becoming apes at one point too. Wow, super confusing.

My mother was the optimal figure of a lady. She didn't drink, smoke or swear. She didn't wear trainers unless in the gym. She wore make-up at all times, hair perfectly preened, skirts below the knee, never showing any cleavage. Mum was guided by my father, who always kept an eye on her behaviour to make sure she was 'perfect'.

My father was a disciplinarian, a local Conservative councillor and a self-made man. In this day and age he would probably be diagnosed with numerous mental disorders, including OCD, bipolar and ADHD. He was (and is) a very charismatic character but with some pretty dark traits. My dad was never boring, though.

He came from a very poor family, who lived in one room in south London. Dad was a naughty boy as a kid but left all that behind him to marry a lady in Wales, only to later leave her with two kids. He got on his motorbike one day and left with just his bike, the clothes on his back and nothing else because, he told me, he had no choice: his wife was a dragon.

My father was also an extremely talented car electrician, who would build cars from scratch just for fun. A genius with motor vehicles, he knew every part of every car inside and out. He said he invented a car part once, when he worked for Ford, but he didn't get paid for the invention as he had to give it to them under the terms of his employment contract. He would read car manuals in bed for pleasure. For an uneducated man he had a remarkable thirst for knowledge, teaching himself everything from chess to geography. Dad seemed to me, as a child, not a nice guy but someone who knew everything.

My father was ambitious and willing to take risks. He was definitely respected in the car trade but was often disliked and feared. No one dared cross him. I thought Dad was fine when he was at work because he had plenty of people to shout at. He kept a tight ship: his garage was always super clean. He had a strict policy of no calendars or posters of girls. Everything had to be in its place and clearly sign posted with Dad's handwritten stickers which he was obsessed with. Unfortunately, this translated into his family life too.

He was my father and I loved him regardless. Take him to a party and he was the life and soul of it but at home he was a hard man to live with.

My sisters were from my mum's first marriage. We didn't ever talk about 'Old Dad', as they called him. Our dad was Dad and we all called him that. My mum married her childhood sweetheart and had two beautiful children. Unfortunately when they were still really young she walked in on him with another woman. Bastard. I heard when I got older that Mum had asked him to stay, as she didn't want the children to be without their dad, but he was in love with his mistress and wanted to be with her.

My mum and her two young children went to live with her mother. In those days it wasn't the 'done thing' to be a single parent so she re-married as soon as she could.

Old Dad would pick my sisters up and go to the park. He seemed nice but being young I didn't understand why I wasn't allowed to go too. I always got so upset that they had this extra dad. Why wasn't Old Dad interested in me too? My middle sister would always be so happy when Old Dad was coming and would say I had to stay at home with 'Him'. She hated my father more than anyone.

Old Dad's visits got less and less frequent, however. We were able to spend most weekends as a family. Yay! No, they were hell.

During the week Dad would be under a car, overalls on, covered in grease. At weekends he would wear suits for no reason other than because he couldn't wear a suit whilst at work and he believed in dressing smart.

At one point we lived over the garage and shop that Dad worked from. We relocated every two or three years because Dad liked doing up places and moving on. Mum hated moving and living in a building site most of the time. I didn't mind, though: the promise of a new duvet cover or something always swayed me.

When Dad had finished work Mum had to have dinner on the table by 6.30 p.m. despite her having worked all day herself. There were special rules at dinner: fork down, sit up straight and *never* reach out for anything – you had to ask someone to pass it, of course. The usual rules applied too: we could only eat once Dad had started and not before. If you did start before him all hell would break loose, to the point that you were sent to your room with no dinner. Portions were stingy too. We were a family of five and always hungry because, like Dad, Mum came from a poor background and seemed to think we were still on wartime rations even though she wasn't even alive during the war.

Dessert was a big bargaining tool. If we ate everything on our plates we could have a dessert, which was most likely one large strawberry each or Angel Delight that had been stretched to serve five people ('Serving Suggestion 2'). Luckily, we had a Labrador so sometimes when we were left for hours forced to finish our frozen peas, potatoes and a lamb chop dinner we could sneak them to the dog. We often ate in silence so this wasn't an easy trick to pull off, especially with a loud salivating Labrador.

Dad liked his home in perfect order but with three kids he was up against it. My mum tried relentlessly to be the Stepford wife, mother and businesswoman but there were only a certain number of hours in the day.

Often Dad would open the fridge for breakfast and a pint of milk would smash on the floor. This would be devastating. 'WHO PUT THE MILK IN THE FRIDGE LAST?' An investigation had just been opened.

We all prayed it wasn't us and immediately looked at my middle sister. You see, my oldest sister was too careful, quiet and clever to do anything wrong. I was too young and spoilt to get the milk out in the first place. My middle sister, well, she was the rebel, the clumsy one and the wild card.

It would all be very traumatic. Mum would be frantically trying to clean it up. Middle sister would be summoned to help as she was most probably the one that did it. Dad would tower over them inspecting and loudly demanding a better clean up job and reminding middle sister how awful she was whilst she scrubbed away on her hands and knees. I, well, I would watch horrified but pleased it wasn't me that did it.

Dad would spend all morning shouting and name-calling until he found his culprit. The criminal milk-spiller would be lectured, shouted at, verbally abused and punished until she cried and wanted no part in life ever again. To him, he was making sure we would never do that again and be more careful. To us, it was the end of the world and we would rather sleep in the street for a month than deal with one of his tongue-lashings.

The rules in the house were strict and if you broke them you really would regret it. Like any family, in the morning the one bathroom was at a premium. God forbid if you spent more than your allocated time, especially if Dad needed the bathroom. He would bang his fist on the door or, worse still, if you left it unlocked he would come in unexpected, thinking it wasn't occupied. The humiliation of sitting on the toilet whilst he shouted at us for not locking the door chipped away our self-confidence. Dad had a unique way of making you feel small and inadequate. His rants would go on for hours, days, sometimes even weeks.

His fierce temper made us all live in fear but there was another side to him. The side that played card and ball games with us, the side that meant when he would have an argument with Mum or one of my sisters he would say, 'Sarah, do you want to go to Tesco and rifle through the bargain bucket with me and get out of this awful house?' – that side. The man who lit up when he found a ten pence packet of bread rolls in the Tesco bargain bucket. That was the side I loved and no matter what he did to me, or my beloved mother, I forgave him.

Dad didn't allow my mum to cook cheese straws, as he said it stank out the house and he didn't like the smell, but we kids loved them. Now and then Mum would rebel and make them anyway when she thought he wouldn't be around but she always seemed to get caught. He had a nose like a bloodhound. Dad would storm out and leave the house until she had adequately Febrezed the building to get rid of the smell. That's when he and I would go through the bargain buckets.

Mum wasn't allowed to cook with garlic either but if one of us had eaten something with garlic we would have to stand in the garden, even in the rain, eating parsley until we could pass his breath test at the door. I remember eating parsley trying my best to digest as much as possible because, to me, having garlic breath felt like I had just murdered a family member.

Dad had a temper on him too. If he got too angry he would smash and throw things. Your room had to be tidy on inspection and God forbid something was still on the floor. He would point and push us until we got the message. One time he came in there was a water bottle on the carpet in the room I shared with my middle sister, which made Dad so angry he jumped on it. Water went everywhere, it was almost funny but you couldn't laugh. I remember thinking this man, who I loved because he was my father, was maybe the devil.

I remember one Christmas when we all knew what to expect but were in denial. Every year we made the mistake of looking forward to the holiday season – of hoping for presents we knew deep down we wouldn't get because they were either 'plastic crap', not educational or a 'waste of money', as Dad would put it. If we did get the presents we wanted they would be taken off us anyway.

Dad would often start soon after waking up over breakfast. Someone might have failed to put the lid back on the ketchup or to properly clean it, or traces of toast might be detected in the butter. These were serious offences and it took at least forty minutes to 'drum into our thick little heads' the exact severity of it. Dad ranted about anything and everything.

That Christmas my father decided Mum had not cleaned the door knobs properly. Despite the fact she was preparing a meal for thirteen people, he insisted she clean the brass door knobs before the guests arrived, which she dutifully did, panicky, desperately trying to get the perfect shine that would meet Dad's approval, kneeling with her yellow rubber gloves in her best frock, trying not to cry. I hated seeing her so scared, so frantic with worry, so used and abused by him. Dad was a bully to whom my mum was kind to a fault. So we spent early Christmas morning cleaning door knobs and then the skirting boards before, finally, it was present time.

That was a nightmare too. If we ripped the wrapping paper, which was supposed to be carefully taken off and recycled for the next year, we had our presents taken away. Nine times out of ten this would happen. If we did not seem grateful enough that was another offence, entitling Dad to take back a present. So my sisters and I never really got the 'plastic crap' that we had as presents as he knew these were the presents we really wanted and would use these mistakes to take them back from us. To be fair, we did always get one or two 'pieces of crap' toys, as Dad would put it. Most of our presents consisted of globes, encyclopaedias, Swiss Army knives or rounders bats which I really didn't want and was most ungrateful for, until I'd finally open the present that I really wanted: a Barbie caravan. Dad would be disappointed and, looking back, I can understand why. Most parents want their child to have a desire to learn but I was only interested in Barbie's world and I did not appreciate the educational toys. I learnt to be a great actress, as I had to show real passion for the globe and look thankful. In my mind it was all about the fold-out Barbie caravan but I would pretend to care about the dictionary and the globe that lit Dad's face up: I would pretend it was the caravan that Dad would complain about whilst helping me to assemble it, protesting it was 'flimsy, shoddy, and a piece of overpriced crap'. I think they call that method acting.

Dad believed the best place to shop for us kids was Millets, as camping equipment lasted a lot longer than 'novelty crap'. We were discouraged from having anything to do with fashion. Our trainers were Dunlop Green Flash, our trousers had pockets on the sides and our school bags were camouflage army equipment. We would try to rip them in the vain hope of getting a replacement with a Barbie, or any other doll, on it but my father was right, the bags were hard-wearing.

Shoes were strictly Start-rite, which we called 'handicapped shoes' – the thick ones with the T-bar across. I had unusually slim feet and I would be so excited to get new shoes. A forever optimist, I believed each time that somehow I would get a nice pair of shoes – forgetting, like a goldfish in a bowl, what my last trip to the shoe shop had been like. Every time the woman would measure my feet, nod her head worryingly and come back with two, possibly three, pairs, if it was a good day, of the worst, ugliest, thickest shoes. I wanted white shiny slip-ons but I got T-bars with thick soles and big straps. They were 'Coco the Clown shoes', as my sisters would say. My middle sister would tell me that I looked like a golf club.

If I dared to say I didn't like the new shoes my dad would be angry and would tell me not to be so ungrateful. I was a girlie girl and I wanted patented shoes. I couldn't catch a ball and I liked dresses, not what Dad wanted in a daughter at all.

On one occasion we took the carefully-fitted shoes home but a week later my feet were blistered. Dad stormed back into the shop, making an almighty scene, showing where the shoes had blistered my feet, demanding to see the manager and to get a free pair of shoes – and he got them. It was these acts that made me realise that his heart was in the right place. He cared, and cared passionately about our feet.

Shoe shops were not the only place Dad would cause a scene: he was very good at it. If we ate out during one of our UK camping holidays, nine times out of ten we would get a free meal. Dad would complain very loudly about the food being too cold, undercooked or the service too slow, anything that got us a free meal. He figured if he started complaining really loudly the restaurant management would be embarrassed and shamed into giving us a free meal or something, and it would usually work: when it came to a battle of wills he always won, he had no shame in his game. Mum did, though: she would hang her head low in embarrassment as Dad would stay standing up until he got his free meal. If he didn't, he would storm out of the restaurant.

Mum and my sisters always thought Dad's shameless tactic of getting a free meal or go was deeply humiliating. I, on the other hand, felt proud that my dad was bold as brass and stood up for what was right. Dad had tactics, though, to ensure the meal was never 'right': for example, he would order steak medium-rare in the motorway Little Chef or local

Harvester, so they would hardly ever get this to his liking. My sisters and mother would beg him not to walk out and if they did have to leave they would scurry along, head down. I, on the other hand, would proudly prance out of the restaurant, ignoring the stares from the onlooking diners and enjoying my moment of glory.

Make-up was forbidden as were heels, scruffiness, tie-dye, hair that wasn't tied back, piercings, tattoos, dangly earrings, nail varnish, watches that were not 'sensible looking', fashionable clothes, soaps on television, plastic toys and books that contained 'mindless fiction'.

Dad wanted us to be cultured. Growing up, he had had very little schooling but had educated himself to move to the next level, becoming a fairly wealthy man. Like any good parent, he wanted us to be better than him: to play chess, to be knowledgeable and to be a good citizen. He wasn't the man he used to be and was trying to better himself and his family. The trouble was, he was a man of extremes.

My middle sister dreamed of getting away, of having what she thought would be a normal family. She would tell me enviously about other kids' families. On the other hand, if I went to a friend's house and saw how relaxed things were in comparison, I thought the rules were not strict enough. It just seemed too lax; how could they function effectively when there was no order?

Don't get me wrong, I did watch families on TV and thought the fictional families looked lovely – but it wasn't realistic. Dads were strict, we needed order and that was that. I did miss feeling loved and safe, though. I certainly didn't feel safe, no one did, but I would not have swapped Dad, then or now. He loved us, he brought us up as boys because that's all he knew and, in fact, that taught us some valuable skills we certainly wouldn't have got from playing shops or dolls.

My older sister was the closest to feeling safe because she did nothing wrong. She played by the rules, buried herself in books and kept quiet. She later went on to become an EEG technician and to lecture doctors from all over the world. She never had kids and lives a very eco-conscious life.

With Dad's rants, and two sisters to share a room with, I did not have much time to myself but I did have one escape: Barbie. Barbies were my life. I collected them, I combed their hair at least three times a day and I kept them in pristine condition. When things went wrong, when I was in trouble or scared, I would retreat to my room to be comforted by my Barbie collection.

Barbie was everything I wasn't: happy, successful and pretty. She had nice clothes and she had Ken. It was a standing joke in our family that I wasn't the pretty one. I was very thin and fragile, with permanent dark bags under my eyes and frizzy, fine hair. I wasn't talented in any way. I wasn't tall, like one of my sisters, or have thick, beautiful blonde hair, like the other. It was accepted by all of us, and most importantly by me, that I was ugly.

The older I got the more I wanted to be like Barbie. When most kids were ditching their Barbies as they grew out of their toys, my obsession with them just grew and grew.

The trouble was, I felt more like Sindy, the unfortunate sister who just didn't have it going on. It was Barbie, with her long blonde hair, big blue eyes and Jeep Wrangler, who got the adoring boyfriend Ken, the wardrobe and the success. She had perfect long legs, big boobs and a tiny waist. Her white teeth were always smiling so happily when she was with Ken, and amongst her ever-growing group of friends who, with their second-rate hair and figures, could only wish to be her. Just like me.

My middle sister would find my Barbie obsession sad and funny. She would tease me and often cut the hair off my Barbies to make me cry for days on end, until my mum would feel so sorry for me that she would allow me to wash the car for weeks to earn enough money for another Barbie.

In fact, my Barbie obsession impressed no one. My parents were worried that my doll fixation was going on too long and I was investing too much time in a useless exercise. How little they knew that my enthusiasm for Barbie would turn into a lifetime obsession to try to replicate her. I was lagging behind with my school work and was crap at sports.

Dad tried really hard to make my sisters and me sporty. He tried teaching us rounders, cricket, football and car racing. We were not focused and he got frustrated with us very quickly. Thus we were a family of 'cack-handed girls' that couldn't catch a ball. The disappointment and anger we saw on his face when we didn't make a catch or understand our homework were devastating. He would shout and rage and then storm off, sometimes smashing up whatever it was we didn't understand. In this day and age this would be called 'anger issues'.

CHAPTER TWO

Good Girl Gone Bad

AT TEN YEARS old my parents pulled me out of state school. I wasn't progressing, I was still obsessing over my Barbies and I was getting bullied. My parents saw no alternative other than to send me away to a boarding school in nearby Petworth. Surely I'd get the best education there; after all, my parents had to pay so much for it. They thought this was the only way to make me 'grow up' and ditch the Barbies. My parents did not understand that this would only force me out of my imaginary world of Barbie and into a world where I would concentrate on working on myself in the most unimaginably destructive way possible.

I attended the school with the likes of Jodie and Jemma Kidd. Jodie, who became a supermodel, and Jemma, now a successful make-up artist, came from a family of earls and duchesses. The school was reputed to be one of the top private establishments in the UK, but, most importantly, it took anyone whose family could pay its really expensive fees.

I didn't want to leave my mum or my sisters and I felt too young to be sent away, but the decision was made and off I went.

Mum and Dad weren't super rich but they did well. They certainly sacrificed nice holidays abroad and clothes for themselves to pay for my education and that of my sisters. Totally wasted in my case, I might add.

My middle sister was also pulled out of state school. She was sent to a convent, all-girls of course, where she said the nuns tried it on with the pupils and hit them. One nun was so old she would fall asleep teaching in the class.

When I got to my all-girls school, with my bag in hand and a pristine uniform three sizes too big (so I'd grow into it), I saw the unruly children. It was more like St Trinian's than anything else. From the start it disturbed me that they didn't have to wear the correct colour co-ordinated hairbands, but it got worse: they dyed their hair crazy colours; their uniform consisted of skirts hitched up, jumpers with holes in the sleeves made by a hole punch, socks scrunched down; they ran through corridors screaming and shouting. I was horrified, I hated it instantly and asked Mum to send me somewhere else or to let me go home then and there. She said I would be fine but, oh, how wrong she would be.

I begged her to take me with her, not to leave me with these girls. I could see the heartache on her face as she left her skinny little ten year-old in her new, oversized uniform. I stood at the door shouting 'Come back!' as she got in her car, trying to be tough and not cry, and then drove away. That was it: I was stuck there. I turned around, looking down on the floor, and slowly walked back to my 'dormitory' trying to work out which way to go in the maze of corridors and doors, nearly being run over by over-excited screaming rebels as they ran past me whilst chasing each other.

I got sick the first week I was there, with an unexplained stomach upset. I was violently sick for weeks, with a temperature, sweats and in agony from pain in my side and stomach. I was a stranger in this awful place, very ill, and my mum didn't come to collect me because I was too unwell to do the car journey home. Kids would run into my room in the sick bay to look at the new 'sick girl' – a great start. I was super shy, I hated being around people and now I was the freak show, the sickly one.

After three weeks my doctor worked out that I had glandular fever, which had affected my liver and kidneys. I was very weak and ended up with months off school, still in the sick bay. By this time pretty much the whole school had rushed into my room and run out again to look at me whilst giggling. Some were brave enough to introduce themselves. I never gave a response, I was too sick and to me they were too naughty. Who was controlling these kids? I thought soon as I was better I would get Mum to collect me from this awful place.

This wasn't the best start and things were about to get a lot worse.

Amongst the unruly kids, who really seemed to do what they wanted, was a Spanish student exchange girl called Umar. She spoke hardly any English but we bonded. I loved how she was so laid-back, non-judgemental and not like the other girls at all.

I tried to join in the classes but didn't get a thing that was happening. That's when this good girl started to go bad. In the beginning I kept putting the effort in. Some teachers thought I was deaf, others thought blind and, eventually, after several hearing and eyesight tests, I was tested for, and diagnosed with, dyslexia. Back then that just meant extra time in exams. They didn't factor in that I didn't have a clue what was going on in class so would not even need the extra time, as I didn't know the answers in the first place. I wanted to learn, I wanted structure; I got neither.

It was becoming more and more frustrating, which was paired with the fact that I no longer had a strict father around. There were no consequences for my actions, so I figured out I could do exactly what I wanted. Plus I was ready to give up. If you can't beat them, join them. Like a child who had never tasted sweets before let loose in a candy store, I went crazy.

Umar and I decided we preferred to play tennis every day than attend classes, so I would make our own timetable. Even my rebellion had to have structure. The timetable consisted of what time *we* wanted to get up, go for a jog (which included trampling over the headmistress' daffodils in her garden), grab breakfast, sign in, go to church then tennis, have lunch then more tennis, followed by table tennis.

We got pretty good at tennis, as we practised sometimes for six hours a day. It was a pleasant life and only now and then would we get into trouble for not attending classes. When this happened we would show our faces for a couple of weeks before going back to doing what really mattered to us – playing tennis. I loved having freedom, doing what I wanted and not feeling ashamed or stressed every day. I knew I wasn't learning anymore but I put that to the back of my mind. For once, I was being me, I was free and I was going to enjoy it. I wasn't afraid of anyone.

We treated school as one big holiday. We carved holes in our bibles to put our cigarette packets in. We would wander off to the local town to buy sweets or even to go out for the evening.

We made St Trinian's look mild. We would organise group smoking sessions, burn banana skins (someone told us you could get high off them), and meet the local boys in the field opposite the school. Any night of the week you went into that field it would be scattered with pupils from both schools making out.

Being at an all-girls school we were all obsessed with boys. It was a prized possession to have a boyfriend and something to be admired. As a gangly kid in state school I hadn't had much luck with boys. The boys that I was interested in were the wrong ones and they certainly didn't like me. They wanted the girls with the boobs. I knew I didn't have any, which is probably why I tended to keep my distance. I did find an odd, spindly boy to call a boyfriend but I really didn't care much for him, probably because he was a kind boy. That shit didn't fly with me. I could only love the bad boys, but I didn't know that yet.

Our behaviour as a whole was horrific. The worst thing we did was when someone gave me the details for a credit card and said you could make free calls on it, so I did, plenty of them. I then passed the number onto others; before you knew it went round the whole school. The Chinese kids were phoning China and calls were made to Africa, Vietnam, Japan, you name it, for hours at a time. Someone got the idea to buy a car with the card. That's when the police turned up. They must have been monitoring the card transactions: the *People* newspaper ran a piece on it which couldn't have helped the school's reputation. They couldn't suspend the whole school so there wasn't much they could do but lecture us. They tried to suspend the worst culprits but we all stuck together and no one told on each other, which was good for me, as I had already been suspended quite a few times by now.

They had to close down the tuck shop as it was getting robbed too often, and the stationary cupboard, as they called it, for the same reason. It was only the day girls, who were fifteen percent of the school, that didn't steal, cheat or lie. As boarders we all stuck together. We believed our parents were paying so much that we were entitled to the odd free pencil or Mars bar, not that anyone kept the Mars bars down for long.

Weekends we would attend parties. I was officially a weekly boarder so my absence was not really missed. The school seemed to give Umar a wide berth too, as she was only there for a year.

It was a far cry from the stressful, strict home life I had been used to. I wasn't born bad but that school certainly taught me how to be bad. It was probably the worst school in Britain that my parents could have sent me to: they got super unlucky.

I started to get better at sport and I pushed myself to run miles every day. This didn't go unnoticed and the sports teacher asked me to join the running team and the lacrosse team for the county. I would politely decline: after all, I was on holiday. I only liked the pressure I put on myself. I wasn't good in competition, unless I was in competition with myself. I was a hard one for me to beat. I didn't treat myself so well and I demanded only excellence in what I was doing. Competition meant someone else could win and I couldn't run that risk, so avoided it at all cost.

But one thing was emerging: I was self-motivated. I could punish myself and drive myself to the limit.

Mum gave me pocket money, which was supposed to be for sweets and treats but as I was hardly eating anything, I spent it on more productive things, things that would change how I looked. I bought tanning pills from those dodgy adverts at the back of magazines, hair dye and slimming pills. This was the start of me changing myself. I didn't have my Barbies anymore but I could work on myself. I would be my own imaginary person. I would make myself into Barbie.

By fourteen years old I was completely uneducated. I didn't know where anything was on a map of the world and I couldn't say my alphabet, add up or tell the time.

I had also been suspended six times at this point, for everything from not attending to putting drawing pins on the teacher's seat cushion. I had become a rebel and taken it to the extreme, even more than the rest of the girls. I liked doing what I wanted and resented being told what to do but, more to the point, when they told me off or put me in detention, it was nothing compared to the fear I felt with my father. I could handle anything after him. Besides, I had learnt a trick that protected me from everyone. I would simply shut off, pretend I was Barbie and float away to another place. Their strong words were wasted on ears that were closed.

The headmistress tried everything. After the sixth suspension she said she would only keep me on at the school if the whole family attended counselling. This infuriated Dad, as he was forced to do what he didn't believe in and 'attend a lot of mumbo-jumbo from a bunch of do-gooders', as he would put it. He seemed to really hate 'do-gooders'. If you came round our house with a collection box you would live to regret it.

Counselling was a disaster. Dad shouted, I sat quietly and my scared mum cried. The counsellor concluded that Dad 'only saw in black and white', which, thankfully for me and Mum, turned Dad's hate to her, so she got it next. I have never seen a counsellor reduced to tears but she was. She asked us to find another counsellor. It was awkward, to say the least.

Two weeks later, I was expelled from school for drugs. I had stupidly written a letter to a fellow classmate asking her if she wanted to buy a spliff for £2.50, as my sister had given it to me and I didn't actually want it. Officially, I was a drug dealer.

The school also went through my bag and found tanning pills and vitamins. They decided these were Es too but, obviously, they weren't. My parents fought with the school to keep me on, asking them to prove the pills were Es but the school didn't and said they had been 'disposed of'. To my parents this was serious. It meant I left school with no GCSEs. They needed a good lawyer but they had spent most of their money on school fees so couldn't really afford it. They knew their immature, not-so-clever little girl was no entrepreneur and that I wouldn't take or deal drugs, but there was nothing they could do about the school's decision.

My poor parents were distraught; I was devastated, as I now had to go home and face the worst music of my life so far.

Dad said I should keep out of his way and I wasn't allowed to eat at the same table as him, as he could not bear to look at me. He would regularly have shouting outbursts to show his disappointment, explaining I was talentless, ugly and a waste of everyone's money. He said I was doomed now and a good for nothing waste of space. He was probably right, and this was the only way he knew how to react to it, but I needed help. I needed a cuddle. It had all gone horribly, stupidly wrong and I needed my parents to help me get back on track.

I felt awful. I contemplated suicide at this point to escape the pain I was feeling. It wasn't the first time. I had been rushed to hospital a few times at school with suspected overdoses. I, of course, denied they were suicide attempts, explaining that I had had a headache, and therefore took lots of painkillers as it wouldn't go away.

I also had an eating disorder off and on, which started at boarding school when another girl taught me what she called 'the secret to having a great figure'. I would go from anorexia to bulimia. Eating disorders at my school were rife: we all seemed to be in competition with each other to see who could starve herself the most and be the skinniest. It is hard to remember a girl who didn't have an eating disorder; I would say eighty percent had one. Back then no one did anything about it unless you got so bad you needed to be hospitalised. Most of us were at it and it was only a few of us who took it to the extreme – the ones who had the most control over themselves, I believed.

After contemplating suicide as a way of escaping the verbal abuse of my father, and the punishment I was about to get, I needed a Plan B. I would run away to London and sleep on the streets. When Dad would be shouting at me I would dream of me (as Barbie, with my flowing blonde hair) sleeping happily on the streets of London. I just needed to save up for a really warm sleeping bag and a flask. That would take some time.

Mum and Dad tried to get me a new school but the nature of my expulsion for drugs meant no school wanted me. So Mum decided I could teach myself. She would send me to the local library to learn stuff.

I actually enjoyed this. I would read my biology books and, for the first time, I became fascinated with what I was reading. I wasn't being forced to do it so I did it myself, and it was fun. I decided to put running away on hold: things were bad but not that bad yet.

I actually did learn more teaching myself than I ever learnt at that school. I was one of those kids that suited being self-motivated. I taught myself, as I hoped to go back to school to do GCSEs. Dad was still fighting the school to allow me to go back just for my exams.

Later the school actually closed down. Maybe that's why they let us all run riot, who knows, but let this be a warning to you: when you send your child to a school do your research!

I needed some guidance with my education, ideally for a tutor to come to the home, which I didn't get. Mum was too busy, and so was Dad. Neither of them could bear to be around me; they had sacrificed holidays, been careful on food shopping, clothes and even heating. Their anger was understandable. I don't know why they didn't get tutors in, maybe they were too expensive, or maybe at that point I was a lost cause and my parents were exhausted with me. I realised there was just too much to learn in too little time, it wasn't realistic. So I soon lost interest and found the local hood-rats from a nearby housing estate. I lived in an idyllic five-bedroom house on a private road, surrounded by fields, but within walking distance was the local council estate, where I soon found some unruly friends. That was the start of an even bigger problem and the end of my education for good.

I dampened down my privately educated accent to blend with the locals' Sussex slang. In no time at all I was drinking, smoking, was introduced to drugs for real this time and spending all day at the local youth club, stalking boys who weren't interested.

I was getting into trouble with the police and often came home in a police car. I was so unhealthy that I developed epilepsy. I started having seizures almost every day.

I remember the day when my mum brought me to the doctor, as I had had a fit and, again, injured myself. My injuries included breaking my two front teeth. The doctor said: 'If we don't get this epilepsy under control it will be unlikely for her to see her thirtieth birthday.'

'Wow,' I thought, 'this is serious.' If I had a fit on a metal escalator, or even just at the top of the stairs, it could be fatal.

Dying young never fazed me. I kind of thought it was my destiny. I remember when Mum and Dad treated me to a gypsy card-reading I really wanted at a fairground. All I can remember is my dad having a massive argument with the tarot card reader and storming out of her caravan with us.

Being the drama queen that I was, and given the extent of my dad's anger and upset, I presumed she said I would die young, so when the illnesses piled up on my skinny frame I took it as a step towards my destiny and fully accepted it without fear.

My mum didn't know what to do with me. I refused to take medication for the epilepsy. I carried on drinking, smoking and partying till the early hours. Mum wanted to please my dad, who was disgusted by my behaviour. Because my parents were regular churchgoers and Dad was still a councillor, my family were part of the local community, so it really mattered to Dad what people thought of us. Coming from a small town, and Dad being so charismatic and respected and running his garage, he feared people would talk. The façade of the perfect family would look flawed and we couldn't have that. I had become every parent's nightmare.

So there was one thing for it. Mum wrote a letter to the local council and said I no longer had a home as soon as I turned sixteen. I didn't want to live with Dad anymore anyway and he certainly didn't want to live with me. I spent a few months in hostels and with host families before I would come back home to give it one final try.

CHAPTER THREE

Teen Mum

MY SHAME ON my family wasn't over, oh no. I hadn't put the cherry on the cake yet.

Whilst on one of my clubbing nights I met a tall, dark, handsome man. I thought I'd fallen completely in love, or should I say in lust, with him. I met him in a club. I was with my friends dancing without a care in the world; he had come alone. He stood out with his handsome looks and that laid-back, don't-give-a-damn attitude that bad boys have. He danced with an air of coolness. When he started smiling at me and approached me to buy me a drink, my heart melted instantly. He was generous, wild, rebellious and wore a leather coat: I was smitten. He stole my heart when he bought me 20 Marlboro Lights. It was a wild and passionate affair between an older, free-spirited boy and a not-so-sweet-and-innocent good-girl-gone-bad. He treated me like no man had ever treated me. He sent me flowers and thought I was beautiful. Wow, I was his: someone thought I was attractive?

I decided this man would be my love forever. I had finally found my home, my security, my family and the happy-ever-after that I desperately craved. The day I gave him my virginity I felt so happy; this to me was everything. I felt loved and, most importantly, I felt pretty.

I hadn't had periods for that long but I knew they came once a month. So it was strange when mine didn't arrive. In the back of my mind I thought there might be a possibility I was pregnant: I felt like I had less energy, I was feeling a strange sensation in my stomach, and I was suddenly getting hot flushes. I didn't worry too much, though, as I had heard missing periods was normal. I put it down to poor diet and too much partying. My period didn't come for three months and I noticed I was putting on lots of weight; I was feeling really bloated. Again, I put this down to diet, despite hardly eating anything. I was still slightly anorexic and bulimic.

Eventually, I did a test. My suspicions were growing but I didn't want to face up to them. I was in denial but the two blue lines clearly told me I was pregnant. Sat on my bathroom floor, wide-eyed, my hand over my open mouth, in shock I stared at those little blue lines that would change my life forever. I was young and careless, living from a backpack, with no foundations, no money and no future. Oh shit, Dad was going to kill me.

I sat and stared into space for hours. I kept checking the blue lines, in case they would go away or I was somehow seeing things. I had no idea what I was going to do. I couldn't look after myself, let alone a baby; but, on the other hand, I was strong. I thought I loved the baby's father, who was living up north at that point. I finally could have my dream of a happy family I could belong to and be loved in. Someone was going to love me unconditionally, no matter how ugly I was. Barbie had found her Ken, and little Shelly was on the way. Great, I would have the perfect home and could finally escape the unsafe, mad house I was raised in. I decided the idea of having a baby didn't seem so bad.

Soon as those blue lines appeared I stopped smoking. I had only started to fit in with my council estate friends. I had also been drinking excessively but put an end to that episode of my life for good; besides, I was feeling so tired and sick I couldn't have gone out drinking anyway. It was time to move on, I decided, to the next chapter of my life. My mind was made up: I was going to keep my baby.

I knew I had to tell Mum at some point. I couldn't go round in baggy hoodies for the rest of the pregnancy. I really did not want to and dreaded the moment. I would have done anything to avoid it but I had to say something. So, whilst she was doing her ironing one day, I told her. Her face dropped, she carried on ironing but more furiously. She immediately panicked and her mind went to what Dad would say whilst manically trying to iron Dad's shirt cuffs to perfection. Mum was just as scared of him as me. She tried desperately to keep the peace but it never seemed to work. Kindness is wasted on bullies.

The next morning, Dad at breakfast said, 'Keep out of my way.'

Enough said: he knew, Mum had told him. He packed his bags, left them by the front door and said to Mum it was him or me that went. In a way, I thought that was great. I wasn't getting shouted at, ground down with humiliation and Dad was going to leave, a good result.

But Mum had no choice, she wasn't going to leave Dad. Looking back, I'm sure she had Stockholm syndrome, where you fall in love with your abuser. I didn't want to see my mum hurt anymore and I knew she loved him, so I wrote a letter to them and left.

'Gone to be with my baby's father, I wish you all well, goodbye forever.'

I spent virtually my last money on a train ticket up north, to start my new life. I packed one bag: I couldn't carry too much, as I was pregnant.

On the train up north I gazed out of the window, with a smile on my face, dressed in my best Tammy girl dress that was stretchy enough and baggy enough for me to still wear. I was filled with hope: I had a warm feeling inside me, thinking about my baby and my future as a family. I pictured us all sitting around a log fire laughing, his strong masculine arms cradling his cute baby, smiling down lovingly at his beautiful child. I imagined him looking at me adoringly: we would be a family, unbreakable, supporting each other. The train couldn't go fast enough; I was so excited to get off and start my new life.

I remember the day well, it was raining. I walked over an hour in the downpour to my lover's home, ready to surprise him with my presence and joyful news. I couldn't wait to see his smile when he opened the door. I knew we were young – well, I was younger by about six years – but we would somehow find a way. Love conquers all, right? This was the start of a life of happiness, a real family that loved each other, just like on the television, and just like Barbie and Ken. Finally, I was going to be good at something. I would be the best wife and mother, and finally the constant humiliation and degradation from my dad was over. I had my own family now; I would have another home at last.

I was tired and the pregnancy had made me feel really sick. It had also put me off my food, even more than usual, so I had hardly been eating anything for weeks. But finally I made it to the door. I knocked, the excitement rushed over me, I had butterflies in my stomach, I was smiling with joy. I quickly patted my hair down for any frizz, brought it round to the front to frame my face and put on some lipstick.

Strangely, it took him a while to open the door and he was in his dressing gown with nothing else on. It was early evening and he opened the door only a crack so I couldn't see into the flat. He looked really shocked, not in a good way, and asked what I was doing there.

My lover didn't have the big smile that I had envisioned on his face. I told him I was pregnant, expecting him to wrap his arms around me in joy, just like in the romantic movies and how Ken had hugged Barbie when she was pregnant. He looked gutted. There was no smile, in fact he turned pale and he asked whose baby it was. He wasted no time in telling me to get an abortion. It was too late to even consider that, not that I personally would have anyway.

Then the big blow came. A girl called out his name. As he turned his head to tell her I was 'No one', that's when I saw a great big love bite on his neck.

I felt like the biggest prat alive as I was told to go home and sort things out. He said he'd met someone else and we weren't happening anymore. My world had just been shattered.

I had no choice but to walk away, like a zombie. Suddenly the exciting town of Sunderland seemed grey, bleak and lonely, I walked and walked the dirty streets which I hadn't noticed before, trying to make sense of it all. 'Why?' I thought, 'Was I so unlovable?' as tears silently rolled down my face.

Rejected by my parents, now my dream of having my own happy family had been destroyed. I was also homeless, with very little money left, and I was pregnant.

My mind was a haze of confusion and despair. I sat all night at a bus stop, gazing into space. Drunks came and went. The cold night crept in. I dozed off a few times but I was awake for most of the night. I sat with the morning commuters and old grannies getting the bus, all with some place to go to. How I envied them at that moment. I wasn't getting on any bus but I just didn't want to be alone, I needed to be around people.

I wasn't entirely alone because my growing belly gave me comfort and kept me company. I wanted to eat to give my baby food so later that day I bought the cheapest sandwich I could find. I then used the last of my money to buy a pen and paper to write down my thoughts. By now I was cold, hungry and destitute. Life had battered me down: I felt defeated, unlucky, unlovable. I was feeling sorry for myself, but I knew if I did nothing my baby and I would come to a sticky end, so I decided I had to do something and I decided to fight, to carry on. I found the local Citizens Advice Bureau and told them everything. The lady was sympathetic and kind. I let out a big sigh of relief: for those moments I felt at least one person wasn't out to get me, or to beat me down. She made some phone calls, I sat waiting nervously for her reply, unsure if I would have a place to stay; then she said, 'Okay, I've found you a place in a hostel.' What a relief I felt from knowing I would have a bed that night, as well as warmth and a roof.

I had lived in hostels before but this hostel was something else. It was for battered women but by the look of it they were battering each other. In the communal area chairs were overturned and writing and food were scrawled and splattered on the walls. It was a haven for rogues and hood-rats.

The women showed me around, saying, 'My advice is keep yourself to yourself.' They handed me my food rations: tins of sardines, baked beans and red beans to keep me going until my dole money came in. I was scared stiff of the other girls, who had probably been brought up in the toughest conditions. I, on the other hand, had had what most would call a privileged upbringing. I wasn't one of them and experience told me they would soon find out and discriminate against me for it. I just didn't want to be one of those broken chairs, slung against the wall, left in pieces.

My room consisted of a mattress on the floor, a blanket and a sink. I decided I wasn't going to leave my room. I had four gloomy, dirty walls with a window looking out onto the side of a brick wall building. Somehow, though, I thought life would get better. I was going to have a beautiful baby and I was safe here. To me this was better than being at home with my dad; no one could put me down and tell me I was worthless. This was my space, my home, and I was now in charge of my own destiny. I again was filled with hope, but of course scared as hell.

With my pen and paper I wrote long letters to my baby, telling her how happy I was she chose me and how I would do anything for her. Although I couldn't give her money, or a father, I would love her enough to make up for all of that and I would be both parents for her. It would be just her and me but we would be fine because love would still conquer all. No one could take her away from me. We didn't need men, who only brought pain into our lives. I decided then and there, I would do whatever it took to bring her a good life, sweep floors if I had to. She would be my life from now on.

I was getting skinnier and skinnier, given that I had lost my appetite and stopped eating altogether. My pregnancy was virtually unnoticeable even though the weeks and months were going by. I had no money, no friends and no life. I had tried to get a job but I couldn't: I was pregnant so no one would take me, tough. I would go to bed at 6 p.m. because I wanted the next day to come sooner. I was in survival mode, having to take each day moment by moment, minute by minute, to get through it. I was terribly scared, and totally alone in this big bad world, still just a teenager who hadn't learnt to look after herself yet. My only form of entertainment was my pen and paper; I didn't have a TV or radio, no friends or family to chat to or someone to hug me and say it was all going to be okay. Worse still, I was running out of paper! After over a week of not eating at all I decided I couldn't stomach the water I was drinking from my sink in the room any more, I still hadn't left my room or ventured into the shared kitchen area either so I stopped drinking too.

It was then that I woke up in the morning feeling really dizzy and in pain. I stumbled towards the communal bathroom, holding onto the walls, as I was so weak. That's the last thing I remember.

Someone found me collapsed in the hallway, apparently, and they phoned an ambulance. I was taken to hospital and treated for severe dehydration, malnutrition and a threatened miscarriage.

I don't remember much of this time but I recall having tubes in my arms and being attached to machines that made beeping noises, nurses fluttering around, doing checks regularly on my pulse. It must have been quite serious, as I was later put on a ward with several other women. I stayed there for over six weeks.

I lay for the first few weeks not talking; not eating; just sleeping – too weak even to open my eyes, I barely moved. I was mentally and physically exhausted. My body was giving up on me and fighting for my child, as the baby is the last one to die and takes the nutrients it needs from the mother. The hospital staff told me they got me to hospital just in time. I wasn't sure what that meant but I knew I was frail, as I couldn't even lift my hand.

They nursed me back to health, though. I couldn't believe how caring these women were. Life was harsh and people were cruel, so kindness always seemed so uncomfortable to me. Why were they being so nice to a mess like me? When eventually, after several weeks, I was able to stay awake and start acknowledging my surroundings, I was being told to eat solids but I really didn't want to. I had no interest in food at all. The nurses warned me that if I didn't I would be sectioned and force-fed, so I started eating very small amounts, the least I could get away with. I didn't class myself as having an eating disorder: I just didn't want to eat anymore. Looking back, I now realise this was my way of gaining some control again over my disastrous life – albeit completely subconsciously, as I really believed I had just lost my appetite due to the pregnancy.

At visiting time I would pretend to be asleep, as I obviously didn't have any visitors: everyone else had a sea of flowers, cards and chocolates half eaten. I was immensely embarrassed by my lack of visitors and presents, so pretended to be asleep to avoid eye contact and the sympathy of others, which I just didn't want. I would, however, hear the whispers of patients in other beds telling their guests about the poor young pregnant girl who still had no one to come to see her. They would ask their guests to bring flowers or chocolates for me too and often would share what they were given, especially the woman in the bed next to me. She was defiantly kind, trying to grind me down with her friendliness, seemingly oblivious to my blatantly short answers and lack of engaging conversation with her. A typical Northern lady, I thought, friendly to a fault. I tried my best not to talk to her and ignore her, to answer her in as few words as possible, I didn't want to let anyone else in but she was stubborn.

Somehow her and the nurses' relentless kindness made me stronger, although when I heard their words of sympathy I would silently cry, as I was forced to acknowledge my situation. I also had to accept that not all humans were the same. Some people, no matter how bad you have been, still want to give you a chocolate. I think that was why I didn't want to take their kindness or their chocolates, because the reason I was there in that bed was self-inflicted. I had been a bad girl and I had no visitors as I was so naughty. I had made myself unlovable to all. Why the hell was the lady next to me trying to give me a chocolate? If I refused, and did not talk to anyone, she would stop asking her guests to bring things. She would stop her sharing and kindness and see sense. The nurses were kind but they were doing their job, they had to be this way, so I didn't mind their attention too much.

During my stay in hospital they kept weighing me, but my weight wasn't what they wanted it to be. They kept telling me every day that if I didn't put on weight I would have to go to a special unit where they would force me to eat. They were already pushing their mushy food in front of me on the ward, so I finally checked myself out. They wanted me to stay but I knew I would be okay. I got up from bed one day, put my last remaining drip under my coat, zipped it up and tried to walk off. One of the nurses spotted me, she convinced me to let her help me take the tubes out and told me they could not force me to stay. They also wanted me to sign stuff, which I did. I was feeling strong again and I was finding it harder and harder to pretend to be asleep at visiting time. I was ready to go but knew I didn't want to go back to that hostel.

I was over 'him'. I think I might have had a mini nervous breakdown and just gave up, but time and strangers' kindness healed my sensitive, fragile heart and now I was ready to battle on. The fact I had not had an epileptic fit since I found out I was pregnant was also making me feel more confident: my baby had somehow healed my life-threatening condition. I thought she and I would be a team, making each other stronger; she already gave me a reason to live, and had made me healthier.

I got a train back to Mum and Dad's house but I hadn't thought through my actions. Like a lamb to slaughter, I went back to where I thought I belonged. When I arrived at the station I phoned Mum and told her I had been in hospital, that I had nowhere to live and needed somewhere to stay. How could she refuse? I was pregnant and her daughter. She hadn't heard from me for months and really didn't know if I was dead or alive, especially with my epilepsy, or even if I was still pregnant.

Mum asked Dad, then she came to pick me up.

She was shocked how skinny yet pregnant I was. My stomach was in butterflies when I saw her faithful old Mini car pulling up. It was bittersweet: I had left with high hopes of starting my own life as an adult, having my own happy family, only to be picked up by my mum and told off for not putting my seat belt on. The journey home was awkward, to say the least: it was mostly silence, though we did talk about the weather.

Mum then went on to do what she often does, planning the dinner. She said, 'I'm not sure I have enough pork chops to go round.' I explained to her reassuringly looking her in her eye, 'That's okay.' It was more than a pork chop, it was all okay; I was just thankful for Mum being there for me after all I had put her through. Immediately, she started baking and trying to feed me up. We didn't mention what had happened. I simply said, 'The baby's father doesn't want to know,' and that was that.

'Bastard,' Mum muttered. She knew about being let down by men more than anyone.

Dad could not look me in the eye, I disgusted him. I had to be careful not to be in the same room as him. My pregnancy was shameful and a disappointment to him. I did my best to hide it, to ignore it and not to walk or act pregnant at all, as I didn't want Dad to feel even more sickened by me.

I didn't buy any baby stuff either, as I felt I would get into trouble if I did. Besides, that would be acknowledging it. I never went for any scans or to doctors' appointments. I just carried on as if nothing had happened, but in bigger clothes.

The situation with Dad didn't last long. Mum told me it was best if I found alternative accommodation. I don't think Dad could cope with seeing me on a day-to-day basis and I was rebelling by not complying with the house rules; I was still a teenager and was still acting like one. So I was back in a hostel in Sussex again.

This hostel and my room were not as bad as the last one. It was a hostel for all types of people who would otherwise be homeless and waiting for a council flat. I had a shared bathroom and didn't dare have a shower or bath, as there were often used heroin needles in the bath. I would instead stand at my sink and wash with a flannel; the bigger I got in my pregnancy the longer this took.

I had a mattress and a little kitchen and made use of the charity of the nuns who popped by regularly. The day I moved in I got a knock on the door from the nuns, asking if I needed anything and what I was short of; the next day bedding, blankets, and all sorts were delivered. Using their help and also, secretly, my mum's, I had soon gathered a lot of the essentials. It wasn't much but it was mine. There was no tension in the air. I didn't disgust anyone by simply being there, so I was content; maybe I was happy. Don't get me wrong, I had no intention of staying too long. I wanted my baby to have a good life. I certainly didn't want her to have a life on a rundown estate. I didn't look that far into the future but I knew I was going to be a mother and a father and that meant loving my baby like a mother could and providing for him or her like a father should. I was going to be both, I decided: I didn't want a man in our lives again. This was just a stopgap until I had the baby, until I worked out how to get back on track. I didn't want a council flat like all the others in the hostel did. I just wanted a roof over my head until I moved on again.

I didn't expect much from people at that point. I was very lonely but whenever I felt isolated I would write letters to my unborn baby and then I wouldn't feel so alone.

I remember the Christmas I was in the hostel when I was pregnant. I enjoyed walking past other people's houses and looking in; they would be all lit up, they would look so warm and inviting, cosy and happy. I would see the family in the warm, so I imagined as I stood watching, with my hand on my growing belly, that *that* was my family, that I was there in that glowing house, laughing and sharing food with the others. Seeing that, I would smile, dreaming one day it would be me. I didn't have anywhere to go, or any family to share Christmas with. My sisters had all moved out and drifted away by then and my mum said it was 'best not to be around Dad right now'. The two nuns who had given me all my furniture knocked on my door and gave me a present of a big box of biscuits. I was so delighted they even spent time talking to me. They asked me what I was short of still. I told them cutlery and a kettle and the next day the nuns came again with cutlery and a kettle.

It was these small acts of generosity that kept me going. I will never forget the heart-warming kindness they offered me. I hope they know that that box of biscuits probably gave me the strength to go on. It meant so much to me that someone cared.

It wasn't long, though, until the old saying that 'you sleep with dogs, you gonna get fleas' came true. I came home one day to find my humble hostel room's door was open; the lock had been broken. Immediately my heart sank: I knew I had been burgled. The thieves took pretty much everything I owned, including my kettle and cutlery, my bedding and even my shoes. They had stolen all the baby clothes and blankets I had slowly bought in anticipation of my newborn's arrival. I only had the clothes I was standing in. I was heavily pregnant at this point and it was the last straw. I couldn't face looking at the wreck of my home a moment more.

Crying, I walked, with no coat, as that had been taken too, for two hours to Mum's house. Yet again I begged to stay, as I didn't want to go back to the hostel. I had even left behind my key, so I wasn't going back even if she had said no. I could not go back to that place again, someone had evilly taken all my belongings: they had ransacked the place. I never felt a hundred percent safe in the hostel and was always careful to listen out on the corridor before I left my room so I wouldn't bump into fellow housemates. I knew too well what being in the wrong crowd could do to a girl; now I had my baby on the way I was even more careful to keep myself to myself. I was always scared of getting into fights and being confronted. I often heard fights break out.

Mum told me she would think about it, she needed to ask Dad. Two days later I moved back home. In the meantime, I had managed to sleep on friends' couches. Again, the kindness of others kept me going.

I seemed to have a short memory, as staying with my dad and his disgust towards me was awful. I had shamed him and he still simply couldn't be around me; he found it hard to let things go, and move on. He could not accept it. It was a living hell. Dad had sold his business and expanded to bigger premises so that was stressful and more to take on. Since my sisters had moved out, he only had my mum and me to shout at. The tension was building daily.

It was a strain to be home, as I felt I had let my parents down and was a disgrace. Dad repeatedly asked me: 'What are you going to do with your life? You have no talent and nothing to offer anyone.' I hadn't got a clue. He was right, I was a loser. I was slipping into a depression again. Now thirty weeks pregnant I was starting to panic that I was going to become a mum. My life was a mess, I was a mess. What the hell was I going to do with a baby? Maybe he was right, what could I offer my child?

I had decided I didn't want to be pregnant anymore. It wasn't a good idea. I felt so ashamed of my swollen belly, which left me tired and weak. All I could do was await this baby I had no clue how to look after. Dad was right, I was useless. I couldn't be a mother, I wasn't good enough. Despite my best efforts I was still living with my parents; it seemed I was failing with my life, failing to move forward. In a moment of depression and panic that evening, I downed some castor oil after reading it brought on labour but was violently sick straightaway. I was eight months pregnant. I immediately regretted it, it was a moment of feeling sorry for myself, not believing things would get better and Dad's cruel words getting to me. I was usually so stubborn: I wanted to prove him wrong, but life was getting to me and he was proving to be right.

I hadn't even attended one antenatal class or scan so I had no idea if I was having a boy or girl; if he or she would be healthy or how to give birth. I had never even held a baby before.

My friends wanted to cheer me up so asked me to go clubbing with them. It was nice that they didn't mind the pregnant girl tagging on. I was about to go but Mum said I wasn't allowed. She said she had made dinner and I had to stay in and eat. I was going to go anyway but mum said she would tell Dad. I realised it wasn't worth the hassle or earache I would get, so I stayed in, going to bed early to avoid any contact with 'him'. I rarely sat and watched TV, as that meant time with Dad. Instead I would sit in my room writing letters to my baby:

'Dear Baby,

It's been tough but I am going to give you the family I never had. You're going to be so loved, feel safe and content and never afraid. I might not be rich but I'm going to do anything and everything to make sure you have what you need in life. You are not going to be like me, you're going to be beautiful, strong, talented and happy. You will never feel scared or alone. You won't miss having a daddy 'cos take it from me they're not worth having anyway, they only make you feel pain. With me you just being you will be good enough. Long as you are healthy and happy that is all that will matter to me. You will have my heart forever. I am so grateful you came into my life. I know it was meant to be, God gave me and you each other so we had someone to love us that no one can take away. You are my destiny. The reason I exist. They tell me I won't be able to look after you but I am going to prove them wrong.

P.S. Please come soon as I really am fed up and lonely. I have some lovely clothes for you to wear. I love you.

P.P.S. I don't know how to look after you so bear with me. I am sure it will come naturally though.'

That night I started feeling ill. I went to the toilet several times and obviously had a bad stomach from Mum's cooking. At 3 a.m., Mum came down and asked what was wrong. I told her it was fine but she hadn't cooked the meat properly, as I had a bad stomach. We weren't a family that showed pain and were made to feel ashamed and embarrassed by it (that was for weak people) and I was still hiding my pregnancy as best I could, so I couldn't really admit the pain I was feeling.

Mum went back to bed but after hearing me trot to the bathroom every few minutes she decided it was best for her to drive me to the hospital to get me checked out.

I didn't really want to go, as I needed to be near the toilet. Nothing was happening but I thought I needed the toilet every few moments. With much convincing, I got in the car.

Waves of pain were taking over my body. I simply sang songs or hummed, and clapped to avoid thinking about the pain. When we got to the hospital the night doctor put probes on me and carried out an examination. I took a lot of persuading, as I wasn't expecting something so invasive! It took them at least half an hour to convince me to allow the doctor to examine me. Then I heard the worst thing: 'We need to operate now, she is in labour.'

The hospital staff rushed around and I was injected in my back, the room was crowded with people. They said I wouldn't feel anything but they needed to cut me open and get the baby out. I was 32 weeks pregnant so wasn't due yet, so this was totally confusing. I hadn't a clue what was happening, as the doctors and nurses buzzed around in panic. There were nine of them in the room with my mum and me. She looked on worried, as they prepared my now numb lower body for an emergency caesarean section.

Eleven minutes later I heard the small cry of a baby: this tiny, tiny baby weighing 3 lbs 3 oz, less than a bag of sugar, was put into my arms. Oh my God, she was beautiful and all mine. I counted her fingers and toes and I couldn't believe they were all there, that I had made such a perfect baby. Wow.

I could only hold her for a few seconds because she was eight weeks premature and needed intensive care. They rushed my baby off in a little incubator, shoved tubes up her nose and stabbed her little body with needles to keep her alive. It was touch and go. When I saw her like this I grew scared. I had already fallen deeply in love with her, I couldn't lose her now. She was now my life, my everything.

I wasn't feeling well myself and soon after handing my baby back I went into seizure. This was my first fit since I became pregnant, as if carrying my baby had somehow kept my epilepsy at bay. Luckily, it was also to be my last one.

In the meantime, my precious baby was suffering from jaundice and intolerance to milk. At one point, the doctors didn't know if she would survive; her weight was dangerously low. I didn't leave her side for eight weeks whilst she stayed in the hospital. I was allowed to stay with her, which I hear is very rare. I would sit by her incubator singing songs with her tiny, almost transparent hand clinging to mine.

Back then premature babies often didn't survive but my little girl kept fighting. Despite that she was up against it. She was jaundiced and had no body fat on her but she fought, just like her mother.

The nurses taught me how to bath her, dress her and feed her. I had to ask them to teach me several times because she was so small and the fact I had never even held a baby before made me nervous to carry her. Contrary to what I had expected, it turns out being a mum doesn't come naturally – you do actually have to learn it and you really should read those books.

It was in the hospital seeing her frail body fighting for every breath, aided by tubes and probes, that I decided I was going to change my ways. No more reckless living, no more drinking, no more clubbing. I wanted to come good for this little person that was fighting so hard to live and be with *me*!

The day I brought my daughter home was the happiest day of my life, I feared that day would never come.

I made a vow, there and then, not to allow my daughter to have Barbies. I didn't want her to be at all like me.

My child was just like a little doll: tiny, with blonde hair and big blue eyes. In fact, I had dolls bigger than her. I had hardly any baby clothes either so I often used dolls' clothes to dress her!

Mum and Dad instantly fell in love with this perfect little girl. As she seemed to be my Destiny that's what I wanted to call her, but Mum said I wasn't allowed to call her that. She said it sounded like a lap dancer's name, so we called her Georgia instead, and used Destiny as her middle name.

CHAPTER FOUR

Attacked

GEORGIA CHANGED MY life. Miraculously, the fit I had after giving birth would be the last I ever had. My baby seemed to cure me. She really seemed to be my Destiny, here to put me on a new path, a better path – a path that would lead to my survival, unlike the one I had been on. She for the first time gave me a sense of belonging, a reason to carry on, and had taken away that feeling of loneliness.

I started going for job interviews. I got one working in a hairdressers: a start to my career path and I was getting back on track. I walked two miles every day for a YTS scheme paying £35 a week whilst living in a hostel. Mum would look after Georgia for me whilst I worked long hours. However, this didn't last long, as I got caught shoplifting for my lunch on my one day a week at college. That was the end of that job. The only good thing that came out of it was my hair. I now had bleached blonde hair, just like Barbie. Well, it was a bit shorter and thinner than hers but I was working on that.

I started obsessing about my body when I lost my job. I taught myself how to dance and became a club dancer which was well paid compared to the hairdressers and I got to have fun whilst earning money. I was missing out on all the fun my friends were having being a teen mum, so this was a great way of combining that. I still wasn't happy with myself but being a performer gave me confidence and, most importantly, some money. I was working nights so I could take less sleep and look after my baby during the day. I worked really hard, often five nights a week, and was only catching on average four hours' sleep a night.

Despite the attention I was getting at work, I still wasn't happy with myself. I didn't feel beautiful like the other girls I was dancing with, so when I saw an advertisement in the back of one of my magazines, which showed a picture of an everyday, slightly unfortunate-looking lady transformed into a gorgeous Barbie lookalike, I thought, 'If only I could look like her, then I would be successful and happy.' The ad said I could look just like this doll-like woman with the help of something called plastic surgery.

Soon as I found out that plastic surgery existed I thought this was what I had been looking for. I could create the perfect woman and make poor Sarah Howes, the loser, into someone new. I believed this could be the start of the 'new me'. I used my humble savings to send off for the book, to find out how I too could become Barbie.

So the infatuation I had with Barbie dolls had transformed into an obsession with my own body. I started working on diagrams and making drawings of the perfect woman I was going to create. I cut out pieces of models' and celebrities' noses and mouths that I liked and pieced together the plan that would form me. I made a folder: it was 88 pages long. This project was going to make men want me, so my beloved baby would have a father, we would be loved by him and I would be successful. Plastic surgery would stop this run of bad luck I was having, forever.

I was handed a leaflet as I climbed off the train into London, where hopes and dreams were made... well, for a country girl like me it seemed that way. The leaflet read, 'Special offer on veneers'. Smiling back at me from the advertisement was a really pretty girl with straight and perfectly whiter than white teeth. Barbie had really white teeth and I wanted the same. This was how I was going to start my transformation. So I phoned the number and soon signed up for the veneers.

My teeth were pretty straight and white anyway but not paper-white. This was certainly a good idea, I thought.

I sat in the dentist chair. It was a humble-looking dental practice off the Fulham Road. The dentist numbed me before drilling away at my teeth. I hated the sound and started panicking. Tears were running down my cheeks, the dentist was getting frustrated and flustered with his dental nurse and me. He seemed new to the game of dentistry.

The drilling seemed like it went on forever. I was then given temporary teeth to wear for a week.

When I went back I had the white veneers fitted. They were white alright. They were also far too big for me. In fact, they looked like joke teeth, or piano keys stuck in my mouth. They were terrible but what I could not believe was that as I walked out with my new joke teeth, two of the front ones fell off before I got down the Fulham Road.

I went back with my teeth in my hand only for the dentist to tell me off. 'What were you doing?' he shouted.

I also glanced at my teeth underneath the veneers and I was shocked to see they had been literally shaved off to stubs of nothing. My lovely natural teeth, on which I had often been complimented, had been ground away and there was no going back. I had destroyed my teeth and replaced them with comedy dentures.

I could barely close my mouth because the teeth were so big. I definitely could not talk properly with them in.

The teeth continued to fall out. I started gluing them in with regular glue in desperation to look 'half normal'. Finally, I went to my local dentist in Sussex, where I was still registered. He referred me to another dentist in London who was a professor specialising in reconstructive dentistry.

The professor was shocked to see the state of my teeth. He said he didn't normally get involved in legal disputes but recommended that I sue. This man had taken far too much of my own tooth away, leaving me with very little natural tooth to the point that one day I would need crowns. I was missing about eight out of twelve veneers at that point. He said it was the worst veneer job he had ever seen and the dentist had destroyed my teeth forever.

To insert veneers, dentists are supposed to lightly sand off the top layer of the tooth. My dentist had carved away most of my teeth. To make matters worse, the veneers were ill-fitting, far too big for my mouth, so fell out regularly. My teeth were floppy and loose and my gums were in a really bad way. I was really worried I would lose my teeth altogether, which I think I would have done if I hadn't found the professor.

I found a no win, no fee solicitor to help me and I successfully sued, which got me enough money to pay for the repair to the damage caused. I had all my veneers redone. This time they were not as white and were much more natural-looking.

Stupidly, I would later get them all knocked out again to have yet another set done to make them whiter. They were no whiter the third time but a lot less straight! This was a great example of someone not learning from their mistakes and knowing when to quit.

I was just seventeen when I had my first boob job. The teeth episode didn't put me off: I was still set with my plan. You see, with bigger boobs I could become a glamour model, then I'd get a boyfriend and a father for Georgia and I'd earn enough money to give us a home. I went to the bank and asked for a loan to buy a car. I had never been in debt, as my parents always taught me to only spend what I had. When my application was accepted I was over the moon!

There was one thing I hated more than anything and it was my flat chest on my skinny frame. I was an A-cup and I hated wearing a bikini. I didn't like boys putting their hands up there because I was ashamed I had never developed like the other girls had. I didn't really need a bra either. My mother took me to Tammy Girl when I was twelve, but that was because I was desperate for a one, not because I needed the support. Mum bought me a crop top style bra. I was so happy, but it wasn't long until I wanted a proper bra. She told me to wait until I had developed more, which never happened. This surgery offered me the chance to finally wear my first bra with straps.

Whilst I was initially excited, by the time of my first meeting with the doctor I was so scared. In my consultation he asked me what size I wanted to be. I said I wanted to be as big as possible. Maybe a double-D? The doctor laughed and said the implants needed to be in proportion and that there was a limit to what size would fit. I had no idea what that meant. He was a surgeon so could make me any size, right?

'Yes proportion ones please thanks.' Any boobs would have worked for me at that point. This guy was willing to give me breasts so, I thought, in my book what he says goes.

I didn't tell anyone I was having the breast enlargement, not even my mother. I faked her consent and got a taxi to the hospital. I remember feeling very frightened: plastic surgery wasn't such a common thing yet. I'd never had an operation in my life and I didn't know if I'd be alright. In that cab ride to the hospital, saying goodbye to my mum and my baby, telling her I was going to work, I didn't know if I would be saying goodbye for the last time!

I sat in my bed in the hospital in East Grinstead waiting for my surgeon for what seemed like eternity. He finally came round.

'So we will be using about 300 cc here. Is that good for you?' I was seventeen years old and uneducated, I had no idea what 300 cc was.

I was wheeled into the operating theatre as a flat-chested, unlucky girl called Sarah Howes. I awoke with breasts, big breasts. I looked down and was delighted! It had been worth it. I determined that these two bags of silicone were going to change my life: I would no longer be Sarah Howes, I decided.

The hospital did not want me to leave alone so I had to pretend my friend was in the lobby waiting for me and off I went. I got a taxi home. I told no one about the boob job,

I didn't need to. I was in my own world, happy and positive that, for once, things would change for the better.

I decided that Sarah Howes was no more. She had to die, she was a loser and nothing good ever happened to her. Sarah Howes couldn't get a break, couldn't get a man and (most importantly) couldn't get a job. My new boobs were the start of something new.

I scribbled away adding to my plan to make me Barbie: first I would change my name, and then I would change my hair, my teeth, eyes, nose, hips, lips, bum, stomach, arms, waist, get a tan...

I set about the crucial first move: changing my name. I was endeavouring to end my bad luck. I had heard that if you change your name you change your destiny. I needed to do that after the fits, being expelled from school, the gypsy palm reader and the rejection by Georgia's father. I wanted to make a big change and I wasn't messing around anymore. Besides Sarah Howes was not a model's name.

So Alicia Douvall was born. I changed my name by deed poll. I chose Alicia just because I liked the name and it was very unusual at the time. I remembered seeing the name Duval on a bottle of champagne but, being dyslexic, I spelt it how the name sounded when I made the deed poll application (D-O-U-V-A-L-L) and got the spelling wrong!

Alicia Douvall, I decided, was going to be blonde, beautiful, tanned and successful.

After changing my name I bought a second hand sun-bed, which I went on every day, so Sarah Howes, the pale country girl, could die and I could be reborn as Alicia Douvall, the golden, tanned babe. Except that I soon went too far and I got addicted to tanning. People started asking me what nationality I was. I started getting patches of damaged skin and my face was rapidly becoming leathery.

I knew this was only the start. I was gaining confidence and, with my new boobs, I didn't go unnoticed. This was not always fortunate. I was from a small town where everyone knew everyone, and I was no exception.

One night I walked into a pub with a friend. I felt an air of frostiness but I didn't care because I was still on Cloud Nine. For once, I had a tight top on and I felt good. I was celebrating my boobs and my new start in life. I wanted to walk upright and proud for the first time in my life.

I spent twenty minutes waiting at the bar to get my half a pint of lager. As I walked off towards my friend, I felt someone grab my hair. Before I knew what was really happening, I was falling all over the place. I was being spun around like a rag doll and was dragged to the ground fast. I briefly looked up to see two girls, one holding me and the other stabbing me in the face.

The girls had attacked me for no apparent reason. The girlfriend that I came with was nowhere to be seen, but one boy that I had seen around town defended me from their further attempted attacks. He pulled me outside the pub for safety.

The boy said to me, 'Don't touch your face whatever you do.'

I was confused and covered in blood. My hair had been ripped out and was falling away in clumps. I didn't know what was wrong with my face so I touched it to see why the boy had said not to touch it. All of a sudden, my face started gushing with blood, which spurted out, covering the crowd that had gathered around me.

I had been glassed with a broken bottle. The broken glass had been twisted into my face, several times. Once I had started bleeding I could not see, there was so much blood: it was streaming out, covering my eyes, hands, clothes, the pavement, my shoes, like a dam released. I screamed with panic from the sheer amount of blood I was losing.

An ambulance arrived and I was rushed into the back. The paramedics were examining me when the police arrived. They asked if I knew who did it. I didn't have a clue but the entire pub knew these people, including the boy that helped me that night. They had a code of conduct and told me to say nothing: the boy, scarily stony-eyed, looked dead into my bloody blurry eyes as he said, 'She doesn't know her attacker.' I was scared and I didn't want to be attacked further, so I agreed to keep quiet and not to press charges. Looking back I really regret that decision, I should have been braver to bring those awful women to justice. What they did was sick and possibly helped set me on the road to destruction.

I was taken to hospital, where I was told I needed plastic surgery to fix my face. How ironic!

The boy who had seemed to be assisting me after the attack had come with me to the hospital. This lad, Jason, wasn't my friend but I knew of him. He seemed to want to help and he was the only person I had right then.

The hospital said that I should come back in the morning for the stitches and sent me on my way. I walked out of the hospital completely shell-shocked. I could not believe what had happened to me. I had a bandage over my face that covered one eye so I wasn't sure if I was going to be partially blind or not. In my traumatised state the one thing I knew was that I was disfigured for life – with the amount of blood I lost I knew this wasn't a small scar – I just wasn't sure to what extent.

Jason suggested that we go back to his house. By this point I was in no condition to argue with him and just went along with it, becoming a robot, saying nothing, just taking direction. I was in a state of severe shock. This, I thought, was all my dreams shattered. My chances of earning money as a model were over and I was now mutilated, all because two strangers didn't like how I looked.

Confused, and dependent on Jason's care, I was driven to his house. He showed me kindness and seemed to want to step up to be my hero. I did not have much idea who Jason was but later found out he was a rogue himself, from a well-known family of gangsters.

At Jason's house, the 'family' gathered. They were a scary lot but were showing me nothing but kindness. They said what had happened was 'out of order' and would be 'dealt with'. I was told that they knew where the perpetrators lived. I later discovered the 'family' did 'deal with it' themselves: I know one of them had someone break into her house with a baseball bat. I also know the other one ended up in prison for attacking someone else.

The family told me I was glassed in the face and disfigured for life because 'They thought you thought you were "it"'.

That was it? Really? More like the girls themselves thought I was 'it', so decided to make me definitely not 'it' ever again. It was a mindless attack for no reason.

Jason said I should wash the blood off my hair and face now that it had dried. My dark hair was now a red wine colour and was stuck together in clumps. Spatters of dry blood covered my clothes and body. My white bodycon top was almost all red; the front had been entirely drenched.

When I was alone in the bathroom I starting crying my eyes out, collapsing to the floor, repeating hysterically, 'Why me? Why me? Someone have mercy on me, please.'

Jason rushed in and knelt on the floor to comfort me, wrapping his arms around me.

'It's okay. You're going to be okay.' I really did not believe him at all.

'I'm disfigured, I'm blind!' I screamed through the tears.

'No, they tried to blind you but they just missed your eye. It's okay. It's just bandaged.'

It still wasn't 'okay'. I could feel a large bandage going across my nose and left cheek.

I was drained. This felt like the walk back from Georgia's father's house. I was done living.

Jason suggested he help me wash the blood out of my hair and off my body. He carefully washed my hair like I was his doll. I really didn't understand why he was being so kind, especially as I looked such a mess.

Jason put the shower on, handed me a towel and left me alone to shower, which I dutifully did. He gave me his T-shirt to put on and a pair of shorts. Still bandaged up like a mummy, I did what I was told, waiting for my next instruction. I wanted to go home, to my mum and Georgia. Jason told me he had sent someone round to my parents' house to tell them I wasn't coming back tonight but that I was safe.

I imagined the trouble I would get in from my father for being in a pub in the first place; I thought it was maybe best to stick with Jason so I chose to believe him.

Jason said I should sleep in his bed. It was a single bed and there didn't seem to be much room for two people but in my zombie, defeated state I conformed and lay down. That's when I felt Jason's hand holding mine. 'What?' I thought: I feel like crap, look even worse... This isn't a great time for me right now.

He slowly moved his hand around my waist and started kissing me. I pulled away. I just wanted to go home. Romance was the last thing on my mind, but he was insistent. Jason just kept going, even though I pulled away several times. I was exhausted; in the end I gave up resisting and we ended up having sex. I didn't want to have sex but I felt obliged. I was so beaten up this felt like just another blow. I didn't care about my body anymore, as someone had destroyed it in a moment. Jason was just using the remains of my body, my soul was gone. I lay still whilst Jason got his way, tears silently falling down my cheeks. I just wanted it over. I knew no one did anything for nothing. This, I thought, was why he was being kind. No one was kind without a reason where I came from.

All I wanted was to get back to my family, now even more so. I didn't sleep that night. While Jason slept soundly, I lay awake next to him, staring at the inside of my bandage. I decided I would spend the rest of my life indoors now that I was deformed; I could not leave the house ever again. Georgia would have to go out with my mum. I would wait to die.

The next morning Jason drove me to the hospital, where I received a mixture of stitches and sterile strips. Most of the treatment was stitches though, all across the side of my nose and part of my cheek. It was horrific. I was beyond distraught. This to me was the last straw in an already very troubled life. My attackers had left an S-shaped scar across the side of my nose running down onto my cheek.

Finally Jason drove me home. He walked me to my door and knocked. I was so scared of the trouble I would be in. Mum opened the door; it seemed that Jason had been true to his word and told her where I had been, as promised.

Dad, predictably, told me off. He said, 'If you are going to go to places like that you are going to get hurt and deserve what you get.' He said I was stupid and it was my own fault.

When I saw Georgia's little face I just started crying again. I wanted to be successful for her. I wanted her to have everything: a home, an education and a father. My attackers had taken that from the two of us in a second.

Tears rolled down my face dripping onto her tiny body. Georgia's little hand clenched mine. I was never going to leave the house again. I had to re-think the modelling and find a job that involved staying at home.

Other than refusing to leave the house, I did what I was told. I had lost my enthusiasm, my spunkiness, my ambition and my smile. I became a shadow of myself and my will to live had faded away. I moped around the house, sunken, destroyed and beaten at last. Probably for the first time since I was young I was easy for my parents to handle; my soul had been ripped out, I had no desire to get dressed or showered in the morning, let alone leave the house or eat. Mum would ask me to help with cleaning around the house; like a robot I would slowly do the dusting, soulless and destroyed. I didn't speak to anyone, my head hung low; even the presence of Georgia playing couldn't put a smile back on my face. Weeks went by without me talking, just taking the verbal beating my father would give me when he would be reminded of my stupidity by my red raw scar across my face. I would simply lower my eyes in shame.

Eventually my mother turned to me and said, 'Okay, let's quit feeling sorry for ourselves. The scar really isn't that bad. I can't see it. You need to go out and meet someone. You need to do this for your daughter.'

That was what Mum thought the answer was for me: she thought a handsome man, a knight in shining amour, would one day want to marry me and have kids making me a housewife. She thought this was my only hope.

Maybe Mum was right about one thing. I needed to do something for Georgia's sake. I summoned enough courage to leave the house and go to the doctors. My doctor prescribed anti-depressants for me, which was the first step to getting me back on track. I stayed on them for a very long time.

I got a job working in a shoe shop. I was happy to be building a life again, now as a shop girl. I learnt that I enjoyed working and selling and soon became one of their best salesgirls. I was earning a living and supporting my daughter. I no longer went to pubs and didn't socialise with anyone, especially not girls: they scared me too much after the attack. I would work then go home to my baby.

I had been employed for four months when I had to get up at 5 a.m. to get Georgia ready and drop her off at the child-minders for my 8.30 a.m. start. I jumped into my old Ford Fiesta car, which I had spent all £350 of my savings on, and strapped Georgia in. That morning it was particularly frosty and I was running late. In my panic I didn't wait for the ice to melt from my front windscreen properly. I drove off, worrying I might be late, looking through a small gap I could just see out of through a sheet of ice covering the rest of my windscreen.

I didn't get very far before I crashed into a parked car. I had been doing somewhere between twenty and thirty miles per hour.

My face hit the dashboard. I looked behind me to see Georgia crying. She sounded desperate and scared in a way I had never heard before. Her chair was on its side but she was still strapped in. A passer-by ran over and helped us out of the car. He dialled 999 and requested an ambulance.

My car had to be towed away, it was a write-off. Georgia and I were checked by the paramedics. They wanted to take me to hospital for my head injury. I was bleeding from a cut but I refused, explaining I really needed to get to work.

Mum and Dad were livid that I didn't have the sense to clean my front car window. They had a point but my life was a struggle. I was always panicking and when you panic you sometimes don't make great choices.

We were living in the countryside at the time and I soon realised that without a car I could no longer get to the shoe shop or to the childminders. My luck wasn't improving;

actually, it was getting worse. In that instance I lost my job, my childminder and any hope I had.

I started reading a paper for entertainers, scanning it for jobs. I still felt unattractive but I had no money and it was costing my parents to keep me and my daughter, which Dad reminded me of daily.

A dancing job caught my eye but it was in Italy. I phoned the number in the job advertisement and got an interview. I thought, 'As soon as they see my disfigured face they won't want me but I'll give it a go for Georgia.' Shockingly for me, I was hired. The pay was better than I had ever dreamed of. The hours would be long but it would get Georgia and me out of this hole I was in.

I told Mum and she told Dad. Their reaction was surprising. They said I needed to get some savings and to earn a living. They insisted they would look after Georgia whilst I got myself back on my feet.

I had not planned on leaving my daughter. My parents didn't believe I was fit to look after her without their help. I wasn't a natural mother, I tried but it didn't come automatically. Love, it turned out, wasn't enough.

Mum said Georgia would be fine. I should go out there and soon as I was sorted I could have her with me. So off I went on a one-way ticket to Italy to dance for my supper. Literally.

When I arrived at Italy, we toured Parma and Rimini. I shared a house with other girls who were also go-go dancers.

In hindsight the money wasn't that good, but it was a lot better than I was used to. The other girls were friendly too and I knew I was going to enjoy my time there.

There was only one problem: I did not speak a word of Italian. I arrived clutching only a tourist book with a few 'useful phases' in the back.

The girls and I were put straight to work. It turned out that this didn't just include go-go dancing. We had to get people to buy drinks but that was a way of topping up our salaries and earning more money. Sadly, I was at a disadvantage only speaking English, especially when most of the other girls had a good grasp of the Italian language. I wanted to say, 'This isn't for me, I was privately educated at one of the best schools in the UK, I don't need to degrade myself to grovelling to some leering men for a drink,' but instead I said nothing and stayed. I didn't value myself enough to justify a walk-out. After all, so what if I went to private school? In the back of my mind was the thought that I didn't even finish my education. And leering men? Part of me thought that with my scarred face I was lucky anyone wanted to sit with me, let alone buy me a drink.

I wasn't pretty enough, good enough or clever enough to have dignity. Being a struggling single parent I certainly could not afford morals anymore. I had to do what I had to do to put my daughter first and provide for her. I decided that the second I had made the choice to bring a child into the world I took a back seat and that child became the most important person in my universe. I had to take a big gulp and get on with it. I was not going to complain as long as I was getting paid. When offered lemons, you make lemonade.

I was determined to do well and to be the best dancer: after all, if I was stuck here I might as well try and be the best and earn the most. I also wanted to learn Italian, even though generally it's hard for some dyslexics to learn a language. It's not considered one of our strong points! All around me people were speaking only Italian. If I didn't learn the language very quickly I would be left behind and not earn the commission that I wanted. I was desperate to do well for Georgia, for her to be proud of me.

I picked up Italian quickly, purely because I was saturated in it. No one spoke English, not even my friends. I soon got the hang of getting the men to buy drinks. They would talk mainly about themselves and not notice my lack of vocabulary. I would offer the odd 'Si' or 'No' and nod approvingly, taking cues from them: when they laughed I'd laugh; when they looked leering and mischievous I looked them in the eyes and gave a sexy, accepting, coy, naughty look back.

Many of the Italian men – I'm sorry to say this, but the cliché was true – were sleazy and put their hands everywhere. I could not understand what they were saying but half the time I did not need to. The other dancers and I were adored by leering men in a strict Catholic town. The longer I was in the cage or on stage, which I looked forward to going into, the better my dancing became and at least whilst I was in there I was safe from the guys' lecherous ways.

I recall the first man who had a wandering hand. I wanted to slap it and tell him 'Vaffanculo', which means 'fuck off' in Italian, but this was a crossroads. I had to decide to change my morals for good, to take the hits and bring back money for Georgia or go home a broke loser. Georgia meant more to me than I meant to myself so instead of telling the sleazy old git to piss off like I wanted to, I patted his hand smiling, before slowly moving it to pour him another drink. I learnt survival tricks, like subtly moving their hands, leaning over to pour a drink to get them off or excusing myself to the toilet when I really couldn't take more.

Luckily, we did 'Show Spectacular' twice a night, where we would dance and a few girls would sing. This was like lame, cheap holiday entertainment but in Italy they seemed to appreciate it nevertheless. It also gave me a good excuse to get away from the men and their octopus hands.

The dancing was all night six nights a week, usually until 6 a.m. The girls were hired out to private parties sometimes. That's when I saw how the other half lived. We drank shots of espresso, whisky and Coca-Cola to take the edge off and keep ourselves awake all night: this was basically our diet. We partied hard and got paid well. I was exceptionally bad. I soon got into the habit of drinking too much, eating too little and taking slimming tablets with speed in them to keep me up all night and keep my thin dancer's body – the alcohol and Coke we drank all night was packed with calories so we all struggled not to pack on the pounds.

One by one the girls would 'need a break' and burn out but I, to be fair, had more endurance. I had a bigger reason to put up with the men and to punish my body through dance routines that really only a trained dancer could be expected to do. I was determined and I would put in the extra practice during the day whilst the club was closed to learn the routines that the other girls seemed to pick up quicker.

Italy was a great place for children. I would walk along the beach in Rimini seeing other mums with their babies, watching mums push their child on the swings happily, imagining having Georgia with me, which I missed so much. I was working nights but had money and living was much less expensive than back home. I saved up for an apartment, in which I made a room for Georgia – thinking I could convince Mum – and got a boyfriend. Franco was an Italian DJ at the club but didn't speak any English.

I begged Mum every day to let me have my little girl but she still didn't think I should take Georgia, despite the apartment and the room waiting for her. I would buy her hair bands and pretty dresses, telling the shop assistants proudly of my daughter who would be coming soon; I would hang the beautiful dresses up in her wardrobe waiting for the day my life would be complete. Mum and Dad had grown attached to Georgia. They were now bringing her up as their own. I think that their judgement was clouded by love for Georgia: all I heard from my mother was that it would not be right for my daughter to join me. I disagreed intensely.

I can see now that my life before Italy was getting worse and worse. My parents did need to intervene and help me get back on track. My mother was a great mum and very caring. They adored little Georgia, who was exceptionally small for her age – the perfect looking baby and toddler, with her blonde hair, blue eyes and easygoing, calm temperament.

I was not going to give up, though, and carried on working on the prettiest bedroom in the apartment for my daughter. I constantly bought toys, a high chair: it was all ready, I thought, for when we could be a proper family. Sadly the clothes never got worn; she grew out of them before I even saw her.

It was not going to be. My Italian boyfriend wasn't what he seemed. Franco soon became the clichéd Italian man: he cheated on me and hit me. At one point he even took my passport away from me. It turned out he had a fiery personality, he was controlling and manic.

It was then I realised that Georgia was not going to join me in Italy so, after six months of dancing, Franco and pleading with Mum to let me have her, I had burnt out. I booked the next flight back to the UK.

When I got home I realised how burnt out I was really was. I had worked every day for six months without a break. I spent my supposed day off learning routines. I certainly did not eat a healthy diet whilst I was away. When I stopped I slept for a week. I had given myself a hernia and I had to come off the ephedrine tablets the other dancers and I used to keep us awake and slim. Although my body was toned like you wouldn't believe, my health was questionable. Mum again had to nurse me back to strength.

This time, however, Mum wasn't angry. I had come back with money – savings for Georgia's future. I had also returned home believing in myself again for the first time since the attack. If anything, it seemed as if I needed those leering Italians to stop me feeling ugly. Without them, my confidence started to fade and my attention eventually drifted back to plastic surgery.

CHAPTER FIVE

Building Alicia

ITALY CHANGED ME. I had more confidence and had learnt with a little determination that I could be someone else. The cack-handed girl with two left feet from Sussex had forged herself a career as a dancer through sheer determination and desperation.

This was the start of Alicia Douvall, who was far more successful than Sarah Howes, but she didn't look like me. My new boobs had taken me so far but I still didn't feel pretty, I needed more... much more. I needed to make drastic changes.

For an immediate alteration I decided to tattoo my face. I read about a new thing called semi-permanent tattoos for the eyebrows, lips and eyes, so, of course, I signed up for all three. I thought it could change my look quickly. The swelling was pretty bad and my lips looked like a plunger for a few weeks afterwards but I saw a difference and I liked it. It wasn't enough but it was a taste.

As soon as I recovered from my Italian episode, now that my confidence was restored, I found work club dancing in London.

I also thought long and hard about my new career path. I was uneducated, so I could do nothing that required brains.

I needed big pay but short hours. Glamour modelling – the scar, I decided, could be retouched digitally: I was going to be a famous model. I went to see a local photographer to have some pictures taken. I sent them off to modelling agencies and to newspapers that featured topless women.

I set about joining every good model or talent agency in London. Most turned me down but I didn't give up. I felt confident but part of me still couldn't believe it when I got a phone call from an agency called 'Ugly'. I did think that their name was not very flattering but the agency said whilst they specialised in character models they took on mainstream models too. They said I needed to come to London to meet them for a chat. Wow, I was going to the city to be a model!

I was so excited about the meeting. I didn't have many clothes but I wanted to impress the agency and look like a real model. I went to a charity shop and found a fake white fur coat, which I thought was perfect. I paired it with pink jeans and my heeled boots. I must have looked very funny in hindsight, but they didn't seem to mind, luckily!

So off I marched to London. Ugly scanned me up and down before interviewing me. They told me I was too short for fashion work at 5 feet 6 but I could do lingerie and bikini modelling. The agency sent me for professional pictures, the cost of which I would have to pay back with my earnings.

Two weeks later, Ugly called me about an audition for a TV show called *Big Breakfast*. I was stunned! I didn't expect my luck to turn around so quickly. When the agency told me of the audition I said, 'I don't understand. How come they want me? Have they made a mistake and got my pictures mixed up with someone else's?'

The lady from Ugly said, 'Yes, we were shocked too but, yes, they definitely want you.'

Big Breakfast was Channel Four's popular early morning show. Denise Van Outen had been the last female presenter. She was a blonde, beautiful woman, not a goofy, dark-haired girl like me. (I couldn't afford to maintain my blonde hair from my hairdressing days so went back to black.) I couldn't understand why a successful programme like that wanted to see me!

The first part of the process was to make a cheeky, funny and topical video and send it in, which I did. I got a call back. The second round was to come in to see the producers, answer questions and comment on topics in the news. I got through that stage too.

So I found myself in the last round. I thought I needed to pull something extra out of the bag. Unfortunately, I didn't believe in myself enough as I was. I dyed my hair blonde and cut it short, just like Denise Van Outen's hair. Surely this would get me the job: I was just like her now.

That was as far as I got. I lost out to the questionably-talented Kelly Brook. Afterwards, it was very painful to watch her on *Big Breakfast*, especially because she was a busty, dark-haired girl! The cut and dye job had been a big mistake. I thought that not only had Kelly Brook taken my job but she also turned out to be crap! The TV critics panned her too and she only lasted for seven months on the show.

In the meantime, another opportunity came: this time with Yvonne Paul, a top glamour model agency. Playboy TV was looking for an early evening fax girl. I wasn't really aware of Playboy in those days and treated it like any other audition. It was a success, and I was delighted to get my first job on TV, which was going to pay £1,000 a week. I would get picked up in a car every week, have rehearsals and my make-up and hair done for me. Playboy back then was a prestigious job.

Sadly, the money did not last long. I was not asked to do any nudity but I was still young and just did not understand the Playboy concept. I didn't understand why I was there, that men would lust after us, and that these weird guys even existed. So when I was asked to read a fax out that was asking 'the gorgeous fax girl to wear some tan tights' I really didn't get the whole fetish thing and completely took the piss. I made the other two presenters miss their cues as they looked on shocked and amused, while I put on the tights, walked 'Mr Bean' style across the studio set pulling the tights up to my chin and making faces, joking about the gusset. I had the other girls rolling with laughter; the director, his face horrified, was not impressed.

On another occasion I was asked to bring in my favourite 'toy' so naturally I brought in the board game 'Guess Who'. The director thought I was taking the piss again when I proudly presented the box after he asked what toy I had chosen to bring in. The producer snatched the game out from under my arm and said, 'Very funny, luckily we have toys here. You can have a paddle.'

A paddle? I thought a paddle was like an oar that helps steer a boat! I was naïve but I wasn't going to fall into that trap again and silently took the black 'paddle', hoping no one would ask what it was for, as I had no idea: it looked like a table tennis bat but in leather. I had no clue what to do with it or how to even pretend to know what to do with it, which became very evident on the show with my vague comments like 'I love my paddle, it's my favourite thing'. So when the fateful phone call came to tell me I wasn't 'needed anymore' I wasn't surprised.

I did get some exposure but it was in an industry, and for a market, that I didn't understand. I was far from media savvy, I just thought glamour models must be glamorous and thus the prettiest. I started to get offers of work in the glamour business, which back then was earning girls proper money.

I started out modelling for lingerie magazines but was soon topless modelling for Page Three in *The Sun*. Back in those days, with internet not as popular as it is now, magazines and newspapers paid a fair amount of cash for a shoot. So I was earning good money whilst building a name as 'Alicia Douvall the Glamour Model' or, as my mum would say, 'the Whore'.

Because my religion and upbringing were totally against everything I was doing, not to mention my stream of bad luck, I kept waiting for my bad karma and, funnily enough, it didn't come. In fact, life had never been better. Being a good girl hadn't paid off for me but being a tacky, shameless and topless model – sorry, but it was really working out well for me.

I had a dodgy boob job, a tattooed face and fake hair extensions, which were blonde and extremely long and straight, the exact opposite of the hair I really had. I figured anything that was as far away from Sarah Howes as possible was good. Plus my hair was just like Barbie's. I was at last wanted: men across the country were potentially wanking over me, which would disturb most girls but was a massive compliment to me. Finally, I was good at something and wanted. The photographers wanted me and men liked me – okay, maybe only once I had been retouched and I was in print, but that was good enough.

I remember shooting with Jenny Savage, who was a famous photographer for *The Sun*, and later the *Daily Star*. She never really took a shine to me. Jenny hated fake tan and I was not about to part with it; maybe that was why.

She said: 'It's not enough to be a Page Three model, you got to be on the gossip pages, out in the clubs, you got to have a personality.'

Actually, Jenny did not tell me this; she was telling the other girl on the shoot, but I was listening. She talked and gave advice to her favourites and I wasn't one; the rest of us she treated like trash, using us like pieces of meat, mumbling under her breath when you didn't get a pose right. The other girl was prettier than me, more confident than me but clearly had no personality, which I knew was one thing I had in buckets – lots of personality! Jenny thought the girl was the next big thing, but I knew better.

I was still part-time dancing to supplement my income as modelling was sporadic. It was while I was dancing that I met Seb. Sporting a Ralph Lauren shirt, chinos and red rosy cheeks he stood out like a sore thumb as the posh boy in the club.

I remember him looking impressed as he stared at me whilst sipping his drink shyly. I wore my American flag hot pants and halter neck bikini top. I sensed he liked what he saw so, as a bit of a show-woman and a flirt, I started dancing even better. I swung on the swing, doing extra backward folds, then did the splits upside down, which I know is what clinched the deal.

When I was done I walked off and caught his eye and smiled at him. He grabbed my arm to stop me and asked what my name was.

The chemistry between us was unquestionable but, at the same time, insane. I was a lowly club dancer and he was an absurdly well-spoken, old-money, English public schoolboy. Sebastian had a crest ring, which really impressed me. My stint at boarding school made me appreciate and feel at ease with privately educated men, and I was partial to a crest ring – a sign of old family money, class and heritage. Something I lacked.

Seb was a strapping six-foot-two, rugby-build, high-cheekboned, smiling goof. He was with his brother; he was autistic and needed Seb to care for him.

'This is Jake, my brother. I look after him,' he announced. I was in love. He had it all: a big heart, a glint in his eye that said he thought I was hot, and the class I had been surrounded by at school but never obtained myself.

'Do you want a drink?' he asked.

'Why not?'

'Champagne?'

Wow, this man really had my heart now. He was already spoiling me and he wasn't holding back.

He ordered a bottle of champagne. The rest of the evening we talked to each other, insanely flirting and laughing. From time to time I would have to go off to dance but he would wait by my side dutifully, loyally and proudly, watching my every move with a permanent smile. That night I danced with all my might, busting out moves I never knew I had, high on love at first sight. His eyes did not leave me for a second.

At the end of the night, or shall we say early morning, I gave Seb my number and said we would talk soon. I kind of knew we would.

At 4 a.m. I left to get in my car and make the two-hour journey home to sleep for two hours before taking Georgia to nursery.

Something surprised me though: I looked in my rearview mirror to see an Audi flashing its lights. At first I thought it was undercover cops flashing me to pull over but then, as the car sped up to my old banger, I saw Seb beaming at me. A text appeared on my phone, from Seb. He had written: 'Just want to make sure you get home okay.'

Then another. 'Do you mind?'

Although it could have been seen as slightly creepy I thought it was romantic and amazing. Seb followed me all the way back to Horsham. We stopped at a gas station on the way and had our first kiss. We were chatting when he grabbed me and pulled me to him whilst kissing me, afterwards muttering like an over-excited child, 'I hope you don't mind me kissing you? Was that okay?'

'Of course,' I proclaimed. If there ever was such a thing as love at first sight, this was it.

Seb followed me in the car all the way home. When I arrived home he flashed his lights and blew a kiss, a true gentleman.

The next day Seb texted me. The relationship became intense very quickly. It was love, we didn't hold back: we quickly became inseparable best friends.

We were an odd couple: a rebellious, wandering single mother with no direction in life and a posh boy with a family business he was set to inherit. Seb would confide in me that he felt the pressure of taking over the family business. He was charismatic but still unsure of himself.

I was the sensible one with money, often lending him cash when he would gamble his wages away or spend too much on drink in bars. He drank too much and gambled obsessively.

Seb was also a relentless romantic – which I loved about him – often making me breakfast in bed, prepared with a red rose. He would sprinkle rose petals on the bed, prepare movie nights with candles and an open fire; he would cook food himself and shower me with flowers daily. In fact I can't remember a day that he didn't get me flowers.

He loved me with all his heart and I knew it. I also loved him with all my heart. Most importantly he also loved Georgia. He was the perfect parent and adored her like a real father. We went on holiday, enjoy weekends away and would spend every spare hour together. We didn't have much money: I was trying to save for Georgia and Seb's gambling and spending frivolously often left us without.

Nevertheless, love was conquering all. I would work a lot, which made the infatuated Seb insecure. Sometimes he would follow me to work and spend all night just standing there watching me. We dreamed about a life together, forever, getting married and having kids. But it could be only a dream, because there was one big problem. His family, whom he aspired to please so much, didn't approve of his lowly choice of girlfriend.

Seb was brought up going to the horse races: it was part of their life as a family. He gambled on the horses and attended almost every race. Our weekends were always spent attending the races somewhere.

He dreamt about giving me his mother's jewellery. This was kept in the family and was set to be passed on to his future wife, but the rift was too great. Seb's mother was adamant she would not tolerate him dating a woman like me. At the races, she banned me from the family and friends' picnics and I was not allowed to go to any family event. Seb would refuse to go too but it caused him a lot of grief. He so craved his family's acceptance of me.

After over a year of dating Seb asked his mum if he could marry me: the dream I was hoping for, with the father I wanted for Georgia. His mum said she would cut him off immediately – which meant his allowance, his flat, his car – and cut him out of the inheritance. His parents had already bought a flat for him and his brother to live in and were paying him a handsome allowance. This was also a wage whilst he learnt every aspect of the family business he was intended to take over.

It wasn't long before this caused a problem. I craved security and a family and Seb's mother had stopped him from giving that. I wanted him to marry me anyway but he was now torn between two women he adored and wanted to please.

The conflict grew but our love for each other was strong: neither of us could walk away. We would argue, make up, passionately kiss and make out. On two occasions, Seb actually said: 'Right, get in the car. We are driving to Gretna Green in Scotland and getting married.'

We drove for hours before deciding to come back home, both of us chickening out and realising the drive was too long.

We discussed marriage so many times. Seb dreamed about a family too and, one romantic evening, we got carried away. He told me we should try for a baby: if it happened there and then it would be meant to be. I didn't think it would happen so went along with the gesture to enjoy the moment. Needless to say, it happened.

We bought one of those pregnancy tests and sat there together in shock when the two blue lines showed up. We both smiled and were happy with the news. He kissed my stomach and swore to be the best father to this baby and Georgia. I felt like my battle, my struggle was over. I had found my family, my home and my happiness. The journey was over, finally I felt I belonged, I had a family, I was safe and loved, I had arrived.

I do not know what happened when he told his mum and dad but he changed his mind over the course of the new few weeks. Seb decided that it wasn't the right thing to do, that we needed to wait till we were married and his parents had come around. He was convinced that his mother would do so eventually.

This was my family. I wasn't into abortion but I also was so scared of the thought of becoming a single parent for a second time. I had gone through hell and wasn't sure I could go through it again.

So I agreed reluctantly to consider aborting our child, thinking he would change his mind. Deep down, however, I knew I couldn't really do it. I remember when we were in the car park of the abortion clinic I clutched onto my tummy and said, 'I cannot do this, this is my baby too and the baby stays.' I had already fallen in love with the baby, and besides, I knew what rejection felt like, I wasn't about to reject anyone, not even an unborn foetus. I refused to get out of the car and demanded that Seb drive me home. After a long negotiation I ground him down and he did. His face was pale with worry. We ended up arguing for weeks over my decision. He wanted so badly for his mum to accept me and his child, which somehow he knew she would not right now.

I wanted Seb to just walk away, to forget the hold his parents had on him and for him to be his own man. Seb wanted to but he couldn't; he would have to walk away from all that he knew and start again. He had never had to struggle like me.

I was nearly three months pregnant and Seb still was in two minds when fate intervened. I started cramping with pain that came and went, then bleeding: I was miscarrying. We both cried as I sat on the floor clutching my stomach every few minutes as we were obviously losing our baby.

I suffered from depression afterwards, blaming myself. Because I didn't have the confidence to make the decision to keep my baby from the start, because I even entertained thoughts of abortion and let him drive me to that car park, I believed I had somehow been struck down by a higher power. For not valuing the chance I had been given I had it taken away from me. Karma, I decided.

Seb and I were not the same afterwards. I resented him for not having the balls to want the baby and go ahead regardless;

I blamed him as well for me losing the baby. I was good at closing my heart by now, walking away from everything I knew and not looking back. I wanted so badly for him to commit now but, again, he was too frightened of cutting ties with his family. The baby was a path he was clearly too scared to go down. I knew there was nowhere else for me to go but out the door. I wanted a family, he was too scared to give me that.

Eventually I walked away for good. In my mind I thought 'I will come back one day', when Seb was more of a man and could face up to his parents, be able to make a decision without their agreement.

Seb was the love of my life. I still loved him but I had to move on. Both I and Georgia, who was getting older, needed security and he couldn't give it to us.

Seb would often sit outside my house in his car or turn up at my house or at work begging to talk to me. I wouldn't see him and I cut him off cold, changing my number so he couldn't call me anymore. It broke my heart to be so cold and cruel to him but I knew I had to try and move on, otherwise I'd be going round in circles.

CHAPTER SIX

The Making of Frankenstein's Monster

LOVE WASN'T FOR me, I was unlucky in that too. I decided instead to focus on my career. Although I had not been modelling long I was doing well, but I knew I wasn't the prettiest girl in the world. Statistics say that better looking people get better jobs, have better relationships and, therefore, have better lives. Surely my efforts for beauty were just? So I decided I really needed to work on being better, on being perfect. That way I'd get even more work, and maybe find a new man who could fulfil my dream of a family and be a father for Georgia.

My nose seemed a good start as it didn't look like a model's nose. I decided to go for a nose job and went for a consultation with a plastic surgeon based in Sussex I found through an advert in the local paper. My nose didn't actually offend me but I knew I could be prettier. The surgeon told me he could 'thin my bulbous nose'. Bulbous nose? I didn't even know I had a bulbous nose! I just knew I didn't look like Gisele Bündchen or Cindy Crawford – or, most importantly, Barbie – so that obviously needed to change.

In hindsight all I needed was for him to tell me I was beautiful and that shading with make-up could do wonders for my nose. He could have said, 'Actually, if I work on your nose you may not be able to breathe out of it, you won't have a better nose, just a different nose and the nose you have got is pretty good. On photos you can shade to make it look slimmer. You're perfect just as you are.'

Instead he smiled sympathetically whilst examining my nose. He sank back into his chair, demanding authority with his body language and pauses of silence and leaving me to fill them in with nervous laughter and explanations as to why I needed to have a better nose.

He declared after his silence, 'Yes, we can do something about the bulbous nose. We can thin it, ever so slightly, on the tip. It is a very simple operation and can be a day case.'

'Day case, what's that?'

'You won't need to stay the night. We'll put you to sleep but you'll be home by the evening. Now you know the dangers, don't you? There's always a very small chance of infection or of you not being happy with the results but, in your case, I don't think there will be a problem.'

'No, no, no problem,' I answered obediently. This man held the key to me being pretty. I had to keep him happy.

So that was it. I checked in, had my nose job and went home, which was now a small bedsit. I sat staring in the mirror, in which I could see two black eyes forming and a bandage across my face, through which I could vaguely see the outline of the nose. It still looked 'bulbous', just not as cute. I hated it, I decided.

I phoned the nurses the next day, explaining I didn't like my new nose. They told me it was swollen; I should not worry about the result for at least three months and that the final result would take a year!

I phoned the day after and the day after. Every day I grew to hate my new nose more. I didn't look like Barbie at all, I just looked like a worse version of me. I demanded to speak to the surgeon but I didn't get to talk to him. I just kept getting patronising nurses talking to me like a child, telling me it was 'too early to tell'.

'Damn you, I know my own mind and I know my own face, it's not too early to tell that I hate my nose *now*!'

Once the bandages came off I hated my nose even more. It was slimmer but it was uglier. It turned out the 'bulbous' nose gave me a cute baby face, a Marilyn Monroe, childlike face, and it suited me. This nose didn't. It made my eyes look all wrong; it put my whole face out of sync. What had I done?

No one told me, 'Your face is in harmony, if you change one thing you change the harmony of your whole face. So when you change your "bulbous" nose, for instance, which, by the way, may be bulbous but makes you look cute and works with your other features, suddenly the rest of your features are disharmonious.'

I did get to see the surgeon but he entered and exited very quickly. He wasn't interested in my unhappiness and put it down to me making my mind up too soon that my nose was still swollen. He brushed me off just like the nurses had, saying it was 'too early to tell' and that I should 'give it a year'.

I wasn't about to go round with my terrible deformed nose for a year so after three months, when the supposed swelling had gone down, I found another surgeon. This time I went to a surgeon promoted by the plastic surgery pioneer Cindy Jackson. When I first rang, I talked for a long time with his secretary for some reason. After that I got to talk to the surgeon himself, who told me I could visit him for a consultation at his house in the countryside.

I drove for hours to see this man, who I felt so hopeful about. I thought he would be the one to finally bring me my dream.

The surgeon reminded me of Einstein. I called him 'Mr Fix-It'. He had curly, crazy hair, buck teeth stained from his pipe smoking, and thick fingers. His office was surrounded by amazing drawings he said he had produced. He said, 'Make sure your plastic surgeon is an artist', because that is essentially what they were doing, drawing on you and sculpting you.

It was weird. I was in his house but he had a table with tools, as if he could operate from his home. The wife was around somewhere.

This eccentric surgeon, Mr Fix-It, spoke to me softly, telling me I was young, too young for surgery but he could see why I needed it. He showed me 'before and after' pictures of ugly ducklings turned into swans. I told him I wasn't happy with my nose. He examined my face and said it was a bad nose job which needed revision. He pulled out a marker pen and drew on my nose before taking a Polaroid picture and showing me how my nose would look with the bone shaved by using his pen to shade away areas. It did look a lot better: I was sold.

He explained it was a lot cheaper to have more than one op at a time: that was what most of his patients did, to save money. He asked me, in his creepy but soft and caring manner, did I have any other concerns?

I looked at this seemingly caring man. He could help me. I thought for a moment: what else bothered me?

'Well, I don't like the scar across my face. Or my last boob job. I think they could be better, I'd like them bigger.'

First he looked at my face, breathing heavily through his hairy nostrils, peering down on me through his spectacles. Mr Fix-It paused before reclining back on his chair and declaring, 'Yes, you need full face dermabrasion which is a wire brush which takes off the first layers of the skin, a bit like when you graze your knee but deeper, which will certainly help the scar and the sun damage. Stay away from the sun beds, my dear, nothing will age you worse.'

Reassuringly, he proceeded. 'My dear, slip your top off and I'll have a look at your breasts.'

That was nice of him, I thought. This man could fix everything, I could tell. So, dutifully, I slipped my top off. He stayed in the room, watching me carefully unbutton my blouse. I sat there, vulnerable and topless, as he examined my breasts.

'Oh yes, I can see, they need a revision too. They are too far apart and could do with being a few sizes bigger and you need "tear drop", you're far too slim for "round".'

He prodded my breasts, disapproving. I didn't realise they were quite that bad! It was clear they needed changing immediately. After hearing the expert tell me how terrible they were I decided then and there they needed changing straight away.

'What do you do, my dear?' he asked, his voice full of care.

'I'm a model,' I explained naïvely.

'This is a financial commitment. If you want to look like *that*', he said, pointing to one of the 'after' pictures of the 'before and after' album, 'then you need to commit to it.'

I wasn't quite sure what that meant but I knew I was very committed to not being Sarah Howes anymore and this guy could make me look like Barbie. I would do or say anything.

'Yes, I am very committed.'

'Good,' he said, touching my knee and beaming a slimy smile. 'I can make you like a little gorgeous doll, my dear.' His eyes scanned all over me, obviously excited. This was music to my ears.

Mr Fix-It scribbled down 'deals' to make it clear I was saving money by having the operations together. I told him I wasn't sure I had that much cash but he said he wanted to help me. He asked me how much I could afford and negotiated from there. It seemed weird haggling for tits, dermabrasion and a new nose but every penny counted. After all, it was coming out of money saved for Georgia, but I had to have it. Without the surgery no one would want me and she would never have a father. Maybe with better boobs, face and nose I would finally meet Mr Right.

He smiled, caringly but slimily. 'Talk to my secretary for dates.' He whispered, 'Don't worry, we will fix you,' smiling excitedly at me as I was on my way out. He walked with me then opened my car door for me.

That was what I wanted to hear. Someone was willing to 'fix me' because I was definitely broken. That made my mind up. Someone finally understood the pain I felt from not being beautiful enough and was, at last, going to help.

I had found my home.

I was not hesitant booking the surgery; it did seem like a lot of money. I knew it could be saved for a house for Georgia but I decided it was a good investment. After all, on the aeroplanes they always tell you in an emergency to put your own gas mask on before helping others. That is exactly what I had to do.

I was far more excited this time than at my previous surgeries. I chatted away to the nurses, one of whom recognised me from the papers. I didn't fear having an operation anymore or dying from the surgery, I was quickly getting used to undergoing procedures. I loved the feeling of the injection that put me to sleep and, after all, the anaesthetists told me it was safer than crossing the road. That's fine then. What could possibly go wrong?

I woke up in a lot more pain than before. The results were nothing less than shocking. My face was red raw, like when you graze your knee, and was covered in what looked like cling-film. I felt that my nose, though still heavily bandaged, was drastically smaller. My boobs were visibly bigger but, again, still bandaged.

It crossed my mind: 'Oh God, what have I done to myself? Have I gone too far? What will my mum say when she sees her little girl, who she brought into the world, like this?' I knew I was chipping away at my mum's heart with every surgery. She would tell me, 'You were a perfect little girl, so pretty, why do you keep doing this to yourself?' Like a stubborn teenager, I would storm off in denial.

The nurses reassured me when I asked if everything had gone okay: 'You look beautiful.'

A handheld mirror was lifted to my face. I hadn't banked on my face looking so horrific. I had to go my mum's home like this! My daughter Georgia would see me! They did not even know I was having surgery. You see, Georgia was still living with my parents and I was staying there whenever I could. I did not want to leave her, no matter what. Having given up the bedsit, I was staying with friends for the rest of the time but in my condition the only place I could go was to my mum, and of course I was desperate to see Georgia.

I managed to untie my drips and tubes and drag them all to the bathroom so I could have a good look at everything. I sat for 45 minutes looking at the new me. I certainly did not recognise the girl in the mirror, imagining beyond the bandages, the swelling and the red bloody rawness a different girl completely. This was a drastic change. When my mind wandered to what the hell I was doing to my young self I thought of the nurse saying I looked beautiful and I kept hold of that. I was not even sure what beauty was anymore or what I was hoping to achieve. Of course, in the state I was in I certainly was not beautiful. I was sore, puffed-up and bruised, but maybe, just maybe, this surgeon had the key. Once all the injuries were healed I finally would be pretty, my luck would change and everything I ever dreamed of would be on its way...

Mr Fix-It came in soon after. I was still in a daze as he held my hand, explaining that he took quite a lot of my nose off. Smiling, he said, 'Your skin is going to be as young as a baby's bottom, I went quite deep.'

Good to hear, although neither were my initial wishes. Hey, I must have needed it! Mr Fix-It said, 'Your breasts went better than expected and look great.' He said I would be really happy, whilst exhaling his stale cigar and pipe smoke breath over me, his face way too close.

Mr Fix-It was so reassuring and happy with his work that it made me feel like it didn't matter my nose was maybe too small now or my face may be permanently scarred or even that my huge breast implants might be too big. Obviously that was all in my mind. He was an expert, after all, and was sure I was fixed so I felt this was 'money well spent'. Finally I could start the next chapter of my life and move on from my reinvention of Alicia Douvall. She was complete... or so I thought.

I had made myself believe in him. I didn't even mind his creepy ways or him holding onto my hand a tad too long to be friendly or caring. This man had fixed me: smelly breath or not, he was my hero.

Mr Fix-It was to become a fixture in my life for a very long time and was maybe another part of the reason for my self-destruction but like any addict I needed a good dealer, and with him I had found one.

Mr Fix-It became my ally: I needed him, and relied on him. It soon became less and less about plastic surgery. I found myself driving to his house almost every week. Sometimes I would call him in the middle of the night to ask him to help me with my 'awful nose' or 'thin lips'. I'd tell him I needed to come in the next day urgently and most times he would accommodate me. He fed my addiction and also soothed my insecurities. He would give me prescriptions for things I knew he was not allowed to but, as I found out later on in life, I seemed to be able to persuade many doctors and surgeons to give me pretty much what I wanted when I wanted it, something that would later work against me.

Mr Fix-It made it clear early on that I shouldn't go to other surgeons and that I was an ongoing project and his vision needed only his scalpel as other surgeons could easily ruin his work. What did Mr Fix-It get out of it? He never charged me for consultations and his hands were wandering. I guess with me he had found a living woman to sculpt just how he pleased.

At the start of my relationship with Mr Fix-It we were both happy but, like a lot of relationships, things can turn sour, very sour. We were both, it seems, self-destructive and did not know when to stop.

After the first surgery, as far as I was concerned I was fixed and I could get on with my life but for Mr Fix-It it wasn't over... it was just the beginning.

CHAPTER SEVEN

'Jordan Ruined My Life'

AFTER THE SURGERY I took a taxi back to Mum's, having pretended to the surgeon that I had a friend to pick me up. Early on I had learnt to be secretive about my guilty pleasure.

Still, I realised I hadn't thought things through this time. I couldn't work or even go out with such a horrific face. I would again be dependent on my already overworked mother, who also cared for Georgia.

I saw Mum's face when I walked in the door. It was a mixture of horror and disappointment.

'What have you done now?'

'Nothing,' I said. 'Just some revision on my scar, it was recommended.'

Mum replied, 'Are you sure? You have a bandage across your nose.'

I was never sure if Mum really was naïve or was only acting but I went for the former.

'Just to help with the dermabrasion,' I said, whilst quickly exiting. I went to find Georgia, who was hiding.

I started to hear Georgia crying. 'What's wrong?' I asked, walking towards the curtain she hid behind. She ran away from me again, screaming with fear.

This time she ran to my mother, crying. She said, 'Mummy is a monster!'

Mum looked at me, sunken. 'Look what you have done!'

'Georgia, don't be silly. Come and give me a hug.' But she was too frightened. It was three days before my own daughter would go near me. She wouldn't even eat with me. Mum did end up having to look after me too, as I couldn't go out like that. I think this was my first real feeling of guilt for my actions.

My skin, although red as a beetroot, did seem smoother and my scar looked less angry and obvious. The recovery wasn't easy, though: full-face dermabrasion meant I could not leave the house for two weeks. I could only drink through a straw, and eat foods like soup, and I did look like a monster. My nose job had given me black eyes so swollen I could not see out of them for days; my boobs were quite painful too.

After ten days, finally, the bandages were off. I still took the painkillers but there really wasn't much pain. I had two black eyes and my face was red, but I was still getting booked for work and I was eager to return to making money again so I took the work anyway. I would turn up to shoots with a bruised and puffed-up face. The poor make-up artists had to work miracles to hide the black circles, the redness and my fragile, swollen features.

After about two months, however, I could start to see results. I didn't look like me at all anymore. Most people might not have liked this but it was exactly what I wanted. For once, I was happy with the result. My boobs did look great and my nose, though far too small, was back to being how it was before: the cute, ski-slope nose that I originally had, just a smaller version of it. Oh, and it turned out I couldn't breathe through my nose anymore, but I figured that was a small price to pay for beauty.

My modelling career was going well by now, despite my destructive behaviour, but I didn't feel like Page Three was particularly rewarding. It didn't seem like an achievement to be featured there. After all, I just had to stand there with my top off looking confused and blank, then someone would airbrush my imperfections away. It wasn't really you. They say modelling is an art in itself but it didn't feel like it needed much talent on my part. I wanted more than to be a 'good glamour model'. Page Three wasn't enough anymore: I needed to be on every other page of the paper.

The photographer Jenny Savage may not have liked my tan but she liked my changing face even less. Still, the advice I had heard her give the other model resonated with me. I did need to be noticed.

By now I had a small basement studio apartment in Knightsbridge where I stayed when I was in London. The long journeys to Sussex on two hours' sleep were getting to me so I needed a base in London. Georgia was still living with my parents. I had some free time in between indulging my fast-growing obsession, I made the strategic move of regularly going to night clubs, a glamour model's stomping ground where paparazzi would stand outside in the hope of catching a drunken female flashing their boobs or getting into a car in an undignified manner. Of course I soon learnt to lose the lady in me and unashamedly grab those tacky headlines. I was working on the premise that all press was good press, which it turns out in the long run is not true...

It was actually at the Sanderson Bar in Fitzrovia that I met a tall, handsome, athletic sportsman. Let's call him 'Mr Athletic': a dashing man, with women all around him, trying to edge their way in with him. It looked like he had a sparkling bucket of champagne beside him, which, to me, was still only for the rich. I hadn't seen much champagne in my lifetime, needless to say.

I was with a friend and we were enjoying ourselves, dancing and laughing, when my friend nudged me. She told me that the tall, athletic man with girls swooning around him was looking at us and beckoning us over. After Italy, I was not about to go up to any man who waved for me to come. I had developed a slight distaste for men after seeing them at their worst, which probably left me with an air of 'take it or leave it'. I wasn't bothered about meeting him, although I found him interesting. I was having a great time with my friend and had no reason to join those other women.

Then two glasses of champagne were sent over, which we accepted, nodding our heads and raising our glasses to Mr Athletic to say cheers. He smiled a gleaming smile then walked towards us with his friend.

Mr Athletic seemed really friendly and gentlemanly, not like the boys where I had come from. This guy was different. He asked me why I didn't have a boyfriend. 'God, if only he knew,' I thought to myself.

We talked all evening; his charm overwhelmed me. He flattered me, complimenting everything from my hair to my clothes. He said I was beautiful and sexy and asked me if I knew who he was. I didn't have a clue and said, 'No.' He didn't mind and told me he played football for Manchester United. I didn't know much about football and had never got into the habit of watching TV. (At home, the living room had been a potential battleground, so best left alone.)

When the club was closing, Mr Athletic got me a car, the poshest car I'd ever been in, with a bottle of water in the back, which I took home.

I felt like a queen. No one had treated me like this before, so when he gave me his number and told me he'd like to take me out I was not going to say no.

The next date was at a lovely restaurant. It was there that I saw how famous Mr Athletic really was. People constantly asked him for autographs and patted him on the back to praise him or just to say hello.

I didn't care about any of that, I was just glad to be with a man who treated me well and thought I was pretty. He would look at my outfit and say, 'Wow, you look stunning.' What girl doesn't want to hear that?

Mr Athletic really was a true gentleman. It felt like a big sigh of relief when I walked out with him, his protective arm around me and his smiling face beaming at me. It seemed like his love was genuine, as was the chemistry that we shared. We were both young, so we jumped headfirst into a relationship.

I started visiting him in Manchester, where he lived a few doors down from David Beckham. We would drive past the paparazzi camped outside David Beckham's house, with their fold-out chairs and flasks, and wave hello. The paps left us alone, relatively speaking. I wasn't really known at this stage and I was happy for it to stay that way whilst I was with Mr Athletic.

I was happy to be Mr Athletic's girl, who he could talk to about his ups and downs and hold his coat whilst he got his picture taken. He was the star and I was happy to let him shine. As long as he loved me, that was all I ever wanted for my life.

We would watch the Discovery Channel together and really learn about things, like wildlife. Neither of us was greatly educated but we had a thirst for knowledge. Mr Athletic was a very intelligent man in his own way, with an inquisitive mind, which I loved about him.

We would play football together indoors. Mr Athletic taught me the basics and encouraged me, saying I was really good at the game. He built me up instead of putting me down and, as a result, I was completely in love with him.

My visits to Mr Athletic's house and staying together in London were getting more frequent. I had practically moved in with him and I was looking forward to the day Georgia could be there too. We could be one big happy family. I really believed I had found my true love, my one and only. My struggle was over. I had found my soulmate, someone who loved me and who I loved. Simple.

Eight months into dating Mr Athletic, with wining, dining and amazing sex, I noticed his attention was waning. He wasn't acting like his usual self.

One Saturday, we had arranged to meet some of his friends, to go out to a restaurant together and then onto a club, but

I had got sick. I was disappointed but there was no way I could go out. I was vomiting and had a high temperature. Mr Athletic decided to go out anyway, which was fine, I didn't mind.

The next day a friend phoned me to tell me Mr Athletic was two-timing me with a model called 'Jordan'. I had heard of her: she was a brash topless model who was doing very well in the glamour modelling world. In fact, she was the best. Jordan wasn't my cup of tea and I didn't think she would be Mr Athletic's type either, so I choose not to believe it.

Then the next day I saw them in the newspaper together. My heart sank. I prayed it was all a big mistake. I was shocked, and my mind manic, as I tried to dial Mr Athletic's number – struggling to even tap the numbers in as I was shaking so much. I asked him, as calmly as any girl could in that situation, what the hell he was playing at. Mr Athletic told me it wasn't true. I remember his words were: 'I would not go near her,' adding, 'Everyone knows she's the local bicycle'. So I felt reassured. Surely what he was saying was true: after all, who would say something so nasty about a girl they were seeing?

Friends kept trying to convince me he was cheating on me. I did not believe it. How could the man that I loved so much and so dearly hurt me so badly? Worse still, how could he turn out to be nothing like the man I thought he was? Surely the love of my life was not a cheater or a liar?

Another article came out, this time with him and Jordan in Cannes holding hands. There was no denying it – Mr Athletic was lying to me.

My friends had been right. This time though, one friend – let's call her 'Pornie', as she later went on to do hardcore porn

– said, 'My friend at the *News of the World* wants to talk to you about what happened.'

I rarely picked newspapers up unless I thought there would be a picture of me modelling in them, and even then I didn't like to see myself in print as I was always so disappointed with my image. I had always presumed, being dyslexic and a logical thinker to a fault, that the *News of the World* was what its name said it was: a newspaper that covered news from all around the world. I was confused as to why a paper like that would be interested in Mr Athletic. I knew he was famous and a big Man U player but I didn't think he was newsworthy worldwide, especially not when the news was just that he had cheated on someone.

I got an unexpected phone call a matter of hours after the conversation with my friend. It was from the journalist Jules Stenson. I was still crying and trying to process the whole thing. Jules sounded very sympathetic.

Looking back, I was naïve. I did not understand the game I was about to play. Jules offered to meet me for coffee and just chat. He claimed he knew Mr Athletic and I didn't see any harm in the meeting. Besides, I could do with a shoulder to cry on.

Jules told me that the *News of the World* would pay good money to hear my side of the story. The money sounded nice but I was never going to sell a story on Mr Athletic. I just wanted my stability, love and dream of a family home back and to mend the pieces he had shattered.

Jules appeared caring and listened intently to me whilst I poured my heart out; he even bought me lunch which I munched through whilst I talked. In hindsight, he didn't seem that bothered about my feelings. He kept asking random questions, like where did we have sex, what position and in what type of bed.

I brushed it off. 'I never saw it coming, I love him so much. What? What bed? Well, we have a water bed,' and that would be it.

I had dug myself a hole I would never get out of.

Jules asked if I minded him taping a phone conversation with Mr Athletic. We planned to see each other again and had not officially finished being a couple: as far as Mr Athletic was concerned we were still together, but after what I now understand to have been an interview – not that I realised it at the time – we didn't meet again. I went along with Jules' suggestion and phoned Mr Athletic, arranging to meet up at some point. He was still denying the Jordan thing and trying to string me along. Jules said I deserved better, that Mr Athletic was lying and I should not stand for it. He said he would always be a cheater.

When I made that call Jules got the evidence he needed. He asked me to do a shoot but I didn't want to. I said I had changed my mind and decided it wasn't a good idea to speak to the press. Jules said it was too late. He was right. The fact I didn't do the photoshoot meant nothing; they had enough stock modelling photos, which they used.

I had never sought revenge before but it did make me feel slightly better, once the initial shock of what I had done had worn off, to get the last kick in. Two wrongs don't make a right but I was tired of getting beaten down by men, so it was kind of nice to do the beating for once.

That Saturday, the evening before the article, I will never forget. Mr Athletic phoned from the locker room. He was devastated that I would do such a thing to him. He said he could not even speak to me before passing me on to his team mates, who one by one asked why I went to the papers and told me what a big mistake I had made.

I didn't sleep much that night; I was feeling guilty and ashamed. I woke up to texts coming into my phone. I switched it off immediately. I knew the story had been published.

I rushed to the newsagent and I was flabbergasted and appalled to see I was on the front page of the newspaper with Jordan. She was one side and I was on the other.

I opened the double-page spread, which read like a Jilly Cooper book. The headline was about the water bed and the article said that I was Mr Athletic's long-term girlfriend, who he had hidden away. By a stroke of bad, or good, luck the paper had found one of my modelling shoots with me wearing gold hot pants and one of Jordan wearing the same. They compared us and it was brutal. I was so ashamed: I didn't want to acknowledge this girl Jordan, let alone be compared to her; the pain of being cheated on was made a whole lot worse by the girl being famous. I was forced to stare right at her. At the same time, this article seemed to launch my career and make me a household name.

I bought as many newspapers as I could and turned the ones I could not buy face down. I figured the fewer people that saw the front page the better. It was shameful and I knew my parents would go mad.

Funnily enough, my parents did not even acknowledge the newspaper article. I'm not sure if it was through sheer embarrassment or if they failed to notice it. I felt bad for my dad; the other guys in the car industry would all have known what his daughter was up to.

My dirty laundry was there for all to see. Mr Athletic was truly out of my life now and I had now got myself a name: the girl whose boyfriend had been taken by Jordan. I felt ashamed and degraded for what I had said. I discovered that what I had done by giving an interview was called 'a kiss and tell'. This was a cardinal sin, breaching the code of honour that said you should never give away private secrets.

Why was I even worried about this code of honour? It had prevented me from getting justice when I had been glassed in the face by the girls in the pub, because 'you don't inform on people'. I was tired of the kids from my home town with their street code. I wasn't going to abide by any code anymore. What if you broke the rules? What would happen? So I lose a guy that cheated on me? So what if I was publicly shamed? The only people whose opinions I cared about had already seen me embarrassed when Mr Athletic was snapped holding hands with Jordan.

I don't think Jordan and Mr Athletic's relationship lasted long. It seems I had a lucky escape.

Well, I had done it, it was too late. I had stuck up for myself and ratted him out, kissed and told and I chose not to care. I decided not to mope around and feel sorry for myself. I thought the press could be a useful tool.

After the break up with Mr Athletic, I had seen that the grass was no greener on the other side. Seb had never left my mind and I wanted him back. I wanted to be with my love and, after two years, I called him.

I was excited and had little doubt that Seb would be pleased to hear from me. During the first eighteen months after we split I would often see him drive past my house. In the last six months, however, he had stopped, so I knew there was a chance that he could have met someone else, but I was willing to take the chance. I was sure that he was the love of my life.

I called Seb's parents' company, bracing myself for abuse, in case the phone was answered by one of his family, and asked for Seb. The conversation went:

'Can I speak to Seb, please?'

A secretary had picked up the phone. 'Who is this?'

'Alicia.'

'Do you not know?'

'Know what?' Oh God, I thought, here it comes. He is now married with two kids.

'He... He died six months ago. I'm sorry to give you this news.' Her voice saddened.

I choked up, was lost for words and felt utterly distraught. 'How?'

'Heart. Sorry, I have to go now.' She was trying not to break down, and that was it.

I sat in shock. I could not accept that Seb had died. I even applied for his death certificate to try and get more answers, partly because I didn't believe life could be so cruel. It read that he had died through 'misadventure'.

I discovered that Seb had died near Cheltenham, I presume at the races. I remember him telling me on one occasion when he was trying to get me back that a friend had introduced him to cocaine. Seb was a man who enjoyed things to excess. He would drink a bottle of champagne for lunch and still seem sober. I thought at the time that cocaine would be a disaster for him and told him to stop. From the death certificate I presume he didn't. I would like to punch the person who introduced Seb to cocaine.

Even now I don't think a day goes by without me thinking about Seb. He was the one that got away. I often think that maybe we have one love of our lives and he was mine. I also think about the baby I lost. If only I had been more careful maybe I would have kept Seb's baby and perhaps he would still be alive. I wonder if he would have chosen a different path if he had a family. I know you shouldn't regret or think of maybes, and friends say the outcome would always have been the same. He was obviously troubled and probably had a weak heart which was undetected, and the cocaine put his body under too much strain.

But I can't help thinking of the love that I lost. Seb was my chance at a normal life. Afterwards, my life would go in a completely different direction to the one I had dreamed of and it would be far from normal. I think when Seb died he took a part of me with him. I decided that he was my family, my man, the love of my life, and now I had to manage without him in this harsh world in which only he made me feel safe and happy. I am convinced that I was the only one that made him feel safe and happy too.

We loved each other so much; apart, we were both lost, self-destructive and caused an awful mess. But I had reached out to him too late and I should never have left.

From now on I decided I was not going to take any prisoners. I was done with love for good this time. I would be the player, the user and the heartbreaker. My faith in love had gone and I decided to quit it forever. I was done with romance: the newspaper story about Mr Athletic and me was the start of a new direction.

Alicia Douvall wasn't going to be anyone's doormat anymore. My kindness was seen as weakness, it really didn't get me anywhere, so I was bolting the doors. My heart was closed.

Jules Stenson did pay me for the article and when the cheque came though I knew exactly what I would spend it on: plastic surgery. The way to heal a broken heart, for me at least, was to have more surgery. It had quickly become my fix.

So off I went to Mr Fix-It and announced to him that my boobs just were not big enough and my nose needed thinning. He agreed but was still firmly in the driving seat. He started planting a new seed in my head: that my lips and eyes could be better.

Going to see him was like having therapy and visiting the school headmaster at the same time. You knew you had to get your ideas signed off and approved. If they weren't he would convince me that actually I did not need that, explaining in a logical scientific way that made sense to me why it wouldn't work and get me closer to my Barbie dream: he was fully on board with helping me with that, but right now I hadn't reached that stage. Mr Fix-It was eager to work on me. He was very attentive and I was fast becoming even more reliant on him, both mentally and emotionally.

Whilst examining my breasts, he kissed one, before he told me to get dressed. I thought this was shocking but accepted it as I thought he was a good surgeon and I certainly did not want to complain and put him off working on me again. I knew I was his special project and I liked the way he got excited to work on me. I enjoyed his compliments and the hope he gave me that I could become perfect in time.

Mr Fix-It worked out a discount again, whispering to me: 'Don't tell anyone, it's our little secret,' as he kissed my hand. 'Goodbye,' he said, staring deep into my eyes. Awkwardly I smiled, then off I went to make the booking with his secretary. I managed to get the surgery five days later.

This time my chest would go from 28D to 28EE, with big, teardrop-shaped boobs. My nose would also be shaved just a little more to make it narrower.

The surgery was getting easier and easier; it was almost like going to the hairdressers for me. Again, the procedures went well. My boobs felt a lot bigger and my nose felt narrower.

Mr Fix-It was becoming more confident around me. His hands started to wander more. The next day when he did his rounds to see patients he came in, examined my boobs, lingering too long on them and again kissing them, then my nose, and told me I was looking even younger. He said again how great the surgery went and how cute I was, this time adding, 'You're my special little girl.' He perched on my bed and whispered how 'gorgeous and utterly edible' I was.

I was like a proud student: he drew and sculpted on me and I got to be beautiful and praised for it, just what I needed. I was just what *he* needed too, because this was a man of extremes, who wanted to sail close to the wind. We were the perfect pair to walk together down the road to destruction.

I had been perfectly happy with myself before Mr Athletic did his thing, which just let me know that I was still ugly. Mr Fix-It had been there all the time, waiting with his knife. I wasn't addicted to the surgery yet but I didn't have a clear plan of what or how I wanted to look anymore. I just needed someone to make things better and this to me seemed the logical way. If I became beautiful and perfect I would not be cheated on again or lied to. I could run the show and not be used by men.

CHAPTER EIGHT

About-Face

OUT OF THE blue one day I had a very strange phone call from a man who claimed to know an ex-boyfriend of mine. He said we had something in common: we had both been cheated on. He asked me to meet for a coffee at a Costa near to where I lived. I didn't have anything to lose and was inquisitive, so I met him. I was late, as the night before there had been heavy rain and my basement flat had flooded. My phone had been on the floor so had got wet. As a result I didn't have a mobile and turned up at Costa half expecting him not to be there.

A slim, 5'8", dark-haired, goofy man with glasses and sharp cheekbones grabbed me as I walked in the door. His smile beamed at me and immediately I felt his friendliness.

We sat together whilst he offered me coffee and 'anything I wanted'. I asked for a chocolate croissant, so he came back with two chocolate croissants and nearly the entire cake collection. He said the others looked so good he thought I might want to take a bite from them too. This guy was eccentric, that was for sure.

He seemed to know a lot about me already from friends and said he had followed my Page Three career. Most importantly, he was friendly and sympathetic to me after the trauma of my break-up with Mr Athletic.

We chatted away and then he asked me for a date. I explained about the flood in my flat and the problem with my mobile to excuse my lateness. He said he needed to get me a new phone straightaway and marched me off to the nearest Vodafone shop. He signed himself up for a contract and gave me the phone. I could not believe this relative stranger had just handed me a phone and was going to pick up the bill. It was confusing, as I didn't really understand why he was being so generous.

On the second date, we dined at a beautiful Italian restaurant. He smoked a pipe but the smell of stale pipe smoke on his breath was weirdly comforting. I had begun to associate it with happiness because of Mr Fix-It.

Let's call this guy 'Sugardaddy', for reasons I will soon explain. He was a lot older than me, in his mid-thirties; he was kind and treated me like a princess. He was not my usual type but that hadn't panned out for me so far. Maybe it was time to try something new.

When we went back to his place, Sugardaddy claimed to be instantly in love with me. He went down on one knee and said, 'Please love me. I'll give you everything you ever dreamed of.' Then he burst into tears, in an Oscar award-winning moment.

He was so keen to be generous to me. I never had anyone give me anything, I wasn't sure why he acted like this but I had heard that giving makes people happy so I went with it, as it certainly made me feel good too.

I knew I couldn't go further with him, as I hadn't told him about Georgia. In my experience men run a mile when you tell them you have a kid. By the third date, Sugardaddy picked me up from my flat. Again, we wined and dined. Things were perfect – except I still didn't really fancy him and hadn't told him about Georgia.

I had to tell him so over our dinner I sheepishly said, 'So, by the way, I have a daughter. She's five years old. She lives with my mum and dad. I wish I had her with me but they won't let me, probably 'cos I'm a hot mess.'

Sugardaddy choked on his food and blinked several times. 'I had no idea. Give me some time to process this.'

I walked away thinking that would be the last I would hear from him. How nice it was to meet such a unique man, I thought, to taste what it would be like to have someone adore you. This, I had accepted by now, wasn't my life. I had resigned myself to being forever single.

Instead I got a call the next evening inviting me to come over to his house. Waiting for me was an over-excited man. He had read dozens of books with titles like *How to Raise Children*, *Bringing Children up with Self-Esteem*, and more.

Sugardaddy embraced the idea of me having a child, he'd never dated a girl with a child before, and was actually excited to meet her. He told me how he had planned lots of trips, to Thorpe Park, restaurants and castles, when I was ready to introduce him to her. He then asked, 'Where is she?'

I was overwhelmed by how kind one man could be about my child, who had been so cruelly rejected by her own father. It's true what they say: men fall in love at first sight; women take longer, they need to feel it in their heart.

I burst into tears. 'She's with my mum and dad. It's terrible, I miss her every day. Not a day goes by when I don't wish she wasn't with me. My mum and dad aren't enjoying the best relationship at the moment, so it's not a great environment for her either. They said I can take her when I have my own place and stability.'

'Simple,' he announced. 'We'll get you your own place and stability.'

I was confused. Did he just say he would give me my own place and stability?

'Look for a house. I will give you a budget. Organise to take your daughter for good and introduce me to your parents.'

I was flabbergasted, confused and astonished. Surely this wasn't real? It was too good to be true. Knights in shining armour don't really exist, do they?

Sugardaddy was handing my life's dream to me on a plate, sorting out all my problems so easily. I had one issue, I still wasn't sure if I fancied him. What a dilemma: this man would give me my dream of having my daughter back with me but I wasn't sure if I even wanted to be with him.

I felt at this point I was at a moral crossroads. I would have to commit to living in this man's house, having him as my boyfriend and I wasn't sure if I could love him like he deserved to be loved. I was already falling for his kind heart, but wasn't chemistry more important? I wanted my daughter back more than anything but I was not about to sell my soul.

I phoned my mum to ask her advice. She said, 'Looks fade, a kind heart doesn't. Believe me, a man that is kind and loves you and has beauty on the inside is far more important than a man with beauty on the outside who you may fancy now. If he doesn't love you enough you will soon grow to hate and resent that man. Always,' she said, 'go for beauty on the inside.'

'Learn from my mistakes,' she added.

So there it was, I jumped in headfirst. I found a house and moved in under Sugardaddy's name. My phone was already in his name and he gave me an allowance, even a car. He said I could give up working nights in clubs for good so I wouldn't be tired in the day any more.

I had everything I had dreamed of, except for one thing. My parents were still making excuses as to why my beloved Georgia could not be with me.

So I asked Sugardaddy what to do. By now he was becoming my go-to man for everything, from whether I should have beans with my sausages to how to get my daughter back.

Thinking carefully, sucking on his pipe, he came up with a plan. 'Get my driver to take you to pick her up for the day and we will kidnap her. Just take her favourite toy and we will buy all new stuff of the rest.'

It was a crazy idea. 'I can't do that! My poor parents…'

'Do you want your daughter back or not?' he asked, seriously.

'Yes, more than anything,' I said, determined and sure.

'Then do as I say. Trust me, it's the only way. You will never get her back otherwise.' Deep down I knew he was right.

It was far from ideal but I wanted her back so much, my heart was broken without her. I knew my parents had fallen so deeply in love with her that they wouldn't give her back. I also knew they would never forgive me.

The journey to my parents' house in Sussex wasn't a pleasant one. As I looked out the window to green fields I thought how I was about to change everyone's world for good. I was strangely nervous: could I be the mother she deserved? I had fought so hard for this moment, would I ultimately fail being the mother I kept telling my mother I could be? But when I picked up Georgia and I saw her face I knew I was doing the right thing. My mum was fussing, telling me what time to be back. It hurt so badly to take Georgia away from her, the child she had so kindly taken on as her own. And now, too, I was going to leave Mum alone with my father. I wanted to take her too but she loved him and I respected that. I also felt so awful about my father, who also loved Georgia dearly but he wasn't in a good place with Mum. I knew this was right for Georgia but it was going to hurt them badly.

Georgia sat innocently in the back of the car, thinking she was going on a day out. She loved seeing her mum and missed me when I was away. A silent tear fell down my cheek, partly from fear, partly from joy and partly from sadness of the unknown. I hugged her and whispered, 'Everything's going to be okay now.'

I had a better life waiting for her. She wasn't going to be in the middle of arguments anymore. Sugardaddy had promised to put her in private school and to get her counselling for the trauma she had endured from not only the transition but also the intense arguments that were now building between my mum and dad, who had discovered after years of marriage that they really didn't like each other after all.

Sugardaddy organised counselling for Georgia and various tests. She was behind with school and very quiet. She was also wetting the bed a lot. We put it down to the trauma she had been through.

The counsellor and educators that tested her concluded that Georgia had self-confidence issues, which we had to build up. After various tests it turned out she was dyslexic, just like me.

We took her to various private schools in London but they all turned her down, as she was so far behind. Sugardaddy even offered to pay double to one school!

So I decided to home educate her, bringing in home tutors but, just as we made that decision, the Kensington Dyslexic Centre, who had helped us immensely, told us of a school for children with special needs, where there were four kids to each teacher. I didn't want to see Georgia as someone who was damaged but she was dyslexic and wasn't really talking at a six year-old level; neither could she read or write. So I was open to listening, and thank God I did.

In the meantime, Mum and Dad were on the phone constantly, threatening me, trying desperately for me to bring back Georgia, but, unexpectedly, when Sugardaddy talked to them they seemed to accept it. I knew I broke their hearts but I also think they loved Georgia enough to let her go and they knew it was now the right time to do that. They just had to have their hand forced to let her go. Even so, I didn't speak to my parents for years after that. I was a family with Sugardaddy and Georgia now.

I soon grew to love and adore Sugardaddy. I fancied him as time went on, just like my mum had said I would, because of his heart. It seemed love really could grow.

Sugardaddy gave me everything I dreamed of, as well as things I had never dreamed of. Georgia and I flew off in private jets on holiday to Thailand, Barbados, Europe and America, all paid for by Sugardaddy.

I wanted him to live with us but he kept us at a distance. Sugardaddy always cancelled holidays after he promised to come along with us, so we would end up going alone.

Now I had Georgia finally with me, I had become a clingy, over-protective mother. I savoured every second with her, I had her sleep in my room, even though she had a designer little girl's dream room of her own. We shopped in Harrods and Dolce & Gabbana for her; I sat patiently outside ballet and tennis classes, enjoying every moment of just watching her. On holiday I secretly, and admittedly selfishly, prayed she would not meet friends to play with so I could keep her to myself. I never left Georgia's side, and years later, in 2012, our strange relationship ended up the basis of a TV documentary called *Glamour Models, Mum and Me*.

Sugardaddy would take me on shopping trips where we would walk into Versace or Chanel and not think twice about spending £20,000 on clothes, handbags or shoes. But that never got me off like surgery did: what I really wanted was to have surgery and with Sugardaddy's deep wallet surgery was potentially unlimited.

I told Sugardaddy about my plans and dreams for surgery, not too much information as I didn't want to scare him off. I knew Georgia was sorted for education and a home so I potentially could now really indulge myself in my dearest, and darkest, desires.

First, he paid for me to get my hair blonder and for extensions costing thousands of pounds, and then he decided to allow me to have surgery. Sugardaddy loved bigger boobs anyway, so he eagerly agreed to that. His P.A. would pick up the bill; he wasn't really interested in the finer details.

What Sugardaddy didn't know was that I was about to have some more work done on my face. I went back to Mr Fix-It, who didn't like the idea of me having a boyfriend, especially someone who could control me in the same way that he did, but once we started talking about more surgery his face lit up like an excited child's. He suggested that to accompany my bigger breast implants I should have cheek implants and an eye-lift. I also convinced him to tweak my nose yet again.

I was so excited driving back from the consultation, this time in my BMW convertible that Sugardaddy had given me. I thought this surgery would be the one; this would be the last surgery and the operation to make me stunning. I would be complete. I would be the girl that other girls envied and would have it all. Looking back, I very nearly did have it all, but I was so self-destructive that I let it slip from my grasp.

I hadn't had a problem with my cheeks or eyes before but, now that I thought about it, I guess I was never the girl with sharp cheekbones and my eyelids did seem very heavy.

I yet again checked into the hospital, anticipating the procedures. By now I knew most the nurses and the fear and anxiety of having surgery had well and truly gone away completely. I would plan my week ahead and carry on the next day like the surgery was just a trip to the nail salon. I wouldn't stop to rest or recover.

After surgery in the recovery room I would always have a panic attack when I woke up, shivering and demanding drugs, before being put out again to wake up later more peacefully. When I came round properly I would be handed a hand mirror to inspect the work before the swelling had time to kick in.

My boobs this time were massive, a 28F. My cheek implants were not that noticeable so were slightly disappointing. My nose job was quite apparent and my eye-lift was drastic, so drastic that I could not close my eyelids properly. It seemed he had taken away too much skin.

When Mr Fix-It came in the next day to talk about his work he told me he made me look 'ten years old again'. I was never after looking ten years old but it seemed that was important to him and, after all, I was his canvas. The surgeon inspected his work like an artist with a sculpture.

Mr Fix-It had convinced me to have the work done on my eyes and cheeks and I went along with it, as I believed he would make me pretty. I remember asking: 'Do I look beautiful now?'

'Oh yes,' he would say, 'I would ravish you myself if I was younger. It's a lucky man who has you. You're my little doll, you look just perfect. Anyone would be insane not to love you.'

Perfect: my ultimate aim. He knew exactly what to say and would often whisper these things in a creepy way. They did make me feel good, though. But let's face it, they were slightly inappropriate.

Again he stroked my arm, but this time caressed my boobs and kissed them beyond anything professional.

'And these are just delightful,' he smiled like a mad toymaker working on his own doll.

When I went back for the check-up Mr Fix-It told me I looked great. He said I might want to make my lips poutier.

I was still bruised as I hadn't really recovered from the last surgery. Things hadn't settled down yet and I still wasn't sure if I was happy with the results, but I was learning fast to move onto the next surgery with haste.

I was concerned that I was not able to close my eyes properly. I also felt one eye was different to the other. However he reassured me that this would be temporary and that I had nothing to worry about.

It took about two years for my eyes to get close to closing properly and even then they still would not shut fully.

My boobs looked good, not great. I was very skinny with very little original breast tissue so huge silicone breast implants never looked natural, and the bigger I went the less natural they were to look at.

My cheek implants made a millimetre difference and weren't worth the thousands of pounds or the scars in my mouth where he inserted them. Mr Fix-It, though, insisted it was money well spent and that I really needed the extra cheek.

I hadn't thought about my lips, as they were always naturally quite full but, obviously, this man was a plastic surgeon, a professional, and knew far more than me. So I attentively listened.

'What I can do, my little treasure, is give you a little pout. Your delightful lips will be even more kissable.' I was still bruised and at his house for my week-after check-up from my last surgery.

I was excited: more kissable meant more lovable, so, yes, I was definitely up for it. 'How do I go about it?'

Mr Fix-It said to save me some money he could do it then and there with local anaesthetic. I agreed but felt worried as I lay down on the medical bed in his home office. When he injected me, I wasn't sure if this was correct but I trusted him by now. I was controlled by him and had become his project, his doll and his puppet. To me he had become my hope, my enabler and my darkest secret that I kept from Sugardaddy and everyone else.

The pain I felt whilst Mr Fix-It worked on my lips was excruciating. He had cut my lip open in four places, inserted what looked like the inside of a Biro pen into my lips to give a permanent pout then stitched them back together again. I could feel the warm blood drip down my neck past the numb areas.

When Mr Fix-It finished working on my lips he wiped away the blood. Whilst his face was closely examining his work he crossed the line and kissed my lips as I lay helplessly on his couch. I tasted the pipe smoke on his tongue as he forced it into my mouth. I was astonished. I had no idea that this was coming at such a vulnerable moment.

I got up, listening to him telling me how to clean my lips. After any inappropriate behaviour he would quietly switch it back to being professional or telling me off for asking for unnecessary surgery. He made it clear that he would be my enabler but at any time he could stop it.

I chose not to tell Sugardaddy who the other man in my life was. I guess I knew he would not like it. Also I liked that even though I now seemed to be controlled by two alpha males I was secretly the one in control.

A few days after the lip implants I was following the aftercare vigorously but it wasn't getting any better. In fact, my lips were swelling up more.

In this case time didn't heal, and day by day the lips became worse and worse. They started to ooze pus from the unhealed stitched edges, whilst the white implants – which I could see in my open wounds – were starting to push themselves out through my skin at both the left and right corners of my mouth. I felt terribly self-conscious, to say nothing of the pain I was in.

I went back to Mr Fix-It, who prescribed me painkillers and antibiotics. This still didn't heal the lips so after a week of worse and worse pain Mr Fix-It took the implants out. He removed them at his house with a pair of tweezers: he literally pulled them out. I felt them rip the muscles, tissues and scars that had grown around them. To say my eyes watered was an understatement.

Mr Fix-It said we needed to leave my lips for a few weeks and then he would put the implants back in again. Unbeknown to me at the time I would have to rely on implants for the rest of my life as their removal would make my lips look feathered, due to the scar tissue that had formed around them.

This was the start of things going wrong. Mr Fix-It would never tell me that there were any problems; he would reassure me it was just a blip. He would say that it was all fine and I would look gorgeous. I was addicted to his hopeful words, just like he was addicted to the money I gave him and to working on me as his project.

Sometimes, and this was one of those times, I would see the worry and disappointment on his face when an operation went wrong. Mr Fix-It was gambling and playing a very dangerous game with a young woman. Did guilt ever creep in? Did he ever worry that what he was doing was actually making me look worse? Did he really believe by hammering and carving away at my bones, blood and skin I really would look better?

It was times like this I saw a glimpse of uncertainty in my ever-so-reassuring puppet-master. It's a shame that same uncertainty did not creep into me. I just thought in this instance I had been unlucky. The fact my eyes didn't close and my nose was so small I could no longer breathe out of it was just a step on the route. A professional doctor who knew exactly what he was doing told me it was fine. I mean, doctors know everything, right? I was too naïve and young to understand that they didn't and that every cut was sending me further down a road from which I would never be able to return.

CHAPTER NINE

The Lure of Perfection

I WAS SPENDING MY days studying my face whilst Georgia was at school. I was still modelling but Sugardaddy had taken away the urgency to earn money so I had the opportunity to look at myself for hours every day. I know this wasn't the most productive use of my time or a humble choice.

By now I honestly could not say whether this was insane vanity or body dysmorphia. All I knew was that I didn't think I was pretty and that needed to be fixed. I wanted perfection and I couldn't see why I was so ugly so I stared into the mirror examining every inch. I had read every book I could on the scientific formula for beauty, like a mad professor measuring out the perfect quarters of my face as if to make it in proportion. I would get a tape measure out, measure the quarters of my face, stare at Barbie and work out how to be more like her. I would Sellotape my face back to give myself a makeshift facelift, even using gaffer tape round my head for a forehead lift and chin lift. This would often rip out half my hair on removal, but I didn't care, I liked fake hair anyway. My heart and stomach ached with the sadness I felt when I looked in that mirror; I would have anxiety attacks whilst making a cup of tea. Being pro-active in organising surgery somehow eased the pain; it was good to know I could do something about my disappointing features.

I would draw diagrams of how I should look and shade photographs of myself. Once I got an idea in my head about what needed to change to make me much better I would see Mr Fix-It; most of the time, he would change it.

Mr Fix-It had his own ideas so sometimes, after I had excitedly and speedily driven to his home with my clear ideas, he would say, 'No, you don't need that,' and he would explain why. Funnily enough, the trips when he would do this and tell me about the positive points of my face made me feel better than the times he did agree to surgery.

It was as if I was saying 'Look, I'm ugly because…' and if they agreed to surgery it meant I needed fixing and I was indeed ugly. When he explained I could not have surgery and that I didn't need the work, that was a big high. It felt like someone saying: 'You are not broken.'

I felt like the only woman in the world that needed this amount of surgery. The more operations I had, the more the papers called me 'ugly' and other names, then the more surgery I needed. Gossip mags loved to print me in their papers; it was starting to get out of control. The press I had started to court as a model with a face and body to envy was turning on me. The papers now pointed fingers at me and said I was ugly, obsessed with surgery and maybe even slightly mad.

I lived in central London so I was often 'papped' with bandages over my face, which always made the gossip mags. They even printed stories about my friends being worried for my life!

By now surgery had become an addiction. I was driving to Mr Fix-It's house or clinic three times a week. It was less about the procedures and more about him making me feel good, either with his words or his knife.

One aspect of my life was going well. After five months together Sugardaddy picked me up in his chauffeur-driven car and said he had a big surprise for me. He took me to a house he was thinking of buying. It had acres of land and a swimming pool. He said we could live there together. After waving my phone in the air in various locations around the house and garden I realised I couldn't get a good reception on my mobile so I said, 'Thanks, but no thanks.' He said Vodafone would soon provide coverage here so that would change. I just couldn't take such a big risk so wasn't convinced.

It seemed like for every step forward Sugardaddy took, I took a step back. Neither of us could receive love in the conventional way: like scared rabbits in the headlights, at every sign of a move forward one of us would run. I don't know if he felt rejected, but in any case I soon picked up on rumours that he was cheating on me. I would take those rumours really badly. On one occasion I drove his car to his house, filled with every gift he had ever given me in black sacks – even took off and chucked in the clothes he had bought me that I was wearing – parked the car outside and posted my house and car keys through his letterbox and walked off. Sugardaddy refused to take any of it back regardless of whether we stayed together or not, which made me love him more.

He was starting to show an unconditional love that even my self-destructive behaviour could not rock. I was also showing him the same unconditional love. We were both very similar in some ways, both dysfunctional, both insecure, but at the same time very different. He was a highly intelligent and successful businessman and I was a girl who traded on her looks. I admired his brains and he admired my boobs.

It was certainly an unhealthy relationship, though. Sugardaddy had what he called 'his demons', though others called it 'downright selfish behaviour'. Basically, he couldn't keep his dick in his pants. This only fed my insecurities, so I craved more surgery.

This time Mr Fix-It suggested a facelift because my face was too round. It didn't matter that I was only 24 years old: he said I would benefit from a full facelift, including a brow lift, to give me smoother skin and sharper features.

At the same time he said he would put that biro pen tube back in my lips, which really needed doing as removing the first implants had left my lips slightly feathered-looking from the scarring.

I suddenly felt very self-conscious about my face. A facelift wasn't something I thought you could have at 24 but now Mr Fix-It had planted that seed in my brain I had to go ahead with the surgery or live with what I now thought was a saggy, round face that needed to be lifted. There was no other option.

I told Sugardaddy it was a skin-smoothing procedure and didn't go into much detail. He paid for it without much question. He could always be counted on to be very generous after a 'misadventure' where the 'demons' had got the better of him. These, I learnt, were always the best times to ask him for surgery.

This time I wasn't feeling as confident as I had before when walking into the north London hospital. By now I knew the drill and the staff did too. I didn't have visitors and I knew the routines and the room, so there was no need to explain how the emergency cord worked or how the bed went up and down. This was like my second home. I even knew which rooms were the best and would often request certain ones.

Mr Fix-It came by before the surgery to draw all over me with his marker pen and to explain what he was going to do. I told him to keep it subtle – but to make me look like Barbie, please.

He said, 'My darling, you will look better than Barbie.' Sold.

When it came to my time to go under I did my usual trick, I would secretly fold the tube so I could feel the anaesthetic slowly dripping into my arm for longer. I had grown addicted to the feeling of the drug sending me to sleep. It had actually reached the point of me searching for places to buy it privately to use myself at home. Shockingly, it did seem available to buy. I would buy IVs and practise injecting myself with them.

When I awoke after this particular procedure I was told by the nurses that everything had gone great. I couldn't wait to look in the mirror. Still in my ridiculously drugged state, I examined the results for the first time.

What had I done to myself? My face was unrecognisable. I had had a full facelift: metal bolts were screwed into my skull all round my head but, worse still, my hair at the sides had been chopped off. Half my scalp was shaved and the remaining hair I had left was red with blood. My eyes were pulled back and the rest of my face looked completely distorted. I was horrified. Wrapped in bandages, I just sat there crying – my face unable to move, or show expression. Tears fell from my swollen black eyes, dripping down my red, swollen, broken face.

I repeatedly pressed the buzzer and started screaming at the nurses, demanding they bring Mr Fix-It to my bedside immediately. They said he had gone home and told me to calm down. The nurses pumped me with more drugs to numb me but somehow I still managed to text Mr Fix-It. He didn't reply. I must have sent dozens of incoherent messages in my doped state, asking him to come to see me and telling him he had ruined my face.

The next day Mr Fix-It appeared as part of his daily rounds. I chucked my slipper at him when he walked in the door and shouted, 'Look at me! This is horrendous!'

He smiled and started examining me. In his soft, controlled voice he said, 'Shhhhh, you look amazing. It's early days, this will settle down and you will love the results. Facelifts always look bad to start with.'

'But I have metal bolts in my head!'

Mr Fix-It said that was normal and nothing to worry about.

'My hair has gone!'

'Very minimally,' he said. 'Nothing I would notice. You will be very happy,' he said whilst backing out of the door to make his escape.

I wheeled my tubes and bags into the bathroom to stare at myself. Usually his words could convince me but this time they couldn't.

When I left the hospital, wrapped up like a mummy, I didn't leave with my usual optimism. I knew I would not be happy this time.

When the day came for the nurse to take the bandages off the full horror of what had been done could be seen. My hairline had vanished and I had no hair at all on half my head! The metal bolts in my skull had left large scars and bold lines running down my hairline over an inch wide. Mr Fix-It had literally cut off my face. My eyes looked stretched and completely unnatural. My thick hair was now thin, with obvious bald patches; it felt like my ears had moved and my hairline was that of a receding 60 year-old man.

I was devastated. I could not grasp the severity of what Mr Fix-It and I had done.

'This is horrific, I look disgusting,' I told the nurse. She looked worried too but kept reassuring me it was just swelling, that my hairline would, somehow, be fine and the bold lines all would heal up. I knew better by now. I was familiar with how I healed and could tell even at that stage what the result would be like.

'Me and him are over,' I thought.

I felt I had destroyed my looks. Like a gambler I had gambled all my chips on black or red and the wrong colour had come up.

A distraction from all this came at this time in the form of my mother, who was in trouble and needed me. I got a call from her: she was distraught and crying her eyes out. I immediately drove to her house, speeding all the way to make the two-hour journey in an hour. I was very protective of my mother, loved her dearly and hated seeing her hurt.

Dad, it turned out, was having an affair and Mum had found out. Dad admitted it and said he wanted to be with the woman in question.

I told my distraught Mum to pack an overnight bag. Dad told me I wasn't allowed to take her but I did anyway. I wasn't scared of him anymore. I stood up to him using the same harsh words he had once used against me.

Mum was a mess and I needed to just take her out of the situation. I drove her away from their marital home of 25 years. She never went back.

Sugardaddy was amazing. He helped me to get Mum back on her feet and moved us into a bigger house, so Mum had her own room.

Mum was obviously depressed; she had never planned to split from Dad. She was now nearly sixty and had never imagined having to start all over again. Worse still, it seemed Dad had frittered a lot of the family money away on other women.

Sugardaddy paid for us to go on a retreat to Spain. The holiday was great, as I got to know my mum again and, for once I had the money to pamper and treat her how she deserved. We ate the finest food, we spent all morning till lunch having endless massages and manicures and soaking in the hot spa. Money in this instance did buy us back a bit of happiness.

After their split Mum kept going back to Dad. He still loved her; deep down maybe he knew he wasn't complete without the one with the real strength in the family. As for Mum, like I said, I was convinced she had Stockholm syndrome. I had to stand by and watch as she repeatedly kept going back to him for the next five years. It was it hard to watch; I could see she was growing as her own person without him, but it was a slow progress.

Dad would put on his charismatic charm for weeks, sometimes months, to get her back, then it would all go bad again and she would return to me. Though I felt bad for her, I was always pleased when she did return. For the first time in my life I had my mum: she wasn't a shivering wreck any more, she wasn't scared to put us first or need permission to help us. She was a kind woman with a heart of gold, who enjoyed looking after others. Unfortunately that had been exploited and was never enough or right, for my dad. Don't get me wrong, on Valentine's Day and her birthdays he would shower her with gifts, his love for her was clear to see; but she deserved better. She gave herself to him and her three children, never caring for herself, and along the way she lost who she was. Heartbreaking as it was to see her keep going back to Dad, I would smile with delight when she would come back: I knew she was getting stronger and putting up with less and less each time. Just as I had broken away and taken Georgia, I knew what she was going through. We loved him, we loved the moments when he would be happy and 'high' and be the centre of attention, but the other side we just couldn't live with.

I was now concentrating so much on my mother that I failed to deal with the facelift that had gone so drastically wrong. I was still recovering from the surgery and by now I was taking painkillers almost every day, developing an addiction to them.

I hid my hairline and scars from my mother: the last thing she needed to see was the horrific slicing-up I had done to myself. Besides, I couldn't even bear to look in the mirror by that stage.

Mum must have seen my face was different but she was too scared of driving me away again so didn't say anything. However, in the blazing heat of the height of summer in Spain, I was starting to shiver. I was cold and getting a fever.

Mum suggested I call a doctor. I didn't really want one and told her not to but over the telephone Sugardaddy picked up that I was sick and also insisted I get a doctor out. I couldn't refuse him so I relented.

The doctor came to see me and could not put his finger on my symptoms to start with until he said with a Spanish accent, 'Please show me your ear.'

Oh God. I was carefully hiding my horrendous scars and lack of hairline as I was so ashamed and embarrassed. I didn't want to look at them so I would use hairspray to keep my hair in place covering my face.

'Why...' I asked, trying to avoid showing my ear.

Before I had time to finish my sentence and refuse to show my ear or make up an excuse, the doctor had pulled back my hair to uncover the hideous truth. The scars on either side of my face had become infected and had not healed. My hair was matted with pus and raw blood and it stank. I had been applying the hairspray and perfume to try to cover up the smell of the infection. I had an open gash showing bone on one side and a wound over an inch and a half wide on each side of my head.

The doctor said I needed to go to hospital immediately. Of course, I underplayed it: we were going home in two days so I said I really wasn't in pain and I would check into a hospital when I got home. He prescribed me some antibiotics and painkillers, which was handy as I was running out.

Mum must have been horrified but she didn't say anything.

When I got back to the UK I decided I had to do something about the loss of my hairline and terrible facelift that Mr Fix-It had given me.

Sugardaddy also knew what had happened, as he had to pick up the doctor's bill. We sat there on his roof terrace and he said, 'Let me see what you have done.'

I said, 'No, it's not something you show a boyfriend.'

'I love you,' he replied, reassuring me. 'Nothing can put me off you.' This was lulling me into a false sense of security.

Begrudgingly, and against my better judgement, I showed Sugardaddy my shocking hairline and fresh scars.

The gasp of horror was exactly what I didn't want to hear. 'Darling, what have you done to yourself?'

Sugardaddy scribbled down the name of a private doctor, who also served a member of the royal family, and told me to get a referral to a surgeon.

I wasn't going to argue, it was a mess. Mr Fix-It had let me down; I was ready to two-time and betray him by going elsewhere, breaking our code of loyalty.

The doctor on Harley Street became my personal doctor for many years. He gave me prescriptions over the telephone, told me off for taking too many painkillers and referred me to a top reconstruction surgeon.

This surgeon – let's call him 'Mr Reconstruction' – would be my next hero.

He examined my botched facelift sympathetically, nodding his head and saying, 'What did he do to you… what a butcher.' He said he could repair the damage and give me a better facelift. He was going to bring hair from the back of my head to the front to give me back my hairline with a large graft, rather than individually transplanting follicles. Most importantly, he was going to repair the gaping open gashes on both sides of my face.

I didn't get a second opinion, or even question his work, I was just grateful that someone was willing to repair the damage. So I signed up.

This time the work was a lot more expensive, as it was complicated reconstructive surgery. Sugardaddy picked up the bill again.

I was in a top London hospital when I woke up from the surgery. I examined the latest bruised and bandaged needlework of my new hero. I wasn't impressed. I really couldn't tell what the result would be but I didn't like it nevertheless. My hairline was back, which was pleasing, but my eyes still looked pulled. I looked like a Beverly Hills housewife caught in a wind tunnel.

So I started writing out the plan for what to do next. When the surgeon arrived during his rounds I even asked him for my next surgery. In my drug-influenced state I asked for a revision of my lips and eyes, not even caring to hear about the result of this surgery. In my mind I had already moved on. You see, if I thought something was fixed I would move on to the next thing. I knew pulled eyes from a facelift would be really difficult to fix so I didn't bother addressing it; I just had to live with looking like a 60 year-old woman in a 24 year-old's body. It was never clear whether I was addicted to the struggle or to the hope of something better.

The new facelift after healing still turned out to be a disaster. My eyes were pulled too much so I had that 'facelift look.' I looked middle-aged, not to mention that I was not yet 25 and yet had already had two facelifts, which was something I was highly embarrassed about.

On the upside, though, my hairline looked good, all the fat on my 'rounder face' was gone and the scars had been cut away with much thinner, sleeker incisions so well hidden away that even I couldn't find them.

Even better, I was no longer potentially dying from the infected gaping open wounds and didn't smell of rotting flesh anymore.

CHAPTER TEN

What Happens in Vegas

LOS ANGELES: I was sitting by the pool with a girlfriend during one of my many holidays, dressed in my red bikini, when a good-looking guy started talking to me. My platinum blonde hair was perfectly blow-dried, as usual, and my red lipstick was pristinely placed, as I tried to make the best of my new middle-aged look. My ginormous breasts meant that I was always a topic of gossip wherever I went, even in LA – although there they tend to presume that if you have big boobs and bleached blonde hair you must be a porn star.

The good-looking guy said his friends were wondering what I did as a job, or whether I was a kept woman. He then asked my age. When I said I was 24 years old he gasped. He didn't believe I was 24 and asked that I take my oversized sunglasses off.

When I did he said, 'You do look young and seem young, but something's off that makes me think you could be 45.' Not the best chat-up line I've ever heard.

Even with my new-found looks that had aged me 20 years I still managed to model. If anything, I was getting more modelling than ever. My body was still that of a 24 year-old while my face very much could have been one of a surgically enhanced 45 year-old. That's the thing with surgery: it can take years off you but if you do it too young it can pile years onto you instead.

It was on this same trip to LA that I heard about another 'misdemeanour' by Sugardaddy. I had decided to stay longer in sunny California and go on a lads' holiday, with five male friends and one female friend. Georgia was going on a school trip so it was good timing and I didn't want to be home alone.

The guys were male models and actors and the girl was also an aspiring model. It was one of those wild trips on which you just forget everything, including any sense you may have had.

LA soon got too tame for us so we decided to drive in a hired mini bus to Las Vegas. Drinking and taking ephedrine to keep us awake all day and night, we hit Vegas very much the worse for wear. We decided to go out straightaway to a club, staying at the impressive Mandalay Bay, in one of their suites, kindly paid for by Sugardaddy. This was his way of saying sorry for being unfaithful.

I was a rebel and this time I was out to rebel in a big way. If I got chatted up I now had a line about being partly of Asian heritage to explain my fresh facelift. I hit the club in a white shirt tied up around my waist showing off my toned stomach and golden skin, a push up bra to show off my bigger boobs and ample cleavage, a cut-off denim skirt and slip-on see-through heels. I was surrounded by my five male model friends; we were already tipsy when one of the lads said, 'Let's play who can pull the fittest bird and bring them back to the bar. Alicia, you have to pull the fittest man.'

'No problem, challenge accepted.' Off I went, grasping my glass of Red Bull and vodka as I walked brashly into the sea of Vegas clubbers.

It wasn't long until I spotted 'Stefan'. It turned out he had been one of Madonna's backing dancers. He was working in one of the shows in Vegas; his best friend was the blonde guy you would recognise from her *In Bed with Madonna* video. He was six feet tall and muscular, sporting an eight-pack, with perfect teeth and sharp cheekbones. Stefan was dripping with girls trying to hang off him. He was the most popular man in the club, with that certain charismatic, suave energy that drew you in. In no time at all, I brought him back to the bar to collect my award for pulling the fittest.

The lads hadn't pulled anyone successfully and all went off to bed so I ended up talking to Stefan now that my friends had deserted me.

Stefan seemed really interested in me. After all that vodka I had really warmed to him too, so much so we continued our conversation in the suite upstairs. We didn't have sex, as I don't give it up too easily but make a man work for it, contrary to popular belief.

Stefan and I became inseparable. He didn't go into work, we ordered breakfast, lunch and dinner in bed. After three days we ventured down into the bar. A drunken man came up to us and said, 'You two are a good-looking couple, you look amazing. Are you married?' It was random but Stefan replied, 'No, but we are getting married.'

Both still drunk, he said to me, 'We should.'

'We do make a striking couple.'

I was happy to find someone who actually liked me for more than sex, who didn't see me as just a sex object. One of the drawbacks of looking like Barbie (or, before you say it, a melted version of her) was that men didn't take me seriously. I wasn't happy with Sugardaddy at the time because it didn't feel like a proper, fulfilling relationship and his cheating was building up my resentment towards him. I had started to miss the closeness and connection I had enjoyed with Seb.

'Would you?' he asked.

'Why not?' I replied.

We started walking to bar number two when Stefan got down on one knee and said, 'Will you marry me?' Every girl's dream... Well, maybe.

'Yes!'

We continued our night happily, safe in the knowledge that we were soon to wed. We were closer than ever, declared undying love to each other and justified our quick decision on the basis that married people know each other for years and still get divorced. Drunkenly, we reasoned wc 'had a connection' and that we just 'knew' it was right.

We made love that night for the first time before passing out. In the morning, I woke severely hungover, reaching immediately for the paracetamol. I looked over at Stefan who was kneeing on the floor busily thumbing through the yellow pages, looking for a place to get married. I had forgotten all about it, but then the night before came rushing back to me.

Stefan kissed me 'good morning' and said, 'You still up for getting married?'

'Of course!'

I really wasn't but played along as I did not think this was real. We were just having fun and wouldn't really go ahead with such a ridiculous, life-changing idea.

Stefan booked a chapel and a limo to take us there before walking me to Cartier to buy rings. It was at this point that I realised I needed to phone my friends to ask if they wanted to go to a wedding later in the day!

The reaction I got was mixed. Half of them laughed and went along with it; the other half thought I was insane and didn't even want to attend.

I kept thinking one of us would back out but the credit card kept paying for wedding things and the clock was ticking down to the time for the ceremony. I didn't really have any intention of getting married and certainly had not thought this situation through.

Somehow I arrived at the chapel, which was someone's living room with a piano in it. We had been allocated fifteen minutes. I borrowed flowers from the bride who was married before me. We sat down so that we could fill in some paperwork. By now I was quickly sobering up and growing concerned about the seriousness of my actions.

I filled the paperwork in hurriedly, as I thought I would rush off to the toilet to find a window, climb out of it and run before this thing got really out of hand. That's when Stefan looked at me, smiling, and said that because the paperwork had been signed we were actually legally married now anyway. The ceremony was just a nice bit of fun. I had no idea. I tried my best to conceal my open-mouthed look of astonishment and disappointment.

'I just need the toilet,' I choked. I sped off to the restroom and put my head in my hands, crying to myself, 'What the hell have I done?'

My friend, the female model, knocked on the door. She had seen my tanned face go white and had come in to comfort me. She said, 'Think about arranged marriages, a lot of them last. Stefan seems nice. I think you'll be great together!'

She coaxed me slowly downstairs to go ahead with the ceremony.

All I could think about was Sugardaddy. This was revenge taken too far. I would have to give up everything for this man and I didn't even know him! Worse still, I really did love Sugardaddy. I wasn't ready to leave him or give up everything, including Georgia's new private education.

I walked down the aisle's stained and moth-eaten carpet in the minister's living room with my friend, who was in jeans, as my bridesmaid. I was greeted by the smiling, but by now also quite nervous, Stefan. We exchanged rings and walked out to the sound of a friend of mine singing and playing the piano.

A reception had been arranged at someone's house. Stefan and I sat sheepishly sharing the edge of a beaten-up old chair, which smelt of weed. We said nothing, clearly both in a state of shock and now stone-cold sober.

We only moved when prompted to cut the cake and to have the first dance, which, by the way, was J-Lo and Jay Rule's 'I'm Real'. Fuelled by wine and vodka we started to relax and go with our new marital status.

We decided to leave the party early and go back to our hotel room. The taxi ride to the Mandalay Bay was awkward;

we just sat there looking out the window and holding hands, tightly clutching each other, hoping that one of us would save the other.

In the hotel room we somehow had to break the discomfort of our drunken actions and played 'our' song, which we slowly and sexily danced to. This led on to kissing, which melted the nerves away. We ended up in bed where the awkwardness disappeared.

Stefan whispered, 'It's crazy but I love you, Mrs Roulston.'

This completely ruined the moment for me as he had suddenly made me realise that I would have to change my name again. I had already changed my name to something I loved and I had become a known model with that name. No way was I about to change it, especially to something I thought was significantly crappier than what I had.

It had also dawned on me that I had married a man after just four days. We decided to get to know each other and travelled back to LA to have a 'honeymoon'. We stayed at a four-star hotel called the Mandarin. It was, as honeymoons go, quite amazing. We had incredible, electric sex, which, I imagine, was newer to us than to most modern honeymooners. There was great sun, a warm pool to frolic in – much to the annoyance of onlookers – and lots of pool parties with plenty of tequila, champagne and vodka-Red Bull.

It was strange to see a ring on my finger but I was really starting to like the man who was now my husband. It also felt great to be committed, to feel 'sorted' and a sense of belonging. I decided I could really make a go of things. Funnily enough, even though he was a complete stranger, I felt really happy. He gave me a sense of security that Sugardaddy could only fill financially; I thought we were going to be a family unit. We would, I knew, have no real money but somehow that didn't bother me.

We decided the best idea was for me to fly back to the UK alone. Stefan would complete his work commitments and join me later.

I didn't expect Sugardaddy to be at the airport to pick me up but he was. He wanted to surprise me and greeted me with a massive bunch of red roses. 'That was nice,' I thought. 'It's great we can still be friends.'

In the car on the way to my home Sugardaddy said, 'I have something to say.'

'So do I!'

I needed to tell him my news and thought he would be pleased for me.

'Okay, you go first,' he said, smiling and excited, taking an appreciative look at my cleavage.

'I got married!' I said, beaming a cheesy grin and showing off my wedding ring.

'What?' he looked shocked.

'I know it wasn't really planned but it just happened. We are going to make a go of things, isn't that great?! Anyway, we need to organise me giving everything back and us finding somewhere to live.'

'No,' he said. 'I don't want anything back, they were gifts, I gave them to you. I'm a man of my word and you had my word I would give you security. Does this man have any money?'

'Well, he won't have a job as he's a dancer but I'm sure he'll get work... Anyway, what were you going to say?' I asked.

'Doesn't matter now.' I saw that his face suddenly looked drained, disappointed and sunken.

It turned out that Sugardaddy had realised whilst I was away how much he loved me. He had made the decision to commit to me and was picking me up to declare this. Sugardaddy had found a house where we could live together, big enough for Georgia, him and me to have our own space, complete with a gym, swimming pool, tennis court and acres of land – and where I could get a signal on my phone.

I couldn't wait for Stefan to arrive in the UK, I counted down the days, but when Stefan turned up, from the awkward moment I greeted him at the airport, the chemistry wasn't there any more. We were strangers, mismatched, and it turned out we didn't have much in common. I was still willing to make a go of it, but I sensed Stefan wasn't happy. It was like any holiday romance when you meet up in your own town to discover the other party doesn't fit into your world at all and you cannot stand each other. After two weeks Stefan made his excuses and I never saw him again. He literally disappeared, with no forwarding address. I was heartbroken for a little while. I always believed that when I got married it would be forever. I wanted to make it work with Stefan; being married, feeling someone was going to be there with me through thick and thin, no matter what, felt so good. When he disappeared I felt like Miss Havisham, left with the wedding cake still in the fridge, the wedding dress still hanging up. Again it reinforced my feelings of not being good enough for someone to love.

It took me years to divorce Stefan. Sugardaddy had to hire private detectives in New York to find him and then get a summons to him outside *Tarzan*, the theatre show in which he was performing as one of the apes.

Sugardaddy waited before he allowed me to get a divorce as he thought all the time I was married to Stefan at least I could not marry anyone else on a whim, but he had been put off marrying me because of this, he said.

At least one side of my life was getting better and better. As a well-known glamour model I started to get invites to premieres, brand launches, drinks events for magazines and private parties held by footballers and rock stars. With my platinum blonde hair and exaggerated figure I was soon attracting guys, including celebrities and rich men.

Before long I was at a swimming pool party with Eminem, while lots of bikini-clad girls were pining for his attention. I was being treated like a queen by Simon Cowell, dining with him in the finest restaurants. I started dating him when he was working for a music label and *The X Factor* was just an idea. I really liked him and wished things had gone further. I would leave his hotel suite and get into his Aston Martin, and he would ask me questions seeking reassurance like, 'Do you like my car?' Our relationship ended when Sugardaddy saw the threat and gave me an ultimatum. That's when, as soon as Simon let me down, I did not even think twice about doing a kiss and tell on him – the trick I had learnt to cut people off for good.

The partying didn't stop. I was dirty dancing in a club with one hard-living Hollywood star before going back to the

Dorchester for an after-party that lasted two days and took place mostly in a four-poster bed.

I partied with P. Diddy, who had a huge entourage. We went from club to club, then to a party, before going on to another party in the recording studio, always with the entourage. This involved lots of standing on tables whilst popping open and spraying expensive champagne.

I still had Sugardaddy but we now had an understanding, so I started dating famous men. The press were also interested in this doll-like girl who was involved with a string of celebrities.

Footballers' parties usually started off in a restaurant before moving onto a club, where they would run up thousands of pounds on a bar bill, then end up in the penthouse suite of a hotel. I've even seen premiership footballers drink and snort coke the night before a game. I have witnessed many married footballers cheat on their wives and, whilst there is nothing new there, it certainly didn't help me have any faith in men.

I had private parties of my own with one 80s pop star I dated – let's call him 'Mr Red'. We relaxed both at his mansion and in the VIP areas of clubs, surrounded by champagne bottles and groupies, who we would pick up and bring back with us for threesomes. We would find a girl I approved of: none of them ever said 'No'. Perhaps they thought they could steal this man away from me but I knew these girls weren't a threat, no girl was, because Mr Red was crazy about me. When I was with Mr Red I realised that the only way to keep my man was to show him such an exciting time that everyone else would seem boring. I was so upbeat, young and sexy I would party all night. No one else had worked out the way to his heart and gave him the excitement that he needed in the same way as I did. The other girl would get irritated when there was more passion between the two of us in the bedroom. We were always polite to the girl – she was our guest – but soon as she realised that she would not be stealing my pop star's heart she would get annoyed. That's when I would have to call a cab for her. It was the perfect plan because the girls would always self-destruct. Mr Red would like the thought of the threesome but almost always the reality was not as good as the fantasy – after all, you can only have sex with one person at a time. More often than not it was more awkward than sex with just the two of us. It felt like a house-guest you had to try not to leave out, which made him appreciate being with me that little bit more. Even when the beautiful and leggy Lady Victoria Hervey danced desperately in front of him in a club one time, he tapped her on the shoulder and asked her to move, as she was blocking our view. Mr Red was definitely my man: it hadn't been a conventional way of making a man fall in love but it worked.

It was only when Sugardaddy again gave me an ultimatum that Mr Red and I split up. I did not want to but I couldn't risk losing everything I had, including Georgia's education, for a new relationship that I wasn't sure was going anywhere. You cannot expect a man to commit to looking after you like that within eight months of meeting him. Sugardaddy was clever and knew I was caught in his net, trapped by his money and my need for Georgia's special schooling.

There were other famous men after Mr Red that I don't intend to write about here but they included a famous chef, a Scandinavian billionaire and a music mogul. It goes without saying that underneath all the silicone I was still just an ordinary girl from Sussex so the celebrities didn't hang around very long.

That's the problem, you see, men are visual. If you go for a man who likes you just for your appearance he will soon like someone else for theirs. You'll find that looks fade for everyone – don't let your pride tell you that your sparkling personality will prevail, because a certain type of man will always have a roaming eye: the most charismatic girl isn't going to keep some men from straying. Sugardaddy was one of those men who always wanted something better. When you're past your sell-by date you're tossed away like a gone-off, shrivelled-up piece of fruit.

I learnt this harsh truth early on in life, doing my first 'kiss and tell' on Mr Athletic. This later expanded to over 30 kiss and tells because I decided, having crossed that line, that it didn't make any difference now if I did one or 100 kiss and tells. It was still morally wrong. Weirdly, the more kiss and tells I did, the more celebrity men I got involved with.

For a long time I couldn't figure out how I so easily got these men. I wasn't exceptionally pretty, I wasn't the life and soul of the party: what was it? I realised that it was their egos. They wanted what they thought others wanted. I think I became a trophy and I built up such an impressive CV of men that others wanted to conquer me to see what all the fuss was about.

Their egos also made them believe they were special, that I wouldn't do a kiss and tell on them. I taught those men that actually they were not so special, that they all were quite similar and no one was exempt. I also taught myself in the process that it was a two-way street: I could be under no illusion that youth and looks would make a man with a roving eye keep coming back again and again. Sure, I could have cooked and cleaned and made myself indispensable by playing the little woman at home and ignoring his indiscretions; but that wasn't me. Cheaters were not passing 'Go' with me or collecting £200. Sugardaddy was only able to get away with it because Georgia was my priority. In some ways I think his cheating put me off trying to find someone else; it made me think all men would be like that. Sure enough, whenever I did look for someone else I picked the wrong guy, so my doubts would be justified!

Of course, there was always a part of me that was a dreamer, that believed one guy would be different and love me for me, inside and out. But it never happened, so the kiss and tells kept rolling on, my reputation grew, and I liked the fact I was known for being a bitch, for being the girl who ratted on her man. I didn't much care for having a good wholesome reputation: coming from a glamour model past, I figured I wasn't going to get to be the face of wholesome anyway.

CHAPTER ELEVEN

Barbie Explodes

THE MARRIAGE SPLIT from Stefan and Sugardaddy's coolness towards me only fed my ever-increasing insecurities. Before I knew it I was driving in my car on my way to Mr Fix-It. He was angry and horrified that I had 'gone elsewhere' for surgery. He told me my face was now too thin and I urgently needed filler to give me that doll-like appearance again that he liked.

Mr Fix-It had found filler that was permanent, which seemed like a cost-effective way of doing things. Then and there Mr Fix-It injected my face, under my cheek, along my laughter lines and under my eyes. The needle hurt badly but it was nothing compared to the pain I felt from the rejection of Stefan leaving or Sugardaddy's waning desire for me. I endured the pain easily by thinking about my abandonment and told myself that each injection would solve this problem for good. Somehow I convinced myself that Mr Fix-It was right and that with a rounder, fuller face I would look younger and would not be left alone again. I would be loved forever.

I also had it fixed in my head that my hands looked old and insisted on filler being injected there too. The permanent filler apparently couldn't be injected there so he used a filler that lasted only three months at a time. I kept this up for years, having filler placed in my hands every week, as temporary filler in the hands disappears quickly.

Mr Fix-It was regaining his power over me and tried to rein me back in, pooh-poohing the 'other man's' work. He told me to be careful, that I was naïve and vulnerable and lots of men would try and take advantage of me. He said I shouldn't go elsewhere, as I might ruin myself.

Somehow I managed to retain enough good sense not to let Mr Fix-It do any major surgery on me again but I kept going back time and time again for filler. This led to me having an overly rounded 'filler face', which made my eyes look even more pulled and small. It even distorted my laugh.

On one of my visits I asked Mr Fix-It to remove some filler. He did, but this left a rather large dent in my face because of a steroid injection, which he said was the only way of getting the filler out. The dent is visible on both sides of my face even today.

I was now deep into my revived obsession with surgery. I could no longer face looking at myself and chose to take down all the mirrors in the house or cover them up with sheets. If I did see myself I would be disgusted and appalled by the image looking back at me. I would end up staring for hours, crying into the mirror, frustrating myself with my own perceived ugliness.

I had decided that I needed urgent and more drastic corrections. Next on my list of alterations were a tummy tuck, bigger lips, my nose shaved, my brows shaved, my ribs shaved and even bigger boobs, to make me a double-G. This I felt would be the one, the dramatic change I needed to remove the last telling signs of Sarah Howes. I would be the opposite of her, unrecognisable as the old me and, at last, the stunning girl I longed to be.

I went back to Mr Reconstruction and gave him my list. The surgeon told me it was too much to do in one go and that we needed to break it down. He said he was close to retirement and asked if I was sure I wanted to have this. I was sure and Sugardaddy was happy too: it meant I would have even bigger boobs, which always went down well. He had started to become excited by my ever-changing bra size as much as I had. I loved seeing Sugardaddy's excited face when I would unpeel my sports bra to show my latest creation.

So Operation One would be a tummy tuck and a lip enlargement, and my ribs would be shaved. I tried to convince Mr Reconstruction to remove the ribs to give me a tiny waist but he insisted that I needed them to keep my internal organs in place. He said shaving was the only thing any surgeon would do. 'Maybe,' I thought, 'I'll find another surgeon who will remove a few ribs and, in the meantime, I'll settle for them being shaved.'

'Make sure you really shave them though. I mean, saw them off rather than shave them if you can,' I said.

I then pulled a Barbie doll out my bag. 'This is my aim. I want to look exactly like her. See her waist? I need mine just like that.'

He explained that Barbie was plastic and not a real reflection of the human form.

'I don't care. I think she looks great, so I want to look just like her.' I was blinkered by my obsession with Barbie and nothing less was good enough.

'Well, I can certainly bring your waist in by a few inches,' he reassured me.

I knew when to push the surgeons and when to settle. It was like a game of poker in that you had to know when to stop – but unlike poker, the last thing you wanted was for your opponent to fold his cards. I needed him to stay in the game.

So I took what I could and I decided a few inches were okay for now; but soon as I could, I would search for someone else to take the whole pesky ribs off. I had heard that doctors in Brazil and Thailand were more extreme. But that needed more planning. An addict takes what she can to get the hit there and then.

Off I went again for surgery. The tummy tuck was the most painful operation I had experienced: definitely the hardest to recover from. I could not see any difference from the rib shave but I presumed this was adding to my pain. My lips, which now resembled a plunger, were massive. Skin had been taken from my stomach, rolled up and placed into my upper and lower lips. Apparently this skin would dissolve in time.

I also had a fat transfer. Fat was taken from my inner thighs and stomach and placed in my face to 'freshen me up.'

Once the tummy tuck had healed I was happy with the scar revision. I had a big scar that sometimes showed above my bikini line from the emergency Caesarean section I had when Georgia was born. (Presumably they had got an apprentice surgeon to do it blindfolded, who thought it was a game of

'Pin the Tail on the Donkey' that had gone horribly wrong, or perhaps they used the local butcher.)

The tummy tuck itself had given me the washboard stomach I desired but my ribs were now sticking out. I couldn't see any evidence of rib shaving, but after time my waist did definitely go in.

I was already planning my next operation though, so I wasn't that interested in this one anymore. I wanted the biggest boobs in Britain. I wanted 1,000 cc implants: these also allowed you to overfill them. Mr Reconstruction had gone to some sort of surgeons' exhibition especially to shop for these implants. He said he could give me 1,200 cc if he overfilled my boobs.

I was really excited, but I had to wait six weeks for the tummy tuck to settle down before Mr Reconstruction would agree to operate again.

This was when Mr Fix-It came in. I would drive to him in the meantime, to feed my addiction, satisfying my thirst to improve myself on a now daily basis. I would demand filler, filler anywhere, my hands, knees, under my eyes, and then Botox everywhere from my forehead to my armpits. We would discuss possible operations that would fill me with excitement, but I always went elsewhere for the bigger operations now.

I also discovered a top dermatologist, who extensively worked on me. I split my time between LA and London; I also had a team of surgeons in LA to whom I would go for advice and who also operated on me. I had a herd of private doctors ready to prescribe me under-the-table painkillers, Roaccutane to get rid of my spots and Latisse for longer

Mum didn't want her pic taken!

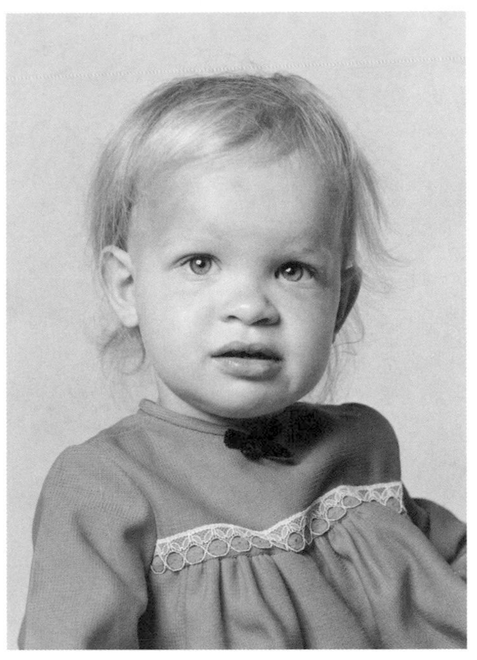

A straggly looking baby me! Apparently I was called 'ET' as a baby.

Donning my homemade dress and bowl haircut. My mum made my sisters' outfits from some of her own old clothes.

The house we lived in above the garage.

Dad the local councillor with Maggie Thatcher!

Sitting in a kit car Dad built from scratch. I often shadowed my dad trying to be interested in cars as they were his passion!

Caravan – Meet the flockers! Misfits! Another UK holiday in a caravan park with prizes for best fancy dress. I think I was Bo Peep here.

Dad loved boats, so I loved boats – always striving to please him.

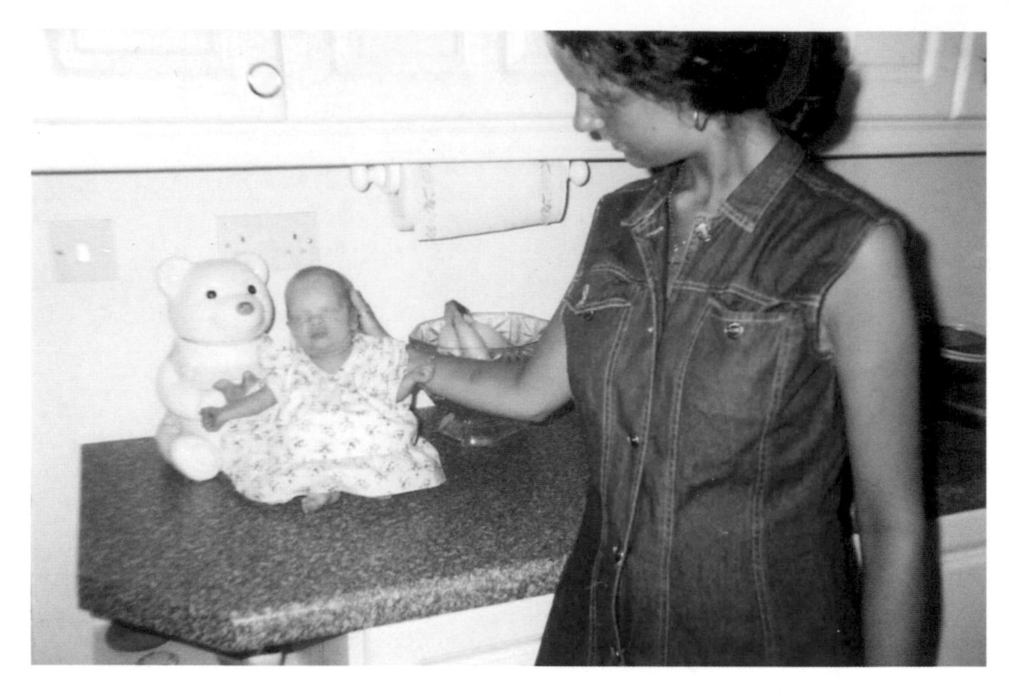

Bringing Georgia home. Look, the biscuit tin is bigger than her!

Georgia put a smile on my face.

Georgia's first birthday!

Now blonde with a few bad nose jobs under my belt in a hostel room, but happy as I'm with Georgia.

Mum and Dad with Georgia.

Up the aisle! A friend walks me up the aisle to give me away on my wedding day!

My band 'Good Girls Gone Bad'. I'm far left.

The Playboy Mansion: I'm left of Heff. My second family!

With old glamour model friends.

Clubbing days and my evolving face. A rare occasion when I didn't have hair extensions in!

One of our many five-star holidays.

The beach in Thailand that nearly took me.

Our little chihuahua puppy called Armani! Too much surgery too!

Happy holidays with Georgia.

I love this pic of me and Mum on holiday: smiling, relaxing and enjoying ourselves, being mother and daughter for the first time. She became my best friend and still is!

My beautiful children: my strength and happiness.

eyelashes. I was also regularly having treatments such as laser skin therapies and peels, as well as further fillers and Botox; I wasn't telling the doctors about the previous treatments. I felt I had built up a team and I needed all of them to feed my addiction. One wasn't enough anymore.

The time finally came for operation number two. I booked myself into a top London private hospital and whilst I was there I thought I would also have some bone shaved from my brow, my lips pumped up, and my nose slimmed (again). I called these 'tweaks', as I thought of them as little extra operations that did not really count.

The 1,200 cc breast implants I was having put under the muscle would give me a bra size of 28HH. With my tiny frame I was set to have 'the biggest fake boobs in Britain', as the papers would later write. This, I thought, would be the one. I would finally be perfect, the optimal figure of a desirable woman: finally I would never be left alone because I would look too gorgeous for any man to turn away from.

Even though I was now being compared to Michael Jackson and Joan Rivers in the press I still thought surgery could somehow mend the problem.

Oh, how I was wrong.

I woke up lying in a hospital bed in the recovery room, drugged-up and confused – and most of all, in pain. This was not manageable pain. This was serious pain, the sort of pain that might mean that I was going to die. In my confused state, I looked down at my breasts, hoping to see beautiful, larger-than-life, Barbie-like perfect boobs. Instead I saw my right breast twice the size of the other, with the veins popping out.

I shouted for help in a mumbled incoherent way, stiff from bandages. My lips felt like they were on fire. My nose was bunged up and bleeding. My rapidly swelling face was stopping me from moving or talking properly. I slurred, 'Boobs bigger, help! I'm in pain!'

The nurse came, 'Out of ten, what is your pain?'

For fuck's sake. 'A billion,' I whimpered before starting to convulse, which seemed to convince her to inject me in the arse.

I was burning up in a pool of sweat, then cold and shivering uncontrollably.

More doped up and even less able to speak or move due to the morphine and who knows what else, I was still in pain, though they were giving me enough medication. By this time two nurses were trying to calm me. They tried extra blankets to warm me, which unsurprisingly didn't work: what they were missing was that I was potentially dying.

I managed to point to my breast and mumble 'Help!' again in between convulsing through the sheer pain and panic I was experiencing.

I remember seeing the nurse's reassuring perma-smile dropping to a worried, wide-eyed, shocked face that she could not hide when she saw my breast, which was getting bigger and bigger by the minute. She rushed to another nurse on night duty and then to the phone.

The other nurse injected me yet again, disabling me even more. I felt helpless, like a stroke victim, with very little movement, or at best like an addict in a scene from a crack den. She explained I had been given the maximum they could possibly give, before her pale worried face rushed off to ask the perma-smile nurse: 'How long will he be? I don't think she has long.'

She rushed back to me to pat my hand and tell me it was all going to be okay, which I had presumed it was until she said that.

Both nurses held my hand whilst saying: 'Hold on, the doctor is on his way back. He will be here soon,' whilst the radio played Dido: 'There will be no white flag'.

Shit, I thought, it's gone wrong, I'm gonna die from a boob explosion. Not cool. Not the way I wanted to go.

The pain made being in labour seem pleasant. I was fighting to breathe, I could not see or speak but I could hear everything: the panic in the room, the beeping of the machines connected to me. I could feel the mask to help me breathe over my face, the jab of another cannula going in to my hand and the constant check of my temperature and pulse.

The nurses were counting down each moment, saying: 'The doctor is ten minutes away now, won't be long.' I'm not sure if they were reassuring me or themselves, but from the panic it seemed it was the latter. I was feeling myself weakening; I knew every second counted as it seemed like I couldn't hold on. Something was taking over my body. All I had to do was breathe and ignore the pain but both were near-impossible. I wasn't being allowed to sleep, but that's all I wanted to do.

'He's here!' said the nurse holding the phone. 'We need to get her on the table.'

At this point all I remember is being awake, seeing the operating table in all its horrific not-glory, with the hammers and instruments lined up that I never cared to believe they used. I was crawling on the bed, my hospital gown blood drenched, the pain throbbing so hard my whole body ached. I was dizzy and confused but at the same time desperate to stop the pain and to live, but my intuition alone told me this was my only hope of survival as pain and growing frailty on this level could only mean one thing. The hospital staff had had no time to put me asleep in a separate room and spare me the terror of seeing the operating theatre.

As they fed into the cannula the substance to put me to sleep, I thought okay, thank God the agony will end either way. If death is the end result least I won't be in pain anymore. I felt my body drift up whilst I closed my eyes thinking, 'Goodbye'. I fought a good fight, now it's fate's turn to decide. But this was only plastic surgery: why was I about to die from it?

When I finally awoke, following what was apparently an eight-hour operation, this time it was a lot less painful. I was still panicky. My drug-induced state made me say: 'Am I alive?' I was shocked to discover that the answer was yes. The last thing I remembered was pain that was surely the agony you feel when dying, the sensation of trying to hold on whilst your body wants to stop fighting. My mind kept struggling and forced my body to keep going. I truly believed I had willed myself to stay alive. I didn't want to die in such a pathetic, unheroic way. I really didn't want my tombstone to say: 'Died through her unstoppable vanity.' So here I was again, living to see another breast job.

Nurse Perma-smile reassured me, 'Looking lovely. Yes, you're alive. Keep lying down please,' as I tried to sit up to examine the new work. I lifted up my (even more) blood-splattered gown. This time I was bandaged. My pillowcases and sheets were also marked where I was still bleeding. My bandages were drenched in blood and leaking through.

In a sick way I was pleased I had managed to squeeze not one but two boob jobs into one day. Madness has no reason.

My boobs felt like I had sliced them off myself with a blunt carving knife and stitched them back on, but they were no longer exploding, nor were my veins popping out. Winning!

The nurse kept checking on my boobs and on me, looking for any signs of further infection or that the silicone which had leaked into my body had not been completely removed by the surgery and had migrated into my lymph nodes or other organs. My temperature wasn't high and she wasn't injecting my arse anymore. These were all good signs.

The beeping of the machine sounded more positive as Perma-smile repeatedly praised me for having 'a regular heartbeat and a strong heart' and said I 'coped ever so well with it all'. Story of my life, I thought.

I did, however, feel like a bus had run me over. In total I had had seventeen hours of operations, with a little break in the middle to almost die.

The nurses' faces were a lot happier this time, especially as they saw I was recovering. They were almost congratulating me for surviving. I thought, wasn't this all supposed to be safe? That is what the anaesthetist told me: that it was safer than crossing the road. I'm not sure where he got those statistics from but crossing the road was a damn sight easier than this, and seemed a lot safer, long as you looked both ways.

'So what happened before?' I asked the nurse. No one had actually told me what had gone wrong and I was really confused.

'Your implant had ruptured, but I'm not sure what happened. I think the doctor will be here soon to explain it all. Don't worry,' she said, still smiling.

'Ruptured? Like exploded, you mean?' I asked.

'In a way, yes.' She sounded like I had asked her to pass the jam at the dinner table. 'Nothing to worry about, it's all fine now.'

Err, excuse me, I think I nearly died. Do we all have to brush this off? Can I please understand how close I was to death, or was the £33,000 I spent not enough to cover an explanation?

I guess they didn't want me to be put off surgery for good. I had seen this before, when private doctors gloss over complications and make out that nothing went wrong. If you're smart you ask for the operation notes so you can read up exactly what happened but, unfortunately, I wasn't.

The doctor came round – an old man, at the top of his game. That game was reconstruction surgery. It turned out he wasn't even a plastic surgeon but saw more money in those procedures and needed a nice tidy retirement plan. He was taking up any surgery that came along, however ridiculous.

'Gosh! That was a close call, wasn't it?' he said as he smiled.

My deadpan face gazed back at him, clearly not amused.

'Don't you look great?' he said, shoving a mirror in my face so that I could inspect myself, before moving his hands down to my breasts.

I was bruised, swollen and bandaged, barely recognisable and clearly not looking 26 years old. I could have been 60.

My lips looked like a plunger. 'Are they going to go down?' I asked, hoping.

'Not too much, I don't think. They look great!'

No, they didn't. They looked awful. My lips overpowered my face and looked like I had got an allergic reaction to a bee sting.

The doctor swiftly moved onto my breasts: like any good salesman, keep it positive.

'I think these turned out really well in the end,' he proclaimed, proudly handling his work and examining them for more problems. 'Obviously, we need to keep you in a bit longer than expected to make sure everything is okay.' No mention of the explosion.

'What went wrong before?' I asked sheepishly. I was always scared to ask the questions they didn't want to answer or to say the wrong thing. That would force them to see I had a problem and not want to operate on me. I didn't want him to think I was fazed by the operation going wrong because I needed him, like an alcoholic needs a drink.

'Just a little rupturing of the implant.'

He proceeded to talk in surgeon-jargon, which completely went over my head, especially as I was still pumped to the hilt with drugs. I had been diligently buzzing the nurses at least every two or three hours for the painkillers, not because I was in pain that I could not handle but because I loved the feeling of the really strong morphine that they injected into me. So I had no chance of understanding the surgeon's complex explanation of what went wrong. I just accepted I nearly died, but didn't. So in my mind there was no harm done and we could all move on.

An incident like this would probably put some people off surgery or at least make them think twice. Some people might think, okay, it's supposed to be safer than crossing the road, but what if you kept crossing a really busy road all day every day for years? Does the chance of you getting run over go up then? I was having surgery every *week* at this point. This wasn't even my first scare: there'd been many, not only ones I knew about but ones I didn't know about until later, like having to have secret blood transfusions, which did really, really creep me out. Sadly, it didn't even cross my mind to stop surgery, or that the law of percentages wasn't on my side. I was gambling with my life and I didn't care.

All I wanted at this point was to go home to my daughter, my bed and my dog (a toy chihuahua) – and, of course, plan my next surgery.

'I'm fine. I can go now?' I asked the doctor, who was doing his rounds at 9 a.m. Funnily enough, I hated hospitals, the very place I was addicted to coming to. They were clinical, the beds were always too hard, there were annoying beeping sounds, the food was crap even when you went private, and you had to rely on a stressed nurse to do everything for you. Not to mention it felt too cold. Plus, I hated rules. Hospitals always had rules, what you could and couldn't do.

I thought I'd convince the doctor how fine I was by sitting up, until I felt a horrendous pain on my boobs, like a forklift truck was dragging them away from my body.

'Careful, you have six drains in your breasts to make sure we filter out any excess blood.' I had only just noticed the tubes that uncomfortably sat inside my breast, attached to bags of drained blood.

'We just need to keep an eye on you. You can go home the day after tomorrow.' Then he walked off. Great. I thought about the horrendous hospital bill for two nights' stay, which made staying a week at the Dorchester cheap in comparison. Worse still, Georgia was due to come home from boarding school. I hadn't even told her I was having an operation. I had to call her, making out that I got tied up with work. I explained that she had to stay at school over the weekend. I could tell from my daughter's voice she was disappointed. It was like a dagger through my heart and, I could tell, through hers too.

I swore to myself at that moment that this would be the last surgery I had. I had nearly died, for God's sake. Why was I allowing my pursuit of beauty to jeopardise my daughter having a mother? I couldn't answer that but I did know deep down I would have more operations, even though the surgery, with each cut of the knife, was taking me further and further away from my dream of perfection. I was turning into a freak, but it was like an addiction to gambling: the next bet would win you all the money back and make you rich. I wasn't a quitter, I was happy to die trying. Not very heroic, I know.

I sat in my bed with the mirror examining every centimetre of my bruised, swollen face and breasts. I hated it all.

Once my bed was wheeled to the private room, and the nurse had closed the door, I did what any addict would do. I gathered up my drains, worked out how to drag them to my handbag and got out the pen and paper I always packed. This was how the ritual went. I started writing a list of what surgery I needed next, what wasn't right with the surgery I had, and how to fix it. The worst thing is, I thought this was my 'best thinking time'. In hindsight, it was my maddest moment.

For starters, the boobs didn't look natural enough. I wanted 28HH, but natural looking. The brow needed far more bone shaved away because the result was *too* natural. The lips were too big and needed reducing, not to mention lifting. As for the nose, I was peeking underneath the bandages and seeing the new shape before the swelling had time to really set in. Beyond the fact I could not breathe out of it, I could see that it looked plastic, worked on and too small. It looked like it was about to fall off at any time, a bit like Michael Jackson's nose. I had gone one nose job too far, I thought, filled with anxiety.

I scribbled away, drawing diagrams and working on my next insane ideas how to become perfect. I need a facelift now, I thought, oh and my eyes bigger to match these lips. I needed to write, to plan and to work towards rectifying the damage I had caused, to give myself a sense of relief, to make it all seem okay again; that this wasn't the best it was going to be, that I still had hope.

I didn't see the doctor again really apart from a brief two-minute call in to try to convince me again how amazing his work was. When it was time to go home I told the concerned nurses that my friend was waiting outside and did my usual trick: walked off down the road to go home.

I liked the long walk alone. It was good to walk off the medication, but at the same time the walk was painless because I was on drugs. I lived in central London anyway and if I felt like I was going to faint I could always hail a black cab. Mind you though, on this occasion I did feel very dizzy and weak, but I still carried on. Maybe it was all part of the pain, the struggle and the torture I seemed to like to put myself through.

Once home, feeling dizzy and ready to faint, I spent the next four hours staring at myself, trying on different clothes (everything you're not supposed to do) and styling my unbrushed, hospital-blood-stained hair to suit my new-found face. It was making me more depressed and frustrated.

This was another part of the ritual, you see. I was never happy with the result and this time I was even less happy. After surgery I always had what a drug user would call 'a downer'. I was so high with hope when I would have the surgery and when the reality dawned that I still didn't look like a Victoria's Secret model I hit a low, a depressed manic low, that only planning more surgery could get me out of.

When I finally saw Georgia she said: 'What have you done?'

'Nothing, why?' I would say this every time.

'Looks like you've had more surgery.'

'Don't think so.'

We'd then go back to watching a film or eating our dinner. She knew not to push me: you can't stop an addict, and they get angry when confronted. They need you to *not* talk about it, to make out everything is fine. The worst thing that can happen is they are forced to see that they may have a problem.

I never spoke about surgery to anyone apart from two people: the newspapers and the surgeons.

The surgeons, I thought, 'got me', so obviously they didn't think I was mad. Besides, they were my enablers, I needed them. The papers, well, they seemed interested in my story. I thought they were exaggerating when they would write their horrifying headlines about me being surgery-obsessed. In my own mind I wasn't obsessed: it was a logical choice to make an average girl above average, so that one day Barbie could find her Ken, and in my case, of course, keep the sugar daddy that I had until Ken came around.

I didn't talk to anyone else about it. I distanced myself from my family because I could never bear my mother's lectures and see her weep at the beginning when she would see my distorted, bruised face and changing body. But she also had learnt, just like Georgia, not to confront it. Whatever state I turned up in, they eventually just carried on as if nothing had changed. This time my boobs were the biggest they had ever been but Georgia didn't even mention them.

The papers ran the story the next Sunday – 'Biggest Boobs in Britain!' I think the headline was. Georgia finally raised the subject and nervously told me that someone at school said I was in the paper: 'Something about bigger boobs.'

'Oh yes, don't believe everything you read, Georgia. You know you are not allowed to read that trash.'

I would brush it off and change the subject. I had banned her from reading tabloids and I hated gossip, even though I fed it. Another one of my contradictions: I was full of them.

My boobs, however, were not easy to ignore. They were heavy, ginormous and my back was soon starting to hurt. I also felt them hardening. I could not shop on the high street so all my clothes had to be altered or made for me. I had to get bras specially made by Rigby and Peller, which cost a fortune but made me feel assured that, at least, my boobs probably were bigger than most people's, paired as they were with my tiny frame and 28-inch back.

None of my family ever mentioned the 'boob explosion'. They couldn't even if they wanted to; they knew better. If any of the family brought up my surgeries without me offering the information, they knew they would not see me again for months or years.

CHAPTER TWELVE

Diagnosed Dysmorphic

THE BOOB EXPLOSION did not put me off more surgery, nor did the procedure that nearly killed me when one of the implants ruptured. I was soon on the operating table again, for more nose, lips, cheeks and peels.

My newest obsession was my eyes. My facelifts had left them pulled, even though when I met Simon Cowell I explained the problem away by saying I had a grandparent from Thailand. This actually seemed to work in my favour, as Simon loved exotic-looking women. I went with my surgery-enhanced appearance because I had to but I was still desperately unhappy with my looks and wanted my old eyes back.

So I went to a specialist, which led me on a road to twelve operations to try and cut the muscles that had been pulled and tightened. This, however, caused my eyes to look uneven; the surgeons just couldn't get the balance right. For a time I had what looked like a lazy eye which, depending on which eye went up further, would change from one eye to the other, so a side fringe was no use. It was a nightmare.

Apparently, your eyes are connected like a seesaw, so if you don't get the balance exactly right one goes further up than the other. Under the care of London's famous and best eye hospital I still couldn't get two even eyes.

I had nearly given up and was trying to get my head round having a lazy eye for life when I trotted to New York City where I met Dr Garcia. I was referred to him by chance from a plastic surgeon in the US, who had offered me another facelift costing £30,000. It seemed the more work you have had, the higher the price tag they put on more surgery. This was for two reasons: firstly, you are basically wearing your wallet on your face, and secondly, it all starts becoming a form of reconstruction surgery, which is more and more complicated and less likely to give good results. Scar tissue which accumulates with every cut builds up after each operation and the results are less and less likely to be pleasing.

Dr Garcia was fairly new to cosmetic eye operations but did want to get into it, so for a bargain price of £8,000 he said he would fix my eyes under local anaesthetic. He also said I needed plastic tear ducts. Apparently I had been unable to cry for years. I obviously hadn't noticed this as any emotion was rendered null and void by the heavy drugs I was prescribed following copious amounts of surgery.

The operation, undertaken whilst I was awake, was not pleasant. I felt no pain but could certainly feel my eyelid being stretched back and the pulling of the stitches, not to mention Dr Garcia's heavy breath down my neck whilst he attempted to repair my eye.

Once the operation was complete I was to rest, so I walked around Central Park with an eye patch on for three hours. I then retreated to my lonely hotel room with a buffet take-out.

I flew home after two days with my newly implanted plastic tear ducts and stitched up eye that, hopefully, would be my answer to even eyes. Dr Garcia had given me exercises to do to gently pull it down if I saw it getting higher than the other eye.

So fresh off the plane from an eight-hour journey I arrived home and looked in the mirror. I noticed the eye was starting to look higher than the other, so I panicked and desperately tried to pull it down, confusing the exercises with the pulling but combining it all...

Suddenly my eyeball started bleeding, the blood dripping onto the bathroom floor. I screamed from the sheer horror of my eye bleeding, not to mention the fact that I was now blinded by blood. It crossed my mind that I may have not-so-cleverly blinded myself in one eye – ultimately for vanity.

In my panicky state I rushed to the phone to call my private doctor, struggling to see the numbers with my blood-blurred vision. He told me to go to hospital immediately. 'Holy melons, this is serious,' I thought. I did not want the embarrassment of sitting in A&E with blood pouring out of my eye, so instead I phoned my old eye surgeon. By now it was late at night but he told me to go to Moorfield Eye Hospital. He fixed it so they would be expecting me. One good thing about spending what was becoming nearly a million pounds on procedures was I could call in a favour or two and get seen without waiting hours.

I covered my blood-drenched eye with a tea towel. Disorientated and still in a state of panic, I hailed a cab to the hospital.

I was seen very quickly but I shocked the physician. He said I had burst the stitches but it would heal. He also said my eyes were in bad repair and I was set for eye problems later in life due to the sheer number of eye operations I had had.

This wasn't my first time at Moorfield Eye Hospital. The earlier operations I had at various places included two laser surgeries so I didn't need to wear glasses for reading. I also had a passion for wearing coloured contact lenses so my green eyes could be blue. These gave me numerous eye infections which led to me ending up in Moorfields. There I was told to stop wearing lenses and messing with my eyes in any way but it didn't put me off. I *needed* perfect blue eyes; Barbie had blue eyes.

So here I was again, with these humble eye surgeons who had a passion for improving sight, who saw people who were fighting not to go blind or for whom they were crafting a new eye. I had not listened to their advice and this time my eye was pouring with blood. The doctors said that my eyes were already damaged and if I didn't stop having these eye operations I would go blind. Shocking as that was to hear, I certainly needed two eyes that matched. I refused to surrender to paying money to look worse than I started. I had invested too much time and money to look perfect to quit now with lopsided eyes.

I bought my ticket to New York City to get what by now was eye operation number thirteen, only three days after my bleeding eyeball incident. My eye was still very red and swollen.

When I arrived in NYC I had to spend four hours at border control persuading them to let me through. They checked with the surgeon that I was indeed having another operation as it seemed that I had been red-flagged by US customs. I can only presume it was because I was passing through the USA almost every week for surgery, and this seemed unbelievable to them, even by LA standards!

I finally arrived at Dr Garcia's office. He inspected my red, angry eye and said it actually would heal completely even. By breaking the stitches I had stopped it rising further. Dr Garcia said I was, astonishingly, going to have two eyes that would completely match. No more lazy-eye!

He was right, the swelling went down. I went back saddened by the fact I didn't have an operation but I did ask him to remove the bags under my eyes, so I wouldn't feel I had left completely empty-handed. Besides, if any surgeon gave me a good result I would find new things for them to do. I realise now this was not a good idea, as it was destined to go wrong in the long run; but my logic then was that this man had made me look better once, so what else could he do to make me look better?

Sadly, he must have heard alarm bells and wanted to charge me £25,000 for eye bag removal. In my experience when a surgeon thinks you are a nut job and unlikely to be content with the result, due to the fact you will never be happy anyway, he over-charges. If you are stupid enough to pay this he will put up with your crap or will see that you're completely addicted and willing to pay any price for surgery.

Georgia had been at boarding school for a while now, and this had left a void in my life. I desperately didn't want her to go, but after Harry Potter she had a fantasy about boarding school and begged to go. Sugardaddy thought it was best she was with the 'experts' who could help her with her homework. Too often Georgia would come to me with questions which I couldn't help her with; I would phone Sugardaddy, but he was too busy. So I felt maybe boarding school gave her something I couldn't, plus that was where she wanted to go. I obviously didn't want her to leave me but she was getting a top private education, which I felt was more important than my selfish motherly instinct to have her with me. They say our children are never really ours, just lent to us for a short time. I had to let her fly or I would hold her back for life.

Needless to say, I now had no one to worry about but myself – oh, and my toy chihuahua, who had far too many coats and Gucci carriers.

I started looking for more and more corrections. Mr Fix-It was putting filler into my hands and now face on a twice-weekly basis, despite his protests about my going elsewhere and ruining myself and his plan for my many other surgeries. He still clung onto the thought of me coming back to him exclusively, but although I needed him to think I would, maybe, come back one day I knew one surgeon was never going to be enough for me now. He also distanced himself from me; our bond had been broken by my unfaithfulness. He no longer tried to kiss me. Often he would pass snide remarks about my appalling surgery by others: if I'd stayed with him I would have been fine, he would say.

The dermatologists were putting fillers and Botox into my face, despite me already having had filler removed.

I had more breast procedures with Mr Reconstruction, who used the value in my implants to fill them up and make my boobs bigger and bigger.

I had my lip lifted, leaving a scar below my nose; I was operated on three times, sometimes just for scar revision.

This is not to mention maybe seven more other operations to tweak my ever-disappearing nose. I would put filler in to plump it out when I went too far, as well as fat transfers. My butt would be put into my face, my hips and inner thighs were used in my boobs and my stomach went in under my eyes.

It wasn't enough. I wasn't happy; something was missing.

I was staring into the mirror, using my black eyeliner pencil to shade in areas in an attempt to try to work out what I needed, when I had a eureka moment. My moles needed removing! They were holding me back: this was exactly what I needed to become perfect.

So I Googled 'mole removal' and found a random surgeon. This time it was a woman: let's call her 'Mrs Mole'.

I asked her for a job lot: the best price to have every mole on my body removed. Mrs Mole said mole removal meant cutting them out, which would leave a scar. Really? There was no other way?

Mrs Mole asked if I would go to a psychiatrist first to seek approval for the treatment. This made it sound as if she would be willing to do the mole removal. Great, I was up for it. Grasping the number of the psychiatrist, who, I later discovered, specialised in mental disorders, I phoned him, not expecting what was to come next.

When I met the psychiatrist he seemed interested in my strong desire to remove every mole. That was because I now believed my moles were making me ugly. I did not want to leave the house until this matter was resolved. This would often be the case before each operation: I would get something in my head, fixate on it, decide that was the major cause of my utterly distasteful face or body and not leave the house until I had arranged for that thing to be operated on.

Often press pictures that graced the newspapers were pictures of me after surgery. I was either covering up bruises or papped showing them 'shamelessly', though the pictures would be taken during the very few times I went out. Sometimes I'd get lucky and would be able to disguise the signs of treatment well.

Anyway, the psychiatrist seemed really interested in my quest for beauty, which seemed perfectly logical. In true Alicia Douvall fashion, I wore my heart on my sleeve and I didn't hold back from telling him my thoughts.

I went home that day confused. I just wanted my moles removed, not counselling! You can imagine my shock when I received a letter through my door containing the psychiatrist's report, which said he had diagnosed me with 'body dysmorphia.' What a bitch Mrs Mole was.

'What a waste of time that was,' I thought. 'The guy's insane and clearly doesn't understand the logic behind my quest for beauty.'

Another blow soon followed when Mrs Mole sent me a further letter refusing to treat me because of this diagnosis and that, in her view, I should seek 'help'. Bloody cheek! I *was* seeking help, for my moles! If she had removed all of them I would have been happy. Instead she had, in my mind, created a bigger problem.

I was now fixated on the small moles on my arms and a few on my legs and face, which I had now no way of getting removed. I was not a quitter. In my book there were no such things as problems, only solutions. There was a way round everything. I trawled the internet until I found a company making micro-dermabrasion machines and mole removal machines in China, which essentially burnt off the skin.

Posing as a professional with a business, I bought the most powerful industrial-quality machines I could and waited eagerly for my packages to arrive.

As soon as they did I got to it immediately. The pain was pretty bad but I soon mentally got round it. I spent hours burning off my moles one by one and viciously sucking up my skin with the micro-dermabrasion machine.

I started ordering peels from eBay, to put acid on my face, more or less. I was now obsessing with *everything*, from the right shade of blonde hair, to my ever-increasing breast size, to my disintegrating nose. I needed to be pro-actively having a procedure every day.

CHAPTER THIRTEEN

Chasing the Dragon

THIS WAS THE height of my addiction. I decided to go for another breast operation as I wanted my boobs to look 'more real' this time, but the operation went horribly wrong.

I went to a surgeon that Sugardaddy recommended. (Obviously one of his bits-on-the-side had received a good boob job from him.) Like always I underplayed the amount of surgery I had previously had when I spoke to the surgeon and in no time at all I was set to go under the knife. I wanted slightly smaller boobs as my breasts were giving me a bad back. I had to do a handstand every day to relieve the pain – and that seemed to help!

By now surgery for me was water off a duck's back. I could also tell what the final result would be by looking at the result straight after surgery. You get a good idea examining yourself before the swelling has had time to kick in. I also learnt to ice, ice, ice – the greater the swelling, the less sure you will be of the result you will have; also never look down and stay sitting up, even sleep sitting up to prevent bruising.

This time when I woke up after the operation I was so bandaged up I could not tell the size, but the shape looked okay. It wasn't until the bandages came off that I saw the true horror of my breasts.

They had collapsed. In the middle of my chest there was no division separating the two breasts. I had asked for a larger, permanent cleavage: surely the doctor didn't mean to do this?

The nurse insisted I wait until the healing had finished before seeing the end result. I didn't need to, I was devastated, and Sugardaddy was not happy either.

I had to live with these breasts for a good few months. I trawled around, trying surgeon after surgeon to repair things until I finally found someone I will call 'Mr Jammy', for reasons that will become clear.

Mr Jammy agreed to reconstruct my boobs, yet again for an extortionate fee. He justified this daylight robbery by saying it would take him all day to do. He also said it was risky, which I think was more to the point.

I signed away any chance of being able to sue if I wasn't happy and again under the needle I went.

At the end of the surgery, my breasts were smaller but the procedure had not been successful. I still had one boob with two implants in it. Mr Jammy said that my breast tissues were just too thin to repair.

So, on his recommendation, I moved onto 'Mr Attitude', a very famous surgeon who graced the papers and was recommended by top high fashion magazines; in his waiting rooms there would always be a sixteen year-old fashion model or two waiting for their noses to be sliced down.

Mr Attitude didn't like me at all but he saw that I had a big problem. He said I needed to downsize to C-cup sized boobs. I wasn't impressed and had no desire for even smaller breasts but Mr Attitude said it was that or nothing, so I took up his offer.

Another overpriced breast job: I surrendered my body to yet another man who would hammer, carve and cut me to his liking.

When I woke up I examined Mr Attitude's work. He was a man of few words, with the bedside manner of Victor Meldrew. Mr Attitude made you feel like he really didn't want to speak to you and if you dared to waffle on in a drug-influenced state he would simply grunt and walk out of the room. He was highly respected in the plastic surgery world, so I guess people put up with this for the sake of a perfect nose or pair of tits, and I was one of them.

I asked him, 'Has the gap gone? Is it fixed? Did you need to move my nipple?'

Luckily, the answer was, 'No', he hadn't needed to move my nipple, and 'Yes', I was fixed. My skin was still young so had bounced back well.

'What cup size am I now?' That was one question too many and then he was gone.

I looked down at my shrunken breasts, unsatisfied. Too small, I thought.

As I recovered I had, in theory, two good boobs. Mr Attitude kept telling me how hard the operation was, even for him, and that I was lucky to have come out of my breast surgery story with, in his eyes, a pretty good chest. His face lit up, showing expression for the first time, when he said, 'No more surgery!' and explained that if I risked one more breast operation I could end up losing my breasts for good. Mr Attitude said I had come to the end of the road. I had barely any of my own tissue left: it was paper-thin when it should have been inches thick.

I tried for a couple of months to live with my new breasts before I was asked to appear on a television programme called *Celebrity Love Island*, on which I was required to wear a bikini on TV and get picked (or not) by my fellow celebrities, who were all Z-list, if they were on any list at all. Brendan Cole from *Strictly Come Dancing* seemed to be the only contestant with an actual job.

Stuck on an island with my small breasts which I hated and felt very conscious of, I soon discovered this TV series wasn't for me. First off I was told to canoe – my hair extensions were not made for water. Then the boys would pick a girl to pair off with. I was picked second to last. The loser, who would be singled out for the week, was supposed to be model Sophie Anderton, but she stormed off into the show's 'diary room' and she threatened to quit the show if things didn't change.

Two days later the 'team' revolted and I was Miss Single Saddo. It was hell on earth and played on my every insecurity. I had to sleep in the only single bed surrounded by kissing couples in snuggly double beds. The presenters said I 'hurt their eyes', as I was so ugly, which was really upsetting. Whatever game this was, it wasn't fun. After only one week I quit and walked off the show. It seemed to me it was rigged shit, playing on people's insecurities and driven by their need to be desired and loved.

I got through it only by the thought of having another boob job. I wasn't picked and I didn't find love on the 'Love Island' but I told myself it was because my boobs were small. The presenters and the show's reviewers showed me no mercy. They pointed out that my face was pumped with too much filler and that I looked 'plastic'. Each cruel word only drove me to want more surgery. I wanted to run and hide, injected by my needle and safe in a hospital, where I would get all the hurt fixed.

That's when I subscribed to boob job number eleven. This wasn't with Mr Attitude, and it turned out he hadn't been exaggerating about the dangers of further surgery. My breasts collapsed during the operation and I woke up to discover I had one breast again. I was so upset to see the appalling result I had paid good money for. I knew I couldn't go back to Mr Attitude. My world of surgeons was narrowing.

By now Sugardaddy was exploring new ways to control me, as he was quickly getting bored of my revolving breasts and different faces.

The celebrity men I had dated were always a threat to Sugardaddy. He knew he had one line of defence: to force me to 'kiss and tell' on the men I was seeing, which would ultimately destroy the relationship for good. This was a routine he had tried and tested many times. I was starting to move away from modelling and increasingly had to rely on Sugardaddy and the stories I was selling.

I fell into Sugardaddy's trap every time and by now I was hardened; I had been let down too many times by men. I felt like by doing that first kiss and tell story about Mr Athletic I had already stepped over the line: I might as well do hundreds. So I did, egged on by Sugardaddy. As soon as the men let me down I let them down, letting them know who was really using who and, in my eyes, having the last laugh.

Even this, though, wasn't enough for Sugardaddy. Sexually he kept pushing me to limits I wasn't comfortable with, like asking to have threesomes with my friends, telling me I was 'boring in bed' if I didn't. I would sometimes phone him to talk and he would snap abuse at me. He was no longer the Sugardaddy who adored me, whilst by now I was completely in love with him. I wanted us to settle down, to get married and have kids together; even if I didn't get a phone signal, I was ready for that house in the country. But the seesaw we were on had completely pivoted. He now held the power and had my heart; I didn't have his.

Sugardaddy started to go off with other girls and have full-on relationships. He told me he would still support me but I wasn't his girlfriend anymore. Despite that he would still ask me to round to his house and we would end up kissing and more. It was confusing for me: every time we ended up in bed I thought we were back on track, but then I'd find another girl's knickers in his drawers and my heart would sink again.

It seemed to be that, yet again, I was in love with a man who didn't love me, a man who verbally abused me and used me. He had power over me, though. I craved security and he knew that. I wanted Georgia to have a good education and he knew that too, so it was hard for me to walk away.

When a new man did come along, Sugardaddy would suddenly reignite his love for me, just enough to make me come back. The first time the new man did something wrong I would do a 'kiss and tell' story and we would be back to square one, with Sugardaddy soon losing interest again, which became soul-destroying.

My crutch was plastic surgery, which I turned to as soon as anything went wrong. I studied my face daily, sometimes all day long. I was always so disappointed in my own reflection. I would go clothes shopping but when I saw my face in the mirror I would be so upset by it I wouldn't buy any clothes, I would simply get dressed frantically, as fast as possible, distraught by my reflection and body and rush home as fast as I could. My thinking was that there was no point purchasing nice outfits when I was so ugly.

At the hairdressers I would read books to avoid looking in the mirror. When I did get a glimpse of myself I would believe the whole hair salon was talking about how disturbingly bad I looked; I would ask the hairdresser to hide my face as much as possible with my hair. Of course this was fed by the media commenting on my 'terrible look'.

It was during this period I met 'Billy' (as in 'Billy Bullshitter'). I was hanging out in a club when I met a smooth-talking music manager, who told me he managed Michael Jackson's guitarist. He said that with his Jamaican roots he had great connections in the music business. Billy had swagger.

He asked me to go for dinner the next day. I was lonely and insecure and Billy was cheeky and charming. The expensive meal at Nobu was a good investment for him and he knew it.

Decked out in Louis Vuitton and Gucci, Billy drove a Porsche. He told me he had offices in Battersea and owned a black male lifestyle magazine. I thought I was dealing with a successful businessman, who showed me attention and saw potential in me. Billy said he wanted to take me to the next level. Little did I know at this point he would indeed take me to another level… down.

It started off with Billy wining and dining me. Things were good for a while. We started attending celebrity parties, which he would arrange for me.

It was when he said he had to move out of his home in north London and needed to live at my place for a while, as he really needed to focus more on me whilst I was 'hot', that I should have been suspicious, but I wasn't.

Billy then told me the magazine was closing down as it wasn't doing well. So Mr Successful was actually left with just a chewed-up old Louis Vuitton bag, some nice designer clothes and a Porsche. He settled himself on my sofa and stayed there for the next four years.

By now Sugardaddy was not seeing me as much but my insecurities and need to feel 'looked after' led me to Billy, I guess. He convinced me I could sing really well. My dad brought us up on country and western music so I had a soulful voice, but it wasn't trained and I was certainly no Adele. I was always brought up to believe I had a really bad voice as when I tried to sing as a child my sisters would howl like dogs and my Dad would screw up his face and put his hands on his ears, asking, 'Stop that, it's not nice for anyone.' So I had never really thought of a music career before.

Billy said I needed to change my look, not take any more glamour modelling jobs and concentrate on my 'career' as a singer. We started off in a studio in the UK. We worked with some respected producers and actually recorded a whole album with an English producer, but Billy mysteriously fell out with him and said the album was, in hindsight, not good enough. Billy said we needed to work with the big guns. He would hook us up with Michael Jackson's singing teacher, Seth Riggs, and record an album with P. Diddy's producers, Mariah Carey's producer Narada Michael Warden and Jamaican duo Sly and Robbie, with guest rappers, like Bounty Killer, performing on it.

It made sense and I was excited. Billy said his finances were being held up and he needed to pay the studio, producers and, of course, flights and accommodation. I had saved up £70,000 from modelling. I figured if Sugardaddy pulled out of paying for Georgia's education the money was here, held securely, to pay the fees myself. So I lent Billy some money from my nest egg.

We flew all around the USA. First, we were off to LA, where we hired amazing cars and stayed in five-star Beverly Hills hotels whilst I had singing lessons with Seth Riggs. We recorded with Narada, P. Diddy's crew and other professionals in New York. We were making great music with the help of the heavy hitters; it was like a dream come true. I felt like it was a foolproof plan that couldn't go wrong. Although I wasn't pitch perfect they all seemed to say I had a soulful voice and had it in me to make it. I was starting to dare to dream of bigger things than being a glamour model. Besides, Billy kept reminding me glamour modelling didn't last forever and was a very short-lived career.

Billy said he had great contacts with the likes of Sony and Universal. With big producers on board it seemed impossible to fail. So when Billy said we needed five more songs and should fly Sly and Robbie into the UK to record with us it made perfect sense. There was one problem, he said: his finances were still held up. Billy could give me back my money within two months and wrote that promise on a piece of paper and signed it.

Billy had already ploughed through my life savings of £70,000. He reassured me I would get this back but with interest. My mum was now living with us and she had £30,000 in savings for her pension. Billy suggested he borrowed it. My mum had a big heart and trusted me so she allowed Billy to drive her to the post office, in her lunch break whilst she worked as a PA to Jaguar in London, to take out her pension money. It was all she had in the world.

We did record with Sly and Robbie. This was exciting: the music only got better and better. But Billy was starting to act shady. When the album was complete he made excuses about when it could be delivered. He was very vague about exactly when my mum and I would be given back our money. Before long he stopped talking and making plans for the album completely and moved on to talking about a concert he was planning with celebrities like Elton John to save the rainforest.

It became a joke. Billy turned my living room into his office and bedroom. He had a whiteboard and he would write on it: '1 p.m. – meeting Boy George. 6 p.m. – meeting Elton.' It was starting to look like bullshit.

The shadier Billy got the more frustrated I got. Eventually I asked him to leave my home but he wouldn't. I even moved house to get away from him but again he found a way into my new home and just settled himself on the new sofa.

Billy shadowed me everywhere I went. He said I should not go to a meeting alone, as he said people wanted to take advantage of me. He guarded me like a loyal rottweiler dog. I got so used to Billy being everywhere I was that I became totally reliant on him. I would go into Starbucks and whisper to him what I wanted to order and he would order it for me. Increasingly this was how I communicated with most people.

I hated Billy but he had made me rely on him. It was at this point in time that I was heavily featured in the press for my drunken antics, plastic surgery and bad outfits. Behind the scenes a terrible story was emerging of a man who controlled me and would try to destroy me.

Billy asked for more money for a music video, suddenly reigniting his passion for the album. He said we had come so far it would be ridiculous not to finish it now. He had taken all my savings and my mother's so by now the alarm bells had rung and Billy could not persuade me to hand over any more money.

Another instance: Billy's Porsche suddenly mysteriously disappeared overnight. He claimed it was stolen, but my cleaner saw someone get into it using a key. Incidentally my laptop was also in the car; that went too. He kept turning up in different top-end, designer cars. Eventually he started driving the car that Sugardaddy had bought for me. He wasn't insured so I really wasn't comfortable with it. I ended up down-grading my car to a really girlie pink Beetle, in the hope that Billy would not want to drive it anymore, but that did not work; there was no shame in his game. It was all very dodgy and, of course, my so-called 'manager' continued to behave suspiciously and make vague promises to give us our money back 'soon'.

It became a horrible house to live in. I had a very unwelcome houseguest who would not leave. My mum was still depressed about Dad, not to mention her savings were now gone too, so we didn't really communicate about how we might get Billy out, so we ended up living with him squatting on my sofa – and it was a nice sofa, which he ruined with his hair products and toupee glue. Billy would wear an unusual afro toupee, with extra helpings of black hair gel, which left marks on all my Versace cushions.

By now Billy had convinced me to stop modelling. Reality TV was just starting to take off and I was getting offers every week but Billy convinced me to stay true to my music and not 'sell out to tacky TV offers'.

I wasn't one to sit around and wait for things to happen so I decided to join a girl band called 'Good Girls Gone Bad', the UK's answer to The Pussycat Dolls (although *The Sun* would write that we were the ropey, sloppy-seconds version of The Pussycat Dolls).

I worked day and night to learn the challenging dance routines. I made all the outfits, sticking jewels on bras until 5 o'clock in the morning. We started touring around the country but with eight girls working together it soon became a bitch-fest and, as usually happens, the band split up. Music had left me £100,000 down. I had lost all my savings and my mum's, I was by now disillusioned with the industry and I still had Billy Bullshitter living on my sofa, so I decided there was only one thing for it.

I needed butt implants.

I had thought about this idea since measuring Barbie and working out that her bum would be bigger than mine if you were to blow her up to my size. It made perfect sense to get implants in my bum.

This, of course, was before the whole Kim Kardashian-inspired big butt explosion, so large bottoms were not yet fashionable. Back then in the UK there was only one person doing this operation so there was no second opinion to be had: it was him or nothing. The surgeon said that with such big breasts I really needed butt implants to keep me 'in proportion'.

I certainly needed something to take my mind off music. Seeing the milky needle of the anaesthetic was like sitting down with the best hot chocolate in the world. It was so comforting and for me had an instant feelgood factor.

I woke up lying on my front with a serious pain from my butt, but when I managed to see my butt I was delighted: a perfectly round 'J-Lo' arse was staring back at me.

It didn't come without its own problems, though. I had to wear supportive pants for many months and I couldn't sit down for at least six weeks without a rubber ring! Even now long-haul flights are painful, as sitting down for long periods of time really hurts. It is like having a very bad headache in your arse.

One time, I remember, I got to Heathrow Airport after a long taxi ride; my butt was already aching. Usually I would carefully book mid-week in low season so I had more chance of getting an aisle to myself in economy and have a whole row to myself to lie down (I hadn't grasped the whole frequent flyer thing), but this time I found out my flight was full and

I would have to sit up right on my butt. So I decided to not take the trip and walked off home again.

I had gone for the biggest butt implants the surgeon would give me. He said butt implants only last ten years as they were not like breast implants: you use your butt every moment of every day. Ten years seemed forever so I wasn't worried about that. He said they could also flip or migrate, as it was not the best place to have implants! Holy moly! My tits looked like smuggled beach balls covered in a towel and my arse might turn over at any time.

It turned out that the butt implants didn't change my life like I thought they would. Although my arse did look good in jeans the down side was when I bent over you could see the implant and photographers often complained that they could no longer shoot me from the back with my 'weird arse', as usually glamour model poses meant a lot of bending over or being on all fours.

At this time I was still going back to Mr Fix-It, but he wasn't a reconstructive surgeon so wasn't keen to repair the damage I had suffered with my re-collapsed boobs and botched face. He had also fallen out of love with me as a project because he didn't have full control. I felt like a girlfriend whose boyfriend had lost interest in the bedroom; no matter how much sexy lingerie I put on it didn't make any difference. Maybe he thought I had grown too old. When I was young and fresh I had looked like a clean canvas for him to work on and it seemed like I was his ideal girl.

I was as hooked on Mr Fix-It as ever and craved both his attention, once he once gave it back to me again, and what he could supply. He was important to me like a dealer to a crackhead: the bond on my side was unbreakable all the time I was addicted. Every week I would ask for something, maybe fillers, lip alterations. Sometimes I would just sit in his office and ask what operations were new, what did he think I could improve. He would still scribble away a plan, but he didn't have the same passion, and I didn't hold the same trust. I was holding on to a love that had gone.

I felt I had outgrown him in some ways and as I found other surgeons to fulfil his role I saw Mr Fix-It less and less. When I met a new surgeon I would obsessively text, email and call him like a young teenager in love. It was all exciting and new. I could never get enough of them to start with but I would soon lose interest when their work showed me that they had no real magic to offer me.

It took me a long time to fall out of love with Mr Fix-It, despite the disastrous surgeries, and, like a cheating spouse, whilst I moved on to many others I kept him hanging on. He knew I was cheating but he couldn't do anything about it but distance himself from me and make little digs which showed the bitterness and resentment that he tried to hide. Mr Fix-It no longer held any power over me. I had unlimited funds for surgery from Sugardaddy and had found many a man to replace him.

However, whenever things went wrong he wasn't far from my mind. So when one day I was thinking about an idea that would give me better breasts I decided to give Mr Fix-It a call. I had last had direct contact with him about six months before.

I phoned up Mr Fix-It's secretary only to be shocked by what I heard. Mr Fix-It had taken early retirement! 'NOOOO!' I thought. She said he had handed over his patients to another surgeon. I frantically dialled his private mobile only to discover it was cut off. I thought how would I cope without him?

I immediately phoned up another surgeon. Plastic surgeons were a small professional circle, they all knew each other and competed against each other. Some were friends and championed each other; others were rivals. I asked, 'What happened?'

The other surgeon said he thought Mr Fix-It had no choice but to retire. He had too many lawsuits against him and there had even been a few deaths on his operating table! One was a woman who had suffered a heart attack there. I was told that Mr Fix-It had insisted on finishing her facelift to ensure that he got paid. Rumours were rife but one thing was sure, Mr Fix-It was a controversial figure and he himself would admit that he didn't know when to stop.

'I sail too close to the wind,' I remember him once saying, without me ever complaining. 'I overdid your eyes but you will benefit from them for years to come.'

It was because he went over the top and sailed so close to the wind that I liked him as my surgeon. I wanted so desperately to be as far away from Sarah Howes as possible so the more drastic the work the better, and to hell with the consequences.

I felt saddened by Mr Fix-It's 'early' retirement but it seemed like a good thing overall. Another door closed meant another temptation I couldn't succumb to. I thought this was another sign that I should move on. Of course, there was always a surgeon somewhere willing to operate on me but none were ever quite so eager as Mr Fix-It.

CHAPTER FOURTEEN

Holiday in Thailand

SUGARDADDY WAS, AGAIN, trying to make amends. He had decided he was a sex addict and he called his two-timing his 'demons' that were 'out to destroy' him. He told me that we needed to have an open relationship, and that most people would not understand this. I agreed; I mean, after all, even I didn't understand it.

He thought a holiday in Thailand would be good for us after all we had been through. I thought it would be a great idea to cheer my mum up over Christmas and New Year, when she was bound to miss Dad. In previous years Christmas was something we looked forward to so much but it always ended in arguments and tears. This year we didn't have the large family anymore and Christmas wasn't something we were looking forward to. We had grown wise by now to its tendency to always end in disaster so a holiday to the other side of the world seemed like the best way of making it through the festive period. We could sit on a beach sipping piña coladas whilst watching Christmas swiftly, subtly pass us by.

As often happened, Sugardaddy pulled out of the trip, saying work had made it impossible for him to go. I was so excited that he would be there with us as a true family it was immensely disappointing. Still, I had Georgia and my mum so we were going to make the most of it.

Best of all, Sugardaddy had arranged for us to stay at the five-star spa resort Banyan Tree, with the next week at another hotel, as the Banyan Tree was fully booked.

After an arse-aching twenty-one hours of travel to Bangkok and then finally Phuket, we arrived in what looked like paradise. I had been to Phuket once before and had fallen so much in love with the place I wanted to show my mum and Georgia how amazing it was. The clear blue sea, the warmth of the sun, the peaceful and friendly local people, mainly Buddhist; staying in one of the leading and most picturesque hotels of the world, I knew we were set for the holiday of a lifetime, something we all desperately needed.

Mum, however, was getting frequent calls from Dad, begging for her to come back. She said she didn't like the food as it was too spicy. I decided to surprise her and Georgia with a boat trip on Boxing Day four days into the idyllic holiday. I hired a boat and crew to take us out for the day; we would catch our own fish and have the crew freshly prepare it. I was so excited to surprise them with my generous, thought-out gift of a fun, relaxing day on the ocean. However, Christmas Day came around and mum was increasingly unhappy. She didn't like that we hadn't had a Christmas dinner and hadn't even seen a turkey or any stuffing. She felt it took away too much of Christmas, complaining there were no crackers, decorations or a Christmas tree. To her it just didn't feel like Christmas.

I thought the boat trip would really cheer her up but Mum said she just wanted to relax on Boxing Day and do traditional things, like let Georgia play with her toys, eat cold turkey sandwiches (or, in our case, green curry sandwiches) and play Monopoly.

We were in Thailand so it wasn't going to be traditional and that was the whole point of it, so I stormed off feeling I just couldn't please her, disappointed I had gone to so much thought and effort to have it so ungratefully received. I was forced to cancel the boat trip, then I ruined Christmas for everyone by sulking for the rest of the day. My poor mother, she was just trying to hold onto something that resembled her life, as at the age of 60 she had lost the husband she had reckoned on spending the rest of her life with and had been left with nothing. She had to start again and, worst of all, she had to rely on her unstable daughter to keep her.

The next day I was still sulking. I couldn't get over the fact that I had lost my deposit and wasn't able to convince my family to get on the goddamn boat. Georgia was backing Mum as she too just wanted to play with her toys. The toys, I explained, would always be there; the boat wouldn't!

I ate my Thai breakfast and told Mum and Georgia that I was going to walk along the beach. I needed to be alone, to just sit in the sun and take myself into a time out.

It was Boxing Day, 26 December 2004.

I started walking alone down the steep stairs to the beach and for some reason it felt eerie. As I got nearer I noticed the ocean had gone. I was confused, not remembering the beach being this big, and swore there was water there before.

I stopped for a moment. My instinct told me to go back, people were running. I was way ahead and further back as the beach was still some walk away.

Before I knew what was happening, children, women and men were running, shouting and screaming, 'Big wave!' I was about to be hit by a tsunami. I climbed the stairs back up towards the hotel and swimming pool.

I was completely bewildered by the sheer panic around me and the sight of a wall of sea, the intense horrifying roar of the ocean like a gang of thugs coming to attack you that you knew you couldn't possibly outrun. Then everything went black. I was hit by the water sucking me into its powerful grasp and thrown around like a rag doll. Suffocating and hit by rubble rushing by, I somehow managed to cling onto a tree which had stopped my tumbling fall. It seemed like forever till the nightmare was over but it was seconds.

As soon as I was out of the water I ran, following the frantic crowds, really believing it was the end of the world. I managed to escape to a hill where local Thai people and tourists gathered. More people turned up, bloody, frightened and lost. Most had lost their family members and were searching frantically; others were terribly injured. One woman was being carried on a broken door, which was being used as a stretcher, as she had a twisted, open wound on her leg, which was clearly broken.

I believed at this point we were the last survivors at the end of the world. I sat on that hill thinking what a cruel creator God was. I was too sensitive for the world as it was and now he had possibly taken my family, ended the world and left me alive in it. I was surrounded by screaming mothers who had lost their children, separated couples who didn't know if their partners were alive and young kids looking for their mum and dad. Almost everyone was injured and covered in blood and bruises. Many had ripped clothes and some didn't have clothes left, as the force of the wave had torn them off. I did, however, see the best in human beings up on that hill, especially the local Thai people. Everyone helped each other, giving up clothes for those who needed them or ripping them up to make bandages, looking after children and older people and doing their best to attend the wounded.

I still had no clue what had happened and I was worried about where Georgia and Mum were. The survivors I was with were warned of 'more big waves' and to stay on the hill for safety but I had only one thing on my mind. I needed to find my daughter. Seeing everyone's terrified faces I realised there was a real possibility that I could have lost my family for good. Had they had survived the world ending?

I didn't care if I was going to die, I decided to find Georgia and Mum. The men there tried to tell me not to go and hold me back but I went anyway. I looked blank and stern-faced at them, as if to say, 'Don't stand in my way'. The man holding onto my arm to stop me walking down to the beach slowly let it go, respecting what he thought was my death wish, not expecting to see me again...

I walked across the seafront, which no longer had pristine sandy beaches. It was a sea of debris, with flattened shops where moments before people had bought drinks or were sitting sunbathing and playing games. It didn't resemble a beach any more, more like a grey dumping yard for old broken wood and junk, while desperate people, like me, tried to find loved ones. They had also ignored the warnings of further waves and would rather be dead than left without their families.

I walked back up to the hotel, stony-faced and fully expecting at any time to be taken away by another 'big wave'. That walk felt like a walk into a boxing ring. As I turned my back on what now seemed like an evil sea I walked boldly, noticing every step I took as I knew at any point I would hear that horrifying roar of the ocean that would once again hit me and suck me into its grasp with all its might, leaving my world blackened and panicked. Only luck would decide if I lived or died. I was willing to fight whatever came along and take a beating or something worse.

Each step up the steep hill back to the now unknown felt like a lifetime but the nearer I got without being taken again by the sea left my racing heart anticipating, scared what I would find. Was I all alone in the world?

When I finally reached the swimming pool of the spa by the hotel I found life was going on as usual. People were still alive and sitting by the pool, complaining there was no ice in their drinks.

When I found Georgia and Mum I ran over, bursting into tears and hugging them. I was never so happy to see them.

Sitting by the pool, with other celebrities, including an *EastEnders* actress who was on her honeymoon, my family had been completely oblivious of the tsunami. They were glad to see me, as I had been away for hours. I explained to Mum that it was the end of the world. She was not convinced but I assured her that if she were to see the beach she would know what I meant.

I was one of the lucky ones and I knew my family had been really fortunate. If Mum had not made me cancel the boat trip we would not be here today.

There had been two waves. Luckily, our hotel was also on a hill. The beach had been a fairly long walk away and there was also a small, rocky island that took a lot of the impact of the wave on our section of the coast. That day 227,898 people died in the tsunami but only eleven people from our hotel were killed.

The three of us were due to go to our next hotel later that day. We decided we would go the next day instead, not realising the severity of it all. When we finally got a taxi to the new hotel we realised it no longer existed. When we pulled into a destroyed town, the taxi driver pointed to a pile of bricks and mess. People were searching for friends and family they prayed were still alive amongst the spookily flattened countryside, which continued as far as you could see.

The Banyan Tree allowed us to stay there for a further two weeks, which I paid for. I volunteered to help out, where I saw some horrifying images that will stay with me for the rest of my life. One hotel, which was exceptionally large, had the breakfast area in the basement, very near to the sea. Everyone who was sitting at breakfast at that time died with nowhere to escape. It was a shell of a hotel, blackened; the basement, where hours before families had sat happily eating their breakfast, was now thick with dark water.

The Thai people didn't have specialist equipment, they would simply dive into the water searching for the bodies. Others used long sticks to find bodies. When they found one the Thai men would dive in, tie a rope around the stiffened, swollen body and we would all help pull the body up, respectfully placing it in a white body-bag. There were no survivors in that packed breakfast hall. I will never forget the distinct smell of rotting corpses.

Dad convinced Mum to come straight home. Georgia went to the Kids' Club, which had now been turned into a day nursery even though it no longer had any children in it. Most of the time, Georgia was the only one there.

My job whilst volunteering included searching for and tagging dead bodies. Whilst this was hideous work it was the first time in ages I felt as if I was making a small difference. Seeing the faces of the local people, whose livelihoods and homes had been devastated by the wave, when they were given food to feed their family for the week felt better than any cosmetic surgeon with his handy knife had ever made me feel. For once my hair, my face and my boobs didn't matter. Maybe looks were not as important as I had thought?

As the days went on and rotting bodies continued to be found, we were no longer searching for people to be rescued, hope was fading: families by now only hoped to find bodies of loved ones so as to get a little bit of closure. There was a growing concern that insects might spread disease. I still wanted to help but when Georgia had an allergic reaction to a bite the British Embassy insisted we go home after ten days of volunteering.

It was a Christmas I will never forget. The disaster put things into perspective and I realised that family meant everything to me. I saw the humble Thai people getting on with their lives and being so upbeat despite losing everything:

their homes, their jobs and even family members. They didn't have the same help as the tourists did, and not only from their embassies. Foreigners seemed to be looked after better than the local people, perhaps due to concerns about Thailand's tourist trade.

Surviving the tsunami reminded me to be grateful for what I had and that maybe my ugly face wasn't that important in the scale of things. I felt grateful that I was still alive and more importantly so were my loved ones, that it wasn't my time to go yet. It made me realise how easy life can be taken away from any one of us at any given moment, how silly it was to argue over petty things, and how every day should be gratefully savoured. I thought about why it had not been me dead that day. Buddhists believe everything happens for a reason and I knew deep down that I still had something to do here and, shockingly, that wasn't to achieve a pretty face. Surely I could contribute more to the world than pictures on Page Three and boob explosion stories?

CHAPTER FIFTEEN

Bad Romance

BEING IN A tsunami changes you forever. You might not think the effects would last, but they do.

I started to crave more out of life. I was missing my soulmate. I really loved Sugardaddy, but he kept me at a distance. I made it clear I would have married him, had ten kids and lived happily ever after, through thick and through thin, but it seemed that this wasn't what he wanted. It turned out that what Sugardaddy preferred was a harem of girls, whilst I was craving cuddles and romantic country walks. I was contemplating a National Trust membership but he was considering sex parties and threesomes. Our worlds were getting further apart and I was getting lonelier.

Of course, I still had Billy on my sofa but that was no consolation.

I had been invited to a charity ball, to which Billy naturally insisted on coming with me as my manager, to fend off 'people taking advantage' and to make sure that, with my open heart, I didn't 'say too much'.

It was at that dinner I met Yusuf. He was a strikingly good-looking, short but muscular Asian man who insisted he was Brazilian. Yusuf sat next to me and immediately we started chatting. I could tell he knew who I was and was impressed. When I asked what he did he said he used to be a footballer but now was in sales. I can always smell a bullshitter when they claim to be footballers. First off he was the wrong build – far too bulky – and secondly he seemed too keen. Yusuf wasn't a man who projected a sense of accomplishment.

However, despite knowing Yusuf was a bullshitter (and by now I was collecting them), I found him entertaining and charismatic. Billy tried hard to keep Yusuf away, having smelt the bullshit too: as they say, it takes one to know one. What neither of us realised, sadly, was how sinister this man really was.

The seemingly fun-loving Yusuf dragged me up to dance and made me forget for a moment how ugly and lonely I was, so when he asked for my number I gave it to him.

Billy was really annoyed and he said I gave my number out too easily. Yusuf started texting me immediately after I left the ball, which made me feel a little uneasy. His texts didn't stop and he bombarded me with them, insisting that I go on a date. I didn't think there would be much harm to it, so I agreed.

Yusuf picked me up the next day in a Porsche four-by-four, dressed top-to-toe in new designer clothes. He took me to Hakkasan in Hanway Place, which was one of London's top restaurants. We talked and laughed all night. I was starting to warm to this seemingly friendly guy who was slowly easing me out of my rigid, controlled world and forcing me to be fun again. Maybe he was the answer to my lonely heart?

We became close very quickly but Yusuf was growing increasingly angry with the problem I had with Billy on my sofa. My mum had met a man and decided to move back to Sussex so when Georgia was back boarding at school it was just Billy and I living at my house.

It got so bad that one night that, when Yusuf came back to drop me off, he ended up getting into an altercation with Billy. Billy pulled a knife out. It was scary so I phoned the police. The police turned up, arrested Billy and took him away.

My 'sofa lodger', of five years by now, was finally and suddenly gone. I broke down and cried about how horribly it had ended; I cried because, at last, I had my house back; I cried because I was afraid to live without the man who had been managing my life. Yusuf was confused. He thought he had done the right thing, and in a way he had. But at the same time I had seen a side to him I really didn't like.

The police asked if I wanted to press charges but I didn't. They also told me that Billy had changed his name and had been convicted three times of fraud. It turned out he would target men and women like me, scam them for hundreds of thousands of pounds before leaving the country and changing his appearance and name. The picture the police showed me of Billy looked nothing like the man I knew. It explained his love of wigs!

It hit me then that I was never getting my money back or my mum's life-savings. I had to start again from scratch. This man had put his own selfish and superficial needs before my daughter's education and my 60 year-old mum's pension. I wanted to kill him.

I tried to find Billy after I had spoken to the police so that I could go after him with lawyers but he had already fled the country. The last I heard he was still living in LA, where I dare say he is trying to find new victims. Hopefully, no one else has been as stupid as me.

So it was good that Billy was finally out of my life. For the first time in five years I drove my car myself and spoke to people on the phone. It was shocking to talk to people who it turned out had stopped being my friend or working with me because of 'that creepy manager guy that controlled you'. The only person Billy didn't try to get in the way of was Sugardaddy, but I see now that this was because he had been living off him, through me.

With Billy out of the picture, Yusuf soon started to change. His behaviour became increasingly worrying. He would have outbursts if I came to his house later than agreed and start breaking things. One time, when I asked him to look after my chihuahua, I came in to see the poor little dog tied up to the banisters.

Things went from bad to worse. It started with Yusuf smashing his own apartment up, then he began destroying things of mine too and soon started pushing me in fits of anger.

Yusuf was Muslim and had some strange ideas. He said it was his fantasy for me to wear a sari. He told me I was dirty when I had a period. Yusuf wanted me to meet his mum but said that when I did I had to kiss her feet when she opened the door and say, 'Salaam Alaikum,' which I wasn't down with. I was Alicia Douvall, not a sari-wearing, feet-kissing girl.

After just three months the ever more unstable-minded Yusuf organised a party for his birthday. I thought nothing of it but when I turned up I felt something was going on.

You can imagine my shock when Yusuf got down on one knee in front of all his friends and family and proposed to me. He told me that we would have two weddings, an English one and one traditional Indian.

I really wasn't ready to get married to him; it had only been two months. Besides, he was acting very strangely. Because of the embarrassment that I felt with his friends and family watching and waiting for my answer I could hardly say 'No.' So, I ended up engaged to a nutter.

It wasn't long before Yusuf had one of his terrible tantrums. This time it involved him demanding his ring back, which he threw out of the window. The next day he did go looking for it but he either didn't find it or took it back to the shop to get a refund and didn't tell me.

Yusuf threw a lot of things out the window. On another occasion he had bought a twelve-pack of doughnuts. When I politely said I didn't want one he lost his temper, shouting and screaming then throwing the doughnuts out the window. By now the poor flat below must have had quite a few items in the garden.

As a result of all this I wasn't engaged anymore, which was great news, but Yusuf's behaviour was getting worse. He knew I had reservations and needed to hook me back in, in a way I couldn't get out of.

After another one of his rages, Yusuf sat outside my house, with his usual dramatic performance, which involved threatening to lie in the road and get run over if I didn't talk to him.

When I did he told me he wanted to drive me to a romantic dinner for two to make up. I had nothing else on, and Georgia was at boarding school, so off we went.

It turned out that Yusuf had booked a hotel overnight and insisted we stay. I didn't have my pills for contraception with me, so I asked him to go back. He wouldn't but he assured me that there would be no nookie.

Yusuf had said in the past that, due to his religion, he didn't subscribe to contraception. My pills kept disappearing: he would hide them from me from time to time or throw them away.

That night, after too many glasses of wine, we went upstairs. I wasn't so drunk that I couldn't tell him I didn't want sex as it wasn't safe, but he started kissing me and taking off my clothes. I started protesting more but Yusuf didn't listen. I thought he was joking when he said, 'Just shut up, you stupid slag.'

'Oh, I'm not cool with that kind of sex talk.'

I wasn't into specialist sex stuff. I had heard of men who really got off on demoralising a woman whilst having sex but that definitely wasn't my bag.

'Seriously, stop now.' I was starting to get worried. He didn't stop and became more and more aggressive and we had sex against my wishes.

Afterwards, Yusuf changed completely, crying and starting to tell me his life story. He said he was born a twin but, sadly, his brother inexplicably died and Yusuf was taken away from his mother, as the authorities feared that she was to blame. He said he had been sent to several foster homes before returning to his mum as a teen, only to be sexually abused by an uncle. I did feel sorry for Yusuf and thought that this explained his behaviour, but knew I had to get away, for Georgia's sake. He had become a ticking time bomb waiting to explode at any moment; he had crossed the line and abused my body. I just wanted out.

When I finally arrived home I sent a text to Yusuf explaining I needed 'time alone'. This didn't go down well and I was bombarded with texts and phone calls and times when he would randomly turn up at my door. He threatened to firebomb my house if I didn't see him.

By now I didn't feel safe anymore so I decided to move house. My mum was living with her boyfriend, and Billy was finally off the sofa, so it was just Georgia, the dog and I left. We moved to a gated development in Chelsea, which I chose purely for the security. Usually I was a daredevil and wasn't afraid of anything or anyone but something told me Yusuf was not someone to mess with: he was mad.

Yusuf again convinced me to meet him for a chat. Don't ask me why but I went. He drove me to his house afterwards. I was tired and decided the drive home was too long so I thought it would be best to sleep over there, rather than travel home that night.

As I started to fall asleep on my front I felt an almighty thump: he had hit me in the back. Yusuf was in a rage and punched me repeatedly. He pulled my hair to lift my face up so that he could punch me there too. It was all a blur; I just remember trying to protect myself but failing, thinking I wasn't going to get out of this alive.

Yusuf was furious because I had gone to bed early without him. He had completely lost it and was throwing punch after punch at me, using all his strength. At the time I thought he was trying to kill me.

As I lay whimpering on the bed, begging him to stop and trying to make sense of what had just happened, I started to realise I could no longer move my left arm. I was in excruciating pain. I tried to reach for my phone to call the police and an ambulance but Yusuf caught me doing it. He stamped on my phone then threw my mobile out of the window.

I tried to shout for help but he quickly put his hand over my mouth and told me if I screamed again he would kill me. I was shocked that the man I thought I loved was now threatening to murder me and had possibly broken my arm.

The pain was by now unbearable and I begged Yusuf to take me to a hospital. I told him I promised I wouldn't tell them what happened but he refused. He then locked the room and barricaded me in. He knew now he had gone too far and he was in a state of panic, going from telling me he loved me to saying, 'You deserved it, you bitch.'

All I could think about was, what the hell was I doing in this mess? I was a successful model and had worked myself out of living in a homeless hostel only to voluntarily drag myself back into the gutter with a no good son of a bitch like Yusuf.

The truth was, I discovered, that when you have been verbally abused you often cannot tell what is and is not abuse. The warning signs go unnoticed, as you put up with a lot more than most self-respecting women would, but you are literally blind to what is, and what isn't, acceptable behaviour. Sometimes it takes the man going too far for you to see you're with an abusive person. Now, I had a broken arm, a swollen black eye and was bloody and bruised all over. There was no question that this was abuse, as I would never let a man hit me. The moment they did, I was gone.

The problem now was that I did not know how to get out of there. Yusuf was keeping me captive, knowing full well the punches had taken away the last positive feelings I had for him.

I kept begging Yusuf to take me to hospital. The painkillers he was giving me were making me feel sick on an empty stomach and were not working. By now it had been five hours and the pain, swelling and bruising were getting worse. I was getting weak with crying so much.

It was late at night before, finally, Yusuf said, 'Get in the car, I'll take you.'

When we rolled up at McDonald's and he ordered a Big Mac and fries I was slightly confused. Were we going to the hospital after he had eaten?

Yusuf ordered two Big Macs with fries and gave me a burger and two Nurofen. He said that I should eat the burger first to keep the painkillers down. Wow, I felt such a fool and guilty for putting myself in a position that had allowed a man to go this far. Most of all, I feared for my life. I actually thought that if I didn't escape this man I would be leaving his house in a bin bag. Thoughts of never seeing my beloved Georgia again rushed around in my head.

Yusuf took me back to his flat and kept me locked up. I couldn't fight him, as I only had one arm and was certainly not strong enough. Besides, I couldn't even drive home, as I could not use my left hand!

Hours passed and Yusuf's mood went from remorseful to angry when I would not forgive him. He said he was going to kill me and feed me to a pig farm, as pigs eat everything, so there would be no trace of my body. Oh my God, this man had it all planned out!

Later Yusuf came down with a kitchen knife, saying he was going to kill himself. He forced my hand with his onto the knife and said he would stab himself with my fingerprints on the weapon, the police would think I did it and I would spend the rest of my life in jail.

Okay, this guy was seriously messed up and dangerous. I was all for risk and bad boys but this one was a complete nutcase, violent to the core. I had no doubt that Yusuf would kill me. I had to get out, somehow. I went into survival mode and hatched a plan. I would agree with him and forgive him and then make a run for it to my car, putting on the alarm.

But luckily, before I could put my plan into force, a neighbour had heard my frantic screams and phoned the police. That's when I thought I would be saved. They turned up and buzzed the flat from outside. When Yusuf said all was fine over the intercom, they asked to speak to me. Yusuf put his knife to my stomach and told me to say everything was good and to make it sound convincing.

I really wanted to be saved but I followed his direction, praying that the police would sense in my voice I really wasn't okay and was being forced to say it, then come up and rescue me. They didn't and left.

At 8 a.m. Yusuf finally fell asleep. That's when I saw my opportunity and I ran. I got in my car, started driving and moving the clutch and gears using only my right hand. It wasn't easy and I knew I could have crashed but I also knew it was my only hope of ever getting out of that flat in one piece.

I started crying in my car but they were tears of relief. Strangely, I drove to Sugardaddy, who immediately got me checked into a private hospital. I got an X-ray, which confirmed that I had serious injuries. I had fractured my shoulder blade and torn and damaged the muscles of my back. The older doctor said it looked like I had fallen off a horse at high speed. He was shocked and held my hand, whilst I tried not to cry again. The doctor said, 'Please love yourself and don't let anyone do this to you again.'

I felt beaten up, drained and embarrassed. How could I let this happen to me?

Worse still, I also found out I was pregnant.

The hospital scanned me and said the pregnancy was not healthy and that I would miscarry soon. I presumed the baby had stopped living at some point and I just hadn't noticed I was pregnant.

The police were also called and they took my clothes and swabs. My injuries were undeniably bad so they immediately went round to Yusuf's house to arrest him, but he had already fled.

The police were amazing. They put a search warrant out for Yusuf, guarded my house and gave me an escort to pick up Georgia from school and even to take her to her ballet class!

They said Yusuf was dangerous and it turned out that he also had a police record, including two reports of rape, both of which had been dropped.

Within forty-eight hours, Yusuf was found and was brought into the police station for questioning. They managed to get an extension, so he was kept in for another forty-eight hours behind bars. I felt safe again.

I miscarried the baby. Afterwards, I had to go to the hospital for an operation because I was told that 'bits remained' inside me. This only added to the trauma of it all. I received treatment for my injuries for almost a year afterwards. To this day I have a bad back that serves to remind me to be more careful who I let into my life.

CHAPTER SIXTEEN

Tried to Make Me Go to Rehab

I NEEDED TO GET on with my life. I wanted to forget this deeply embarrassing, shameful event had ever happened. I needed to pick myself up again and not let this nutter bring me down. My arm was still in a sling, bruised and battered, as I went about organising myself some bigger boobs, the pick-me-up I thought I needed.

This time I really put my heart and soul into it. My collapsed boobs were a mess but no one in England would touch them. Following a recommendation by a UK surgeon, I decided to contact Dolly Parton's surgeon in Nashville. He agreed to see me for a consultation. Apparently if this guy could not sort me out then no one could and it would be time to throw in the towel. The surgeon had an internationally good reputation for his work with breasts and had even invented and manufactured his own implants. I was confident that I had found my new man.

Within two weeks, as soon as I was out of my arm sling, I flew to Nashville to get new boobs. For me this was a way of getting my power back. I was taking control of what was making me unhappy, working on myself and flying halfway round the world alone to do it.

The surgeon 'mmm'ed and 'ah'ed for a while during the consult before telling me that it would be a hard job, maybe an impossible one, but he would try. I had to sign extra documents agreeing to the possibility that the operation might make me worse off. I was told that I might wake up with implants of any size or potentially none at all. I signed because at that point better breasts seemed like the most important thing.

The surgeon said it took him twelve hours and that he nearly gave up halfway through, as my breast tissue had completely gone. It was the hardest breast operation he had ever seen. He had to use human tissue, which was only legal in the USA. I presume this came from medically donated bodies, which isn't a great thought. I have always believed you take on someone else's soul when you transplant part of them into you.

It was made very clear to me that if I touched my breasts again I would not have any breasts to worry about. There would be nothing he or anyone else could do. This was my last breast operation, which made me sad. Surely he was 'egging' it up?!

When I took a sneaky peak at my boobs under the bandages I saw that my once botched breasts were pretty much perfect. I was a happy customer!

The surgeon gave me exercises to do at home so I would not lose movement in my arms. I was also hooked up to six drains, which drained blood and tissue fluid from my breasts. He said I had to have them in for at least two weeks. What? I needed to go home! I had to be there for Georgia, so he agreed I could fly home and that he would arrange for another surgeon to care for me back in the UK and take the drains out. It meant flying home whilst attached to drains filtering blood. It was slightly embarrassing going through the security scanners, where I clearly looked like I was trying to smuggle something under my baggy jumper.

When I got home I received a call from my loyal agent of five years, who said he wanted me to come in for a meeting. I had to work out how to hide or disguise the six tubes draining my boobs but, with a baggy dress and lots of gaffer tape strapped around my inner thighs, hips and stomach, I managed to conceal them.

At my agent's London office he told me that he had put me forward for a new television programme called *Celebrity Rehab*. He thought I could go in because of my diagnosed body dysmorphia. I said that I would be a fraud if I did, because I didn't have a problem. I still didn't believe the diagnosis that I had an addiction to surgery.

My agent asked me to go in to see the producers anyway, which I agreed to do, so he set up a meeting for me alone and off I went.

I was surprised when the producers confirmed that they wanted me on the show and would get me a USA work visa the next week!

I really didn't think I qualified for rehab. I was not an addict and, even if the diagnosis I received was right, being addicted to plastic surgery surely wasn't a real addiction?

I did not say 'no', though. Following the incident with Yusuf I was feeling really down on my luck and fragile, so rehab in Malibu sounded like a nice escape. The rehab centre was called 'Passages' and it took a holistic approach to healing. It was located in a mansion house with a swimming pool and a jacuzzi. I was all set for a party! I would go just to relax and unwind.

Production company Endemol recruited Rowetta Satchell from the Happy Mondays and *The X Factor*; other members of the Happy Mondays who were there seeking help with alcohol; Leslie McKeown from the 70s pop group The Bay City Rollers; a glamour model called Cassie Sumner with an eating disorder; Rod Stewart's guitarist Robin Le Mesurier, who was also an alcoholic; Jason Sellers' daughter, Victoria; and an American TV actor with a painkiller addiction.

First off we had to get visas at the US Embassy. I still had tubes and drains and was again worried when I went through security that I would set their alarms off and they would do their American drama thing and panic, thinking I was smuggling something under my dress. I suppose I was, but it wasn't anything harmful to them! Luckily, I walked through without hearing any sirens.

I was very quiet and couldn't join in with the other celebrities, who were overexcited, chatting and getting to know each other. I was drugged up to my eyeballs with painkillers and fragile as a china doll. Every time I moved a drain would uncomfortably shift and twist inside me and pull on my stitches, so I sat alone, a couple of chair rows away from the others and drifted in and out of sleep whilst waiting for my number to be called for my interview.

When the UK surgeon finally removed the drains almost three weeks later I was so happy. The drains had been very uncomfortable and made it hard to get on with life – though I did go clubbing with them. I managed to strap the drains to my inner thighs and stomach and wore a baggy dress. Men would chat me up and ask me to dance, at which point I had to somehow make my excuses as I didn't want to explain what the weird lumps were when they attempted to put an arm around me or touch my waist. The results of my new breasts were really good: in no time I was emailing the Nashville Surgeon to subscribe to more surgery from my new man.

The flight to the US was business class so we were able to lie down on beds. For me it was a chance to get some rest. Because I was doing the programme I had checked myself in the week before to get my nose reshaped, fat transferred to my cheeks and to get a skin peel. The procedures had taken a lot out of me and I was tired, I guess because my body was trying to recover.

I was the next seat along from Les McKeown, who really *was* an alcoholic, it turned out. The high-spirited Scot drank his way through the mini bar, whilst singing to the disgruntled first class business travellers, only passing out after asking for one of my strong sleeping tablets.

When we arrived at the rehab centre we could not believe our eyes. It was a grand Californian mansion, with chandeliers, massive bedrooms, all with en suite bathrooms and walk-in wardrobes, a swimming pool that sat proudly in the lush garden along with the jacuzzi, a barbecue area and hammocks. Wow, this was paradise! I was getting paid to talk about myself and lie here in the sun. 'Fantastic,' I thought. 'What an easy way to earn money!'

As soon as we arrived the staff asked if they could search our bags. I say asked, it was more like a demand. They then confiscated all the drugs from us, saying they would administer drugs when we needed them. I really panicked at this; paradise had cracks in it. I couldn't function without my sleeping pills and painkillers. I was experiencing frequent headaches that were so bad only my prescribed, heroin-like OxyContin would get rid of them. I had no choice but to let the staff have them. This wasn't going to be an easy pay cheque after all, I realised.

To start with I was just there to get my money and come home, but I realised I was not going to get away with it that easily. I had to endure a gruelling schedule of counselling and therapy, including group therapy, to break me and the rest of the celebrities down.

My experiences had taught me to be strong and I believed you make your own destiny in life; no matter what has happened to you, you decide your own future. I was still making terrible mistakes in my life, which haunted me, but I still wished I could be Alicia Douvall completely and not let Sarah Howes the loser creep back into my life. To me it was the ghost of Sarah Howes creeping in who found the loser men, who got beaten and used, cheated on and lied to, I wanted no part of her in my life.

The counsellors tried to make me go back to Sarah Howes and I wasn't comfortable with that, having killed her off long ago. They said that no matter how hard I resisted they would get through to me. I tried to explain to them that I had no problem and was wasting everyone's time. Really my place should have been taken by someone far worse off than me but the counsellors wouldn't have it and insisted on helping me.

The therapists told me I was like a house built on quicksand with no foundations and they wanted to give me those solid foundations, the tools to get by in life. They said my life hadn't been working out too well so far and what did I have to lose by listening and taking part whilst I was there?

I did a lot of crying in those 90 days and nearly quit the show at one point. I was knocked down then built up and, believe me, I was a hard nut to crack and rebelled at every turn. When as a 'team' we won a trip out of the rehab centre, I went off shopping and didn't come back for hours. I guess I was trying to maintain a degree of control over myself.

Celebrity Rehab wasn't paradise at all, it turned out: it was my worst nightmare. They kept trying to dig up Sarah Howes: no matter how many times I tried to explain she had passed away, they wanted to know what hurt her to make her want to run away and become Alicia Douvall. They wanted to investigate why I spent so much time and energy into planning and recovering from plastic surgery. It was suggested that I was addicted to the pain and liked punishing myself. The counsellors said I wasn't stupid – to have surgery all around the world like I had required a great deal of research and preparation. They said I liked the struggle and the suffering and I needed the hope it created.

I really didn't want to hear this. It hurt to think I really did have a problem and I didn't want this to enter my mind. How could I face that I had got it all wrong, that my carefully thought out plans were just a way for an addict to get a fix that was slowly destroying me? Worst of all, how could

I admit to myself and to others that pursuing this pointless goal had by now (as Sugardaddy's accountants had worked out) led to me spending over a million dollars on procedures?

I fought and fought to stay away from the possibility of me having a problem. After all, without surgery what did I have? It had become my life, my being, and I was now only famous for my surgery.

Passages slowly taught me to respect and love myself again and they gave me the tools to do that. They said it was important to have a hobby (as long as it was a healthy one). I mentioned that I liked tennis as a child so they helped me get back into that. I was also encouraged to look after my soul and to go to AA meetings. Even though I wasn't an alcoholic I was still an addict.

I didn't realise how little I knew about life and how to survive it before I went to rehab. The cameras stopped filming and after the end of the shoot I stayed at Passages an extra two weeks.

I felt myself getting stronger and was amazed that with just other people's words and wisdom I had become a new person. I walked straighter and I was starting to love the girl I despised. I started feeling sorry for Sarah Howes, who was just an afraid little girl wanting to feel safe and loved. I shouldn't be so hard on her, blame her or dismiss her. Sarah Howes went through a lot and kept going until she made Alicia Douvall because she knew she was too vulnerable for this world. Alicia was her only chance of survival. Alicia was a bitch – and many celebs will back that statement up, having been a victim of her kiss-and-tells! She was strong but was over the top, like a drag queen. Behind the make-up, the fake hair and lashes and her brash exterior lay a fragile, lost girl, who saw a mask as her only way out.

Passages said they often saw celebs, sports people, actors and singers come into the rehab centre. They thought their careers defined who they were, that they were The Actor, The Singer or The Footballer and nothing else, but that's not true. As humans we are amazing. We are not one-dimensional and that part of our career was only a phase of our lives; we can find something else that will become the next phase of our lives. We are more than capable of evolving.

The therapists said I was set on a path to destruction and that if I didn't stop I would die. The painkillers I was on were strong, morphine-based, very addictive and hard to come off. They were giving me other painkillers to substitute for them but it was tough going. I sweated for a night, got fierce headaches, sickness even worse than before and cravings for a painkiller for weeks. You also couldn't drink in rehab and by day five I was craving alcohol. I also wasn't allowed my sleeping pills so you can imagine the detox I was going through whilst coming off all of those!

Passages said it was interesting that I hadn't turned to drugs or alcohol as my main drug of choice, but instead to plastic surgery. To me it had been logical. Even though my addiction had been getting the better of me I had been self-medicating, trying to put a plaster on the pain no different to any other addict.

I was told that my life depended on me finding 'something else.' I thought the counsellors were exaggerating, I mean, who ever died from plastic surgery?

In truth, lots of people have and whilst I was in rehab Michael Jackson died. It was not directly related to his plastic surgery but from the drugs you get hooked on along the way.

So I was a house built on quicksand with no foundation, like they said. The psychologist at Passages said I had no idea how to find a decent man because abuse, in whatever forms it came, felt like home. I had to learn to love myself to be able to love others and be respected and I had to learn not to accept abusive words. I had to change or I would be trapped in this world I had created in my mind.

I had to alter my whole life if this was to work and that meant dumping most of my friends, adopting a new lifestyle and, instead of trawling bars and clubs, I needed to hang out at tennis clubs and in yoga studios.

Their trainers taught me how to eat healthily. They treated me with massage and acupuncture. My periods had stopped coming monthly and I was experiencing pain, but the acupuncture cured this. My headaches also completely disappeared after several weeks.

The other addicts and I saw drastic changes to our looks, our eyes becoming brighter with lighter eyelids, our skin growing smoother and our weight dropping or gaining depending on what had been out of balance. The results we saw on the outside were amazing but the results we felt on the inside were even more so.

After over a hundred days it was time to go home. Counsellors say the time you are most likely to relapse is straight after rehab, as you are cocooned whilst you are inside and someone is there to guide you through every emotion and to answer any questions you have. You are safe in rehab, they give you a timetable, and there is no temptation around. In the outside, real world you don't have that.

Les McKeown kept on the programme and no longer drinks at all. It turned out that he was bisexual and had felt very guilty about it. Cassie, the model, accepted her curvy body, met a guy and got married. Rowetta cut the drink right down and the American actor who came in for painkillers turned out to actually be acting and didn't have a problem with them at all. The rehab centre said he had an even bigger problem because he was addicted to fame and would do anything to stay on the TV screen. Mmmm, I think there are quite a few celebs out there who share that addiction!

Some of the celebrities, however, did relapse. I was one of them, and I did so in grand style.

CHAPTER SEVENTEEN

Relapse

I HAD NEVER BEEN happy with my toes and wanted them to be straighter and smaller. I searched the internet for foot specialist surgeons who did this. I finally found someone, a man in a grubby office in south-east London who treated footballers and athletes for actual foot problems. I felt nervous during the consultation. There I was with a man that helped injured athletes, whose careers and livelihoods depended on their feet; now he was dealing with a busty glamour model simply requesting more even and smaller toes to look better in her Jimmy Choos. I even said my left toe was causing me great distress; it was hard to varnish it because it was so bent from years of wearing high heels.

Anyway, for whatever reason, he agreed to do the operation. He would slice open my toe and cut out some of the bone so they would be shorter, straighter toes. I would be awake but I would only feel a pulling sensation.

This was actually the trickiest operation to get home alone from. I couldn't walk as I would have to use crutches. I couldn't bring a friend because all my friends would think I was mad. So I booked a taxi and when it turned up I pretended that the driver, who barely spoke English, was my friend, come to pick me up. The skinny Asian taxi driver was rather confused when I greeted him with an air-kiss as he opened the door for me to get into the back.

I wasn't sure if going to rehab made me worry about this operation, as usually I wasn't concerned about the outcome at all, or if it was because the procedure affected my feet and, if it messed up, I would never be able to walk properly again. Your toes give you a sense of distance and space so after six weeks of limping and a rather unfashionable foot bandage I discovered that I bumped into things a lot more. I still do even now. I do like my toes now, though – but, to be honest, I hardly ever see the things with the British weather!

I had been feeling a lot more confident when I left rehab but a chance meeting in a bar with a man I shall call 'Mr Blondie' left me craving surgery more than I ever did before; the confidence rehab instilled in me got broken down when a new man in my life made me feel 'not good enough'. I had given my power away again. It was not long until I was on the internet searching for the next surgeon. What was I really looking for? What was wrong now? I wasn't sure, other than I just didn't feel pretty enough.

In Boston I found a surgeon, who had been promoted by a model on the E! TV channel and who, again, turned out to be reconstruction specialist and not a plastic surgeon. I will call him the 'Boston Sadist'.

I emailed him and asked him to give me better cheekbones. I knew it was wrong, and against all I had been taught at rehab, but I didn't care. I was like a dieter who plans to only eat salad all day. Within moments of knowing that you cannot eat something you want it more.

I was excited that the new surgery would make me much more desirable to Mr Blondie. I was in love with him: he was tall, a snappy dresser with striking blue eyes, but one thing was wrong: it seemed he wasn't that into me. I thought this latest surgery would make his heart finally melt for me.

In no time at all I was flying solo to Boston ready for my next operation. The Boston Sadist gave me a consult and the operation on the same day, only hours apart. He said cheek implants were a very good idea but I should also consider a chin implant. I told him I had had one before and it was a disaster. The Boston Sadist said this chin implant would be different and would give me more of an Angelina Jolie look. Then he said I needed nose revision, temple implants and an implant under my nose because my face was concave. I never realised I had a concave face before! Maybe this was why I never liked my face and couldn't put my finger on it? Eureka! It was because I was concave!

Well, Angelina Jolie was a very beautiful woman so this sounded like a good idea. He said he could only do the cheek implants that day but I should book another time for the rest of the procedures. Mr Blondie, I thought, was in for a treat: I was going to come back looking just like Angelina Jolie!

So under the knife I went. I was filled with over-excitement for my new man, the Boston Sadist. I loved that he wanted to change me completely and make my doll face into a blonde Angelina Jolie. I wasn't unhappy with my looks but I wasn't happy enough with them either. I felt like I needed a facelift but the Boston Sadist thought I should consider implants first and then perhaps go for a facelift. In hindsight this was his way of selling buckets more surgery and his own handmade implants, which he was using to try to make a name for himself.

The cheek implants from Mr Fix-It were removed and then the Boston Sadist replaced them with his implants, which were much bigger and not made of a hard porous structure to mimic bone.

Hospitals in America are very different. You don't often get a bed. A lot of the time surgeons there have their own 'hospital', shared amongst a few colleagues. These shared hospitals are much cheaper but they don't keep you in overnight unless you are literally dying. You get woken up, put in a plastic armchair and as soon as you can say your own name and empty your bladder, you are given a cream cracker, or a cup of porridge if it's the morning, and some water before being sent home, dazed and confused. Of course, I walked home, hours after the operation, stopping off at a Chinese restaurant. I was bruised, bandaged and on heavy drugs but I didn't care. I was so used to being bandaged and bruised by now that I just carried on my everyday life. People may stare but, hey, they'll get over it.

I also woke up the next day with some strange books and magazines, including Serena Williams' autobiography, a raw vegan cookbook and a yoga magazine. I must have wandered into a bookstore too but I didn't remember this.

I flew home very shortly after and decided it was a good idea to have a few sleeping tablets on the plane. When I didn't fall asleep straight away I took another couple, as well as my pain medication.

By the time I got to the UK airport I could hardly see or speak. I managed to drag my drug-filled body into the bathroom, where I must have collapsed. I woke up on the cubicle floor, slumped over the toilet. It was at this point I thought, 'Girl, I think people might be right. It may just be that I have a problem.'

I managed to throw my half-dead self into the back of a black cab and asked the driver to take me home. Once back in my flat I dutifully examined my face as usual, staring into the mirror at every angle for hours. I was trying to work out if it was or wasn't a good result. As far as I could see I had some serious cheekbones now but my eyes had been pushed up as a result of the implants, and again one looked different from the other. The implants were uneven, having been placed in different areas of my face!

I immediately bombarded the Boston Sadist with one email after another. I probably sent about twenty emails on this occasion but he only did what he had done from day one. He told me that I should have confidence and emailed me back every time I sent a message to vaguely tell me they were fine, of course, and it was 'a good result'. By email he also sold me more surgery, telling me that the other implants would add much more harmony to my face.

The Boston Sadist convinced me for a short time to live with the implants. Moments after receiving his email to cheer myself up I thought it might be a nice idea to grab a tan. Naturally, the tanning shop wasn't hardcore enough for me so I rummaged in my cupboard for some tanning injections I had found on the internet, which promised that if you injected yourself every day you would get a golden tan. It sounded great and just what I needed to complement my cheek implants. I was planning to see Mr Blondie again as soon as I could, so envisaged seeing him with my new-found razor-sharp cheekbones, a golden tan... I certainly didn't look like Angelina Jolie, though, but this, I thought, would have to do for now. I thought a golden tan would give me just what I needed for my date.

By this stage I had taken twelve painkillers after eight sleeping tablets so reading the instructions wasn't going to be an easy job. I got the first needle out and injected all of the substance into my stomach. Immediately I felt hot, dizzy and sick. I got up to go to the bathroom and my head rushed. Suddenly I fell to the floor and fainted.

What was most troubling was that Georgia was due to come home. Luckily, she let herself in but she was not so lucky to find her mum sprawled on the bathroom floor unconscious. My daughter phoned an ambulance and I was taken to A & E.

The hospital asked me what I had taken. Embarrassingly, I had to tell them about the tanning injection. I was being sick constantly and was unsure if I had caused any permanent damage or would make it to another day.

The nurses gave me saline water to flush the poison out of me and pumped my stomach. When they looked at the tanning injections I had given myself it turned out I had injected 100 millilitres instead of the recommended dose of 0.1 millilitres! They said that because it wasn't FDA regulated and available legally on the market they had no research to tell them what the long-term effects could be.

That evening I took my orange arse home, ashamed of my latest antics, which had worried Georgia and taken up a valuable NHS bed. When I got an email from the rehab centre asking how I was doing I didn't lie. I told Passages I had suffered a major relapse.

They suggested I go back to rehab immediately. I was starting to think I had a bit of a problem so I decided I had better go back soon. As Georgia went back to school I flew out back to the Malibu rehab centre.

This time I had no fellow celebs with me. I was with rich teens whose parents had found them smoking a joint and panicked, sending them to rehab, and hardcore heroin addicts, in there for their fifth attempt at rehab.

The counsellors told those of us who had failed that we were on a journey. Just like it often takes several attempts to give up smoking, the more times you try the more likely you are to actually give up.

They said addicts – including me, who they treated like any other addict – often replaced one addiction with another. It was about finding something that was healthy and productive to be addicted to. They said addicts in their opinion seemed the most interesting of people, they didn't do things in halves and were often very successful. We just needed a little help steering back on the right path.

I have never seen myself as an addict. I always felt I was in control of my drinking and my medication but the headaches I had endured coming off alcohol and drugs had said that I really was an addict and my body needed cleansing.

Just like football is a footballer's life, I would find it harder than I imagined to transition from plastic surgery, which had become my life, my career, my hopes, my dreams and my ambitions. Even my relationship with Sugardaddy had been based on surgery.

It was a hard pill to swallow that I had to walk away from it all but when I left rehab for the second time the message was finally sinking in.

I returned to the UK for just one week. Rehab had given me a new-found confidence; I was fighting again to get my life back on track. I was happy to see Georgia: we played tennis together for hours that weekend, and I made healthy organic meals for us. We sat on the sofa that evening watching films. Georgia was understandably confused by this. Where was her wayward, party-loving mother? Why was I playing tennis with her and not in bed instead, bruised and battered? At the same time I could see she was enjoying having a wholesome mother, one who cooked, cleaned and spent the weekends playing sports. Yes, I was finally changing.

The summer holidays were fast approaching and I was finding it hard to stick to my new healthy and wholesome regime – I was constantly fighting a pull towards surgery, which had been my home for so long – so we thought the best idea would be to spend the summer in LA. This was a place I called my spiritual home, where I felt the happiest.

Bizarrely, I had lots of friends in LA, more than I had in the UK. Hugh Hefner's house, the Playboy Mansion, felt like home. Okay, it was filled with old men and young glamour models; somehow, though, they became my family and closest friends. Spending so much time in LA over the years, I had visited the mansion frequently, becoming one of the regular Playboy Mansion girls. I was even featured in the TV show for the E! channel, *Girls of the Playboy Mansion* (aka *The Girls Next Door*): I was jumping into the pool as an extra! The parties at the mansion were all you think they would be: jello shots, body-painted girls, horny old men, player young men, celebrities and more. The weekends at the mansion were mostly spent playing by the pool while Hugh Hefner played backgammon with fellow old men. We would all watch old black and white movies in the evening whilst eating. These were Heff's favourite, but the girls would secretly complain about this as young 20-somethings hardly want to watch old movies. I got on well with the girls – don't get me wrong, the girls would bitch amongst themselves but in general Hugh was very good at picking a good, stable crowd of girls that would get on with each other. I loved dressing up and spending the weekend at the mansion. Georgia would go to surf school and meet her friends, so it suited everyone.

The sex kitten in me loved lacy lingerie and the whole Playboy scene, however tacky and '80s' it was perceived to be. Strangely enough I loved the family feel of the Playboy Mansion that Heff created.

Dressing up in sexy lingerie was strictly only for special occasions as I usually had to wear industrial-style underwired bras that looked like something your granny would wear. Because my implants were big the wires would often dig into my ribs. I needed the wire in between my boobs, as there was always a risk of my breasts collapsing: I had to wear a bra twenty-four seven, taking it off only for a shower. However, for the flight to LA, I ended up wearing a sports bra after returning from a short two-day trip to the UK to do modelling work. I simply didn't have time to change from the gym in the morning. After an eleven-hour flight returning back to my spiritual home I decided to take a shower. That's when I noticed my tear-shaped left breast was upside down! I screamed in horror: my lovely perfect breasts that had taken 18 attempts to get right were now deformed!

I immediately phoned the surgeon who had performed the most recent operation, still in a panicky state. To start with he didn't want to do anything. I am guessing he wasn't keen on recording that the implant was now upside down as he had made the implants himself and I was part of a study to use teardrops. (Teardrop implants are not allowed to be used in the USA due to the fact they flip too easily.)

With some not so gentle persuasion, threatening him with bad publicity, he agreed to operate again. Inevitably, he made me pay for this again, which wasn't cheap. I took the first flight back to Nashville, Georgia accompanying me, clearly disappointed that her healthy, sporting mum was once again succumbing to more surgery and that I was eating into her holiday and surf camp.

The operation in Nashville took eight hours. It turned out my breast had flipped upside down, and then on the flight to Nashville it flipped a hundred and eighty degrees again and had completely collapsed. All the muscles and tissues had been destroyed. So more dead human tissue was inserted. The surgeon used the same implant as before, which later turned out to be a fatal mistake. You can't open someone up and use the same implant, as it will most likely result in encapsulation.

I immediately saw a difference. I knew the result was not as good as last time but my complaints landed on deaf ears, as the surgeon and his nurses fobbed me off, telling me it was too early for the untrained eye to tell. I knew my body and by now felt like I knew how it would heal, and if I was going to get a good result. I understood how I recovered and could usually see the faults within a week, sometimes within an hour of waking up. I begged the surgeon to operate again but he wouldn't, he had his money. It was like asking British Telecom for a refund.

Unconvinced about the success of my new boobs, we had no option but to return to LA, where recovery took a long time. My body was getting tired of healing. I was determined that this time I would not take the painkillers and risk getting hooked on them again. I was definitely affected by my two stints in rehab. I was at last starting to feel resentful to the surgeons, seeing them as greedy men who had taken advantage of me. I no longer looked forward to that milky needle, or planned the next surgery on my recovery bed. Things were changing.

I was determined to make LA great for Georgia. We dined out in the best restaurants, shopped in Beverly Hills; I watched her surf every day. We started joining yoga classes, which led me down a spiritual path, and got my body looking the best it had ever looked.

When we finally arrived back in the UK Georgia returned to boarding school, which always made me really sad and I think secretly her too. We had never had enough time together when she was young. She seemed to like my spirit and that I had worked out a way to keep going and stay upbeat, no matter what; she loved the 'Rocky' in me, the fighter and the conqueror. I pushed her to be the best she could be; she was the grounded one, the cautious one, who helped me see reason. I loved her calmness and her ability to see things exactly how they were. We complemented each other well. Most teens by now would be drinking and partying but Georgia wasn't, she wanted to be with me and seemed to blend into whatever phase I was going through. I had made a mess of my life but it seemed like I hadn't made a mess of her. Maybe love really had conquered all? She certainly kept me going; through my darkest days when I was at the height of my addiction it was having Georgia that made me carry on, otherwise I know I would have been long gone. I saw her strength, through a difficult, bewildering upbringing, never meeting her father or even receiving so much as a birthday or Christmas card from him and putting up with a mother like me.

When she came home for weekends I would always stay in her room. It was as if I savoured every second with her. I was grateful to have her after such a struggle to get her back; and her being at boarding school, against what I really wanted for myself, made me cling that bit harder to her when we were together.

Plastic surgery gave me hope, an ambition and a dream to cling to. I had used it as the solution to all that was wrong with my life. If I didn't have that, what did I have? Could tennis and broccoli really replace that?

For now, the answer was 'No'. My journey to full recovery was going to be a long one – 'If I make it at all,' I thought to myself.

Maybe I didn't really want to give up plastic surgery, maybe this was the only way a girl as lost as I felt could get by. I was also worried: if I gave up plastic surgery, would I turn to alcohol or drugs?

I ended up going back to rehab again after more surgery with the Boston Sadist, having more facial implants put in on two separate occasions. So it took three times in rehab in total, but each time I was becoming that little bit wiser and stronger.

For the last, definitely not least, relapse I had, I signed up again for more surgery with the Boston Sadist. This time, though, I had more implants, my third operation with him, more insane implants – perhaps the most insane of my plastic surgery journey. This time I really went all out.

Here is an email exchange between myself and the Boston Sadist, in which you can clearly see him talking me into more surgery:

My email:

'I hope you are well.

I look forward to seeing you in Jan/Feb/March for nose revision (and discussion on tummy tuck for later date). I have a question from my previous surgery, I wondered if you could answer? My left top lip does not work as well as the right or look even when I smile. Is this related to the nerve damage on the lower lip that you said was non remediable?

(You heightened it for me using a chin implant for better suspension).

Or is it from the nasal implant and it has yet to work the same as the other side?

I attach a picture (not a great picture) but I think it illustrates the point.

Re nasal implant (behind the nose) – the left side (below the left nostril) has a 'bump,' which I noticed I can feel on the right side but higher up on the right of the nostril and side of the nose. When I have my nose implant revision is it possible to straighten it out? Or does it not matter?

Can you do something about my top left lip? I went to my dentist as my smile looks awful, who referred me to an orthodontist who said the teeth are actually a normal size and the problem is my lip covers too much teeth.

Looking forward to your urgent response.'

The Boston Sadist replied:

'Good to hear from you. I don't think that the lip issue is related to the nasal implant. I would leave the bump alone. If you desired more tooth show when you smile, I could do a small lip lift.

After studying all your pictures, I was struck that your lower jaw area seems considerably smaller than the upper and middle two-thirds of your face. Have you considered building up the posterior mandible a bit?'

This time he said he could really make me look much more like Angelina Jolie. He convinced me into a chin implant, temple implants, two nose implants and an implant under the nose. I also asked him to lower or shave the cheek implants he had already put in.

Off I went again to Boston, this time for more implants in my face than I had ever had before. In my head I was thinking I would come back a new girl, who would look sophisticated and spellbind with her mesmerising beauty.

Boston wasn't kind to me. On a snowy December day I took my fateful walk to the Boston Sadist's in-house surgery clinic to undergo eight hours of surgery.

When I woke up in my foggy state I demanded a mirror to look at myself. Despite all the drugs I was on I clearly remembered my shock when I saw the state of my face. I looked like Frankenstein's monster! I was completely deformed; I just wasn't me anymore. I was a much uglier version of Alicia Douvall and looked like a drag queen that had been in a fight and lost.

I screamed for the nurse and told her there was no way I was going anywhere like this. I hated it! At that moment the Boston Sadist came in and I grabbed his arm with both hands and begged him, now in a hysterical state, not to send me home like this.

'It's horrific,' I cried. 'My nose, you've ruined my nose!'

'What don't you like about it?' he said.

'Look!' I shouted, 'I look like Shrek!'

He had made my nose wider and bigger, which was not a good look. The Boston Sadist told me to go home and think about it, at least give it a few days.

I was still crying so the nurses gave me more drugs to induce a sense of calm and relaxation. I powered through but now with slurred speech; no one was listening to me, though, as I championed my cause, complaining to any passer-by.

I was shown the door as soon as I had eaten the dry cracker and walked to the toilet. I think they wanted me and my loud voice out and away from their other patients, as a complaint is never good for a business. I wanted to get out too anyway so that I could stare at myself in the mirror undisturbed.

I started walking home past a restaurant that a friend had recommended. It was a five-star, fashionable eatery, where celebs and the rich ate. I thought it would be nice to forget for a second how awful I had been made to look and console myself with some fine dining. I also hadn't eaten anything but a dry cracker for the past two days. So I rocked up, bruised, bandaged, dishevelled and disorientated because of the drugs but, amazingly, I got a table.

I sat down but could not read the menu because the medication had caused me to lose my vision. I tried to listen to my waiter when he told me the specials, like a drunk who isn't or can't really listen. I just said, 'Yes, yes, that fish thing, thanks,' after catching the end of the specials.

I ate a stupid amount of bread and had my fish soup, gulping it down with water. Then I stumbled along to the washroom, where I caught a glimpse of my new face. It wasn't pretty.

My emotions ran away with me. I start weeping again, sitting on the floor, with my head in my hands and my arms hugging my knees. What had I done to myself? Why would a surgeon do this to me? I was deformed beyond words.

I knew I had to get myself together before someone walked in and took me away in a straightjacket to the local loony bin. I had one thing on my mind. Like a gambler I refused to lose, I refused to quit.

I looked in the mirror, wiped away my tears, rushed back upstairs and asked for the cheque, which I couldn't wait for. I wrapped myself up in my coat, scarf, gloves and hat whilst hovering over the waitress, who was preparing the bill. I said I was in a rush. Well, I was. I grabbed the bill and left the dollars without waiting for my change. Every second counted and I needed to run as fast as I could back to the Boston Sadist's home surgery.

I ran for twenty minutes back to the surgery in the cold, snowy Boston winter, where I was buzzed in. I could tell from the receptionist's face I was not a welcome guest but I didn't care. I demanded to see the Boston Sadist. When the receptionist refused I said that I had left my stuff and walked through the side door into the resting area, which was full of patients fresh out of surgery. I saw a nurse and, thinking I was Spiderman saving the world, I demanded to see the surgeon.

'This face is awful!' I shouted. 'I will not live like this! He has *ruined my face!*'

I turned to a man who turned out to be a NYC firefighter, who was having jaw implants: 'I wasn't always this ugly, you know.'

The nurses started to panic. They knew telling me that I 'looked great' would not wash this time.

The Boston Sadist came in and asked me to go in the operating room. When we got there he asked, 'What have you eaten?'

I said, 'A small piece of bread and a one bite of fish, that's all,' playing it down, choosing to omit the fact I had scoffed the entire breadbasket and a huge bowl of fish soup.

He said he would operate again then and there. I got undressed and put on my gown go to the loo. Within ten minutes I was asleep. I had won. He took a big gamble operating on me after I had eaten, but I guess he knew I wasn't going anywhere otherwise.

Well, I might have won the battle but I certainly hadn't won the war.

I woke up, this time with curtains surrounding me. No mirror was handed to me. I was able to see my nose, which looked much less offensive, when I went to the toilet for the first time. My nose was still not great and certainly not as good as my previous nose before the surgery, but my whole face was ruined by the implants that had immediately made me look manly. So I decided not to argue about my nose anymore.

Have you ever had a boyfriend you don't want to cut off completely, so you leave them hanging on, never confirming you are not really interested anymore? Well, I was like that with the Boston Sadist. Call it Stockholm syndrome or call it madness, weakness or stupidity. Call it what you will, but I went home after the surgeon managed to convince me my now massive chin and jaw, round Shrek nose, which was less disgusting than before, temple implants that looked like horns and the implant under my nose, which elongated my face between my nose and upper lip, looked great. (Let's not even mention that I couldn't move my face because of all this.) He said it was just swelling and that once the inflammation had gone down I would love it.

Really, Frankenstein's monster was going to turn into Angelina Jolie at any moment? I didn't think so.

Months passed; time healed nothing. Back in London my face was a real mess. I really had gone too far this time. Most distressing of all was that I could no longer move my face, or my lips, as the implant below my nose was blocking my smile. This meant I could not physically smile.

My face was so bad I decided to no longer look in the mirror. I would wear hats and sunglasses when I left the flat and I planned to only eat take out to avoid being seen in restaurants. I sank into a depression, sad I had put the final nail in the coffin: I had destroyed what in hindsight was an okay face. They say you only truly learn to love when you have lost – it's true, suddenly I appreciated my face for the simple things. I used to be able to smile, I used to have a petite 'girly' face, and I didn't look like Shrek crossed with Frankenstein's monster before. My face was completely ruined and I felt ruined too.

When I emailed the Boston Sadist, asking him to take everything out, he said it was very hard to remove implants! Nerves, muscles and tissues grow around them so you can cause more damage and deformities from doing so. He never warned me of this. He had completely changed his tune from when he so casually sold me the implants.

The Boston Sadist said the only thing he would and could do was reduce them. As you can imagine, I jumped at the chance – anything was better than nothing – and I booked myself on the next flight back to Massachusetts.

In the reception room I met a lovely lady who was also from England, let's call her 'Rose.' Rose had also been convinced to have implants. She immediately struck me as a very intelligent and articulate middle-aged lady. I told her I wasn't happy and I had come back to get my implants reduced. As soon as I said that, even as I was finishing the sentence, I was whisked away to another room by a nurse. I looked behind to say goodbye to Rose, who waved, with a very worried look on her face. She put her hands together like she was praying and kissed them.

I was kept in the other room for hours. When it was finally my time to see the Boston Sadist he drew on my face what he said he was going to take away. I asked him to remove it all.

'That's not a good idea,' he said whilst he drew his own plan on my face, which it seemed I did not really have much say in.

Lying on the table, waiting for that milky needle to seal my fate again, I was now fretful, thinking about what was to come. For once I was not filled with hope and excitement whilst waiting to fall peacefully asleep. I lay there dreading how I would look when I next woke up. There was even a part of me that hoped I wouldn't wake up. This was a nightmare that I just didn't want to live through.

I woke up, again with no mirror, and this time the nurses accompanied me to the bathroom and stood in front of the mirror. They said it was because I had such low blood pressure they were afraid I would faint, so I had to be watched. Who knows?

The curtains around me were closed but, as the night shift nurses changed, I opened them, to find myself next to Rose.

I whispered to her, 'How did it go?'

She was heavily sedated, like myself, and started telling me, in a very bizarre way, that nothing was how it seemed. She was worried that the nurses or, worse, the Boston Sadist, would catch us talking. Rose told me to be careful. It turned out she also wasn't happy with her results and was waiting to get her temple implants reduced. Rose said she had a bad facelift and some eye work.

In the early hours, Rose sneaked me her number and said, 'Let's chat. He's trying to make a name for himself with his home-made implants and is using us as guinea pigs.' I was starting to think I had stepped into some mad professor's or sadist's dungeon.

I went home the next day. I had learnt over the years to perfect the art of keeping swelling and bruises to a bare minimum. Just like heroin addicts hide their track marks, a plastic surgery addict needs to hide the bruises. I had got so good at preventing swelling that I did not bruise at all this time, despite having several stitches inside my mouth, nose and under my chin. I stayed upright all night, sleeping sitting up, and used ice continuously. The secret, as I have mentioned, was not to look down even for a moment.

I could see straight away that the procedure had achieved a very slight improvement from the Boston Sadist's 'shaving of the implants', but I still looked like the creature from *Frankenstein*.

For the first time I knew without doubt that I had gone too far. This was it, and it felt worse than when I was attacked and glassed in the face and nearly blinded. It felt worse because I did it to myself and because a man I trusted, a so-called doctor who was supposed to be there to help, did this to me. One attack was done out of jealously and hate. The other was done out of greed. It felt like I had been attacked all over again but this time my attacker wore a white coat and had robbed me of over £60,000 whilst pretending to assist me.

It was like that attack years before in another way: I felt I could not leave the house again. I had to work out how to live my life around my ugly face. I know that looks are not supposed to matter and all that but in my world they did. I had built my world on beauty. Sugardaddy only loved me for my boobs and doll-like face. The press only talked about me because of my appearance. Even my social life revolved round looks: like this I was very likely to not get invited back to the Playboy Mansion. I had paid my bills with my looks but I had chipped away at them self-destructively. Now, it seemed that everything I had built up was truly falling down. I felt like broken bricks, just a pile of rubble, destroyed.

I kept telling myself that it was what was inside that counted and I could find another career that wasn't based on looks. No matter how many times I told myself that I wasn't happy with what I allowed the Boston Sadist to do to me, the shaving had made barely any difference. If I ever caught a glimpse of my face my heart would sink and a rush of anxiety would flow through me, a state of panic through the realisation of what I had done. If I forgot what I looked like for just a moment, soon enough the harsh truth would be staring back at me. I wanted to sit in the corner and cry for the rest of my life.

They had told me in rehab that I just needed to transition into the next phase of my life. After a month had passed, I decided to stop feeling sorry for myself and be constructive with my time. I decided I had to go back on the internet and find a surgeon who could make my face go back to how it was.

CHAPTER EIGHTEEN

Brand Douvall

I DECIDED TO CONCENTRATE wholeheartedly on finding a surgeon to fix me – to fix my smile, in particular. I still couldn't smile as the implant the Boston Sadist had put in was preventing my facial movement. So I spent hours trawling the internet for world-renowned surgeons who could reconstruct a man-made monster.

I manically and obsessively approached nine UK surgeons, who all said they would not touch my face: removing implants was too risky. After each consultation, some of which cost me hundreds of pounds, my heart and soul were sinking.

I stopped seeing Mr Blondie. I made excuses not to see him; I couldn't face letting him see the mess I had made of myself. I had lost so many boyfriends in the past from my revolving face that I learnt to avoid seeing a boyfriend after bad surgery until I got it fixed. I knew I risked him moving on, but as I was I felt too ugly to meet anyone.

I had also developed rosacea from having harsh treatments like dermabrasion, peels and lasers. The dermatologist said it was spicy food and drinking but I knew the treatments had thinned my skin and made it sensitive. I was starting to realise you cannot cheat Mother Nature; you fix one thing and something else goes wrong.

I was losing my last shred of self-confidence. I started walking differently, wore baggy clothes and gave up dyeing my hair. I even stopped showering for weeks on end. I didn't see the point in making an effort any more. I was ugly now: this was it.

I was haunted by what the counsellors had said in rehab, that I should give up men. I had not really followed that advice and was starting to see it was relationships that had helped to feed my surgery addiction. Avoiding Mr Blondie helped me concentrate on fixing my face, but also gave me nothing else to think about.

Despite sinking into a pool of depression, not being able to look at the girl in the mirror, who I still could not associate with me – it certainly wasn't Angelina Jolie either – I knew for Georgia's sake I couldn't give up easily. This wasn't me, it wasn't my face and I was damned if I was going to stay with this stranger's face. I wanted me, and most importantly my smile, back. I decided to fly with Georgia back to LA to ask my US surgeons if they would remove the implants. Georgia was off school so we decided to combine the trip with a holiday.

Because Georgia was there, we went to our usual yoga classes and ate only vegan food, both becoming completely raw vegan. This plant-based diet was supposed to be so amazing that you never got sick and no longer needed deodorant. It would reverse grey hair, make skin clear and glowing; you required less sleep and it even stopped and reversed ageing! Its promises were even more dramatic than those of a plastic surgeon. Certainly, being raw vegan combined with practising yoga made a difference: my hair was growing thicker and I was feeling a lot healthier, with more energy. I noticed the whites of my eyes were whiter and my skin was clearer, though still dry.

Meanwhile, I trawled surgeon after surgeon to find a solution to my face. Each one, however, said they couldn't take the metal screwed-in implants out without potentially causing more damage and they were not prepared to take the risk. Shockingly, some had even heard of the Boston Sadist and said they had seen a few cases like mine; one said the guy was nuts and destroying lots of girls' faces!

Luckily, I had made a good group of friends in sunny Los Angeles over the past 15 years; they, along with Georgia, kept me strong – and, of course, there are some messed up faces in LA, so I blended in well.

It was during this trip that one of my friends, a fashion model, introduced me to Argan oil. I immediately liked the sound of it because it was completely raw vegan. I did not want to consume or use on my skin anything that had been cooked past 104° Fahrenheit (40°C) due to my raw vegan diet. I guess subconsciously I was already replacing surgery with my new raw vegan obsession.

My friend said Argan oil had worked miracles and transformed her dry, patchy skin. I couldn't believe it when it cleared up my own dry skin and even cleared up my rosacea! I started using it as a day and a night cream and all over my body. My skin glowed and was much healthier. I also used it as a treatment and as a serum on my hair, which was definitely becoming stronger, making me less reliant on the extensions that I had used for years. It also worked with my nails, which grew stronger and longer, so for the first time I wasn't reliant on fake nails either. I used it pretty much everywhere on my body and it really was a miracle moisturiser, so simple. I'd spent thousands on expensive creams and serums only to find that something 100% organic, 100% natural worked the best.

Eventually it was time to return to the UK and for a change I was going home empty-handed as far as surgery was concerned. However, I felt better than I had ever felt before. My new-found raw veganism, paired with Argan oil, made me feel on top of the world.

My new healthy lifestyle seemed to lift my depression too. When I was in rehab they told me to cut out alcohol and caffeine, which are depressants. While I was in Los Angeles with Georgia doing my yoga and enjoying a raw vegan diet, I had finally stopped drinking, and given up the painkillers for good as well. Something as simple as Argan oil and a healthy diet had lifted the dark cloud around me, made me realise that there was life beyond a pretty face and that I was a strong woman who could overcome this and beat it for good.

Back in London I wanted to continue my new-found, plant-based, natural lifestyle, so I started by stocking up on raw vegan kitchen equipment including a dehydrator, a Vitamix blender and a cupboard full of nuts and seeds, along with lots of recipe books. I was probably the worst raw vegan chef imaginable to start with, but with a little perseverance the food gradually got better and more edible. I carried on with my new-found skincare regime of using just Argan oil top to toe, but I couldn't find cosmetic-grade Argan oil from a trusted source anywhere in the UK. That's when I realised that we all have a purpose and my journey had been a long, winding one to find an organic, healthy lifestyle – the missing key, it seemed, and the reason I had gone on this long journey. I was always one to learn the hard way: I thought I had to go through this hell, to see what really worked, and what really delivered results. I had pretty much tried everything but after all that it was the organic and natural approach that worked best and made me the happiest.

My new lifestyle gave me the confidence to finally see Mr Blondie again. He was shocked at my face, but somehow it seemed not to matter: maybe, just maybe, he liked what was inside this fierce, determined, elusive girl. My face was clearly less appealing: I could no longer laugh at his jokes or smile when I saw him. Somehow, though, the aura of confidence, of inner content, made me more beautiful to him than ever before.

I knew I was ready for a new chapter in my life. I wasn't going to get employed as I had no qualifications, or experience – funnily enough, glamour modelling and being on the pages of gossip mags didn't get you a 100k a year job very easily. I knew that to close the door on surgery for good, I had to transition into a businesswoman, and at the same time share with others the amazing secrets I had found along the way. I was always being advised to start a plastic surgery advisory service, but plastic surgery had never served me well; I would be a fraud, telling people to have surgery and where to go, when I now knew the best advice I could give was to stay well clear of it, that if you want an amazing body, hair, face and most importantly mind, then a healthy lifestyle, exercise, and natural organic skincare was the only way to go. I decided I was no chef, I couldn't bring healthy food to the world as my raw vegan cuisine was far from appetising – but Argan oil, the missing answer to my dry skin that diet alone couldn't solve, was maybe the key; maybe that was what I had to offer others. Plastic surgery had been my drug of choice for so long, my crutch when I was down or even when I was up. I knew I had to find something else to replace this self-destructive addiction that I had lost myself in for so long.

Soon as I knew Argan oil was going to be my new business, I decided to embrace it like I had surgery, full throttle. I did some research on the oil, learning that it comes from the nuts of the Argan tree, which is endangered. The labour-intensive extraction of the oil is typically done by women; those of south-west Morocco are said to have perfected the process. In 2002, the Moroccan government helped to establish female co-operatives to manufacture Argan oil, providing the women of the rural parts of the country with a steady income, a fair wage and good working conditions, as well as literacy and other educational classes. Perhaps most importantly, the co-ops give women a keen sense of empowerment in what is traditionally a male-dominated society. These programmes also helped protect the Argan forests' limited supply of trees. The best co-ops are dedicated to responsible harvesting practices and reforestation projects, which, along with environmental protection policies, aid in the preservation of the Argan trees.

I decided to go to Morocco with Georgia to find the source of Argan oil. I booked tickets for us to fly to a semi-desert region of the country. Back then Argan oil wasn't really known in the UK and outside the tourist spots, Morocco was still quite a repressed, even backward country. People often got around with a donkey and cart. There was often no electricity in some of the places we would be visiting, and as for WiFi or a phone signal, good luck with that. Georgia, being the cautious one, was more worried than I was about us, two young, non-Arabic-speaking women travelling alone in a Muslim country. Being a single mum and taking a teenage girl with me to do business probably wasn't one of my safest or smartest moves!

We boarded the plane and eventually ended up in a tiny, grotty airport in Agadir. (It has since been upgraded.) As we waited for our internal flight to Essaouira on the western coast of Morocco we began to realise the severity of my actions. With no English on the signs or on the shop it was daunting. We had no idea when our connecting flight was. The airport's chapel was constantly used by Muslim families praying. There weren't enough seats to go round so the families sat on the floor, the women dressed in burkas, the men leering at us.

Georgia wanted to go home immediately; she thought it seemed like a scene from a refugee camp. I said it was an adventure – we were seeing the real country and soaking up the culture. Georgia wasn't an explorer or risk-taker like me, she just thought two single girls shouldn't be here. Plus the toilets were just holes in the ground, which shocked her. The time in between flights to Essaouira was hours, probably about four but it felt more like forty. We sat playing cards when all of a sudden, and by chance, we heard 'Douvalls' over the tannoy. Confused, we rushed to the information desk. Our plane was boarding and we hadn't been able to read the sign to identify this. Luckily staff pointed us in the direction to go in to catch the plane. Waving my hands around, I ran towards it across the tarmac: no tunnel here or bus to take you to it. No, it was literally walk up and dodge the oncoming planes!

Luckily we made it just in time and they waved us on. We boarded the plane with Moroccan businessmen and flew off in the old, rickety plane to start the beginning of my new life. The plane was tiny, holding only about eight people, and there were no toilet facilities. Georgia, wide-eyed, clung onto her seat; she thought the chances of us arriving alive were slim. No sense of adventure!

When we arrived we were immediately hassled and had to wrestle to keep our bags; chancers surrounded us and tried to get us into their cab or carry our belongings for us. Eventually we paid rip-off tourist prices and got to our lodgings, a business hotel which thankfully was okay: soulless but clean and tidy. The next day we bartered with cab drivers. I found a non-pervy one and made a deal with him to take us around for the next two days. I had made sure I packed baggy clothes for the trip: I had heard stories of how single women alone shouldn't be in places like this. I was already terribly protective of Georgia, so when we walked along the beach and they leered at us I snapped at them, even having an argument with a man walking around with a camel. Georgia was even more petrified; she begged me to not answer back, but that wasn't in my nature. She feared they would come after us. Another time we decided to do some modelling pics by the side of the road. A man stopped his car, got out, watched us, then went for a wee. I grabbed Georgia and walked off as fast as I could towards the road traffic cops I had remembered seeing on the way.

The Moroccan men generally hated me: they were shocked by this blonde, delicate woman who had a sharp tongue on her and was protective like a lioness towards Georgia. They didn't know what to make of me; they weren't used to women who answered back. Besides, we wore trainers so if I did push them too far we would run! I also carried a hairspray around with me in my pocket in case anything happened. Being a single mum I had learnt to be the protector and the mother. I never liked to show Georgia I was afraid: I had to be the strong one, the one who protected her.

Doing business with Moroccans was also a tricky thing. Georgia and I visited dozens of women's co-operatives. It was shocking to find so many of them were run by men. Their Argan oil was often smelly, had bits in it, or was contaminated with other oils. We had almost given up when I insisted that our taxi driver take us to two more co-operatives that I had heard of. He didn't want to, as even the taxi drivers were paid off by certain co-operatives to bring tourists to their shops.

However, I am so glad I persisted, as the co-operative we found was actually led by women: happy, jolly, humble, clever women. Their co-operative had just received finance from an American firm. The women wore white coats, spoke English and there wasn't a man in sight. I knew straight away I had found my business partner when I found them. They respected me as much as I respected them.

The women told me their oil was completely pure; they explained why they had the best Argan oil in Morocco, which indeed they did. The co-operative had perfected the extraction of Argan oil by combining modern with traditional methods using no heat or water. (Heat takes away the goodness like it does in cooking, and water contaminates oil.)

I made a deal with them then and there to be the sole distributor of their oil in the UK. I ordered a hundred and fifty litres of pure, uncooked cosmetic grade Argan oil, then I went on my way. Signing the deal made me feel great. I was signing up for a new life, a new chapter and the end to the destructive path I had been on. I had found my power again, my strength: this would be my road to independence, while at the same time giving other people this amazingly simple yet effective miracle moisturiser.

Georgia couldn't wait to go home, but it would not be that straightforward. That day I got a call whilst we were at the local souk shopping, telling me that the plane to Agadir was cancelled and I would have to get on a bus, but that it left in two hours. We got in the nearest taxi and fled as fast as we could to the collection point, over an hour away. We made it in time, but then had to endure a four-hour drive through rural Morocco to Marrakesh. Once in Marrakesh we were put up in a hotel. Barely anyone spoke English apart from a South African man who asked where my 'husband' was. He said he was in Morocco on business; I told him I was as well. He decided I needed a guide and went on to explain: 'Don't trust them, they barter with you, everything here is a bloody barter.' Once at the hotel he warned us, 'I've stayed here before. Check your towels and bed sheets before you settle in as they often don't change them. Don't let them get away with it.' I hoped I didn't become bitter like him.

A sense of relief came over us when we finally arrived back in the UK, not to mention my luggage reappearing after it had gone missing in Marrakesh. I now had to get my skincare business going. I didn't have a company, or any idea how to start one, but I thought that even if I got lumbered with loads of Argan oil it wouldn't matter, as I would just share it with all my friends and family, who could also find out how amazing this miracle moisturiser was. I was a big fan of Apple's clean, simple, chic designs; I wanted to combine that with the organic and natural, making it completely eco-friendly, and producing a skincare range that gave back. I decided I was going to be the Steve Jobs of skincare, I was going to bring Argan oil to the UK, be the best. I was sure no one would be able to rival me, as I would be able to apply the same obsessive behaviour I had had with surgery to my Argan organic skincare.

There is only one problem with starting a business: you need money. Billy Bullshitter had wasted almost all of my savings and most of what I had earned since then had been spent on surgery. My flat was rented and Sugardaddy owned my car. I had managed to pull together £20,000, which was all I had left in the world.

Once I was back in England I decided to invest that last £20,000 in setting up a business. I set about registering my company, locally sourcing the packaging and finding a laboratory to develop other Argan-based products. I didn't have much money so had to start by bottling and storing the pure

Argan oil in my London flat. It wasn't long until my home resembled a factory. Georgia and I could hardly move for boxes everywhere!

CHAPTER NINETEEN

A Mum Again

AFTER THE SUCCESSFUL trip to Morocco and sensing that a new chapter in my life was emerging, I noticed I was starting to feel very sick. It began on the flight back from Morocco. Normally I wasn't someone who suffered from travel sickness – you could put me in a fishing boat on a choppy sea and I still wouldn't feel ill – so this seemed very strange.

Then, after arriving home I started to realise that I was putting on weight. My very slim frame was developing a little tummy. At first, I put it down to my new diet. Raw vegans say that you eventually find your perfect weight. I was rather partial to the odd raw vegan dessert, which despite using no sugar can still be fattening as they contain honey or agave syrup. Or maybe I was just meant to be bigger after all?

I also noticed that I had missed a period. That wasn't unusual for me: since my miscarriages I had been diagnosed with endometriosis, and by now I had suffered from it for quite some time. But when I considered the missed period alongside the other changes in my body, it started entering my mind that maybe I might be pregnant.

Georgia was now 17 and as far as bringing her up was concerned, it felt like I was nearing the finishing line. On the other hand, I had a messed-up face that still needed fixing. If I was having a baby, how could I cope being a single mother again? That is exactly what I would be. All I could think was, 'Please don't let me be pregnant. Don't let me be stuck with a face like this.'

I sat alone in the bathroom with that little white stick, just like I had 18 years before, and, just like 18 years before, those two blue lines appeared. I was pregnant.

I smiled, thinking that I had always wanted a bigger family. I did not believe how this could have happened to me again. It wasn't an ideal situation, though. I had always envisioned being married to a loving man, having a mortgage and stability. Maybe that life just wasn't meant for me, maybe I was destined to struggle alone. Abortion was never an option: I considered that even to be pregnant was a miracle after my encounters with Yusuf, which had left me in a bad way internally.

In the beginning I didn't want to tell Georgia. I knew that if I were to tell her I had gotten myself pregnant, again unplanned, I would be told off. As she had grown up our roles had reversed. I was still wild, making stupid mistakes, and she was the sensible, practical mother-figure, guiding me through life and trying to steer me out of trouble. Unfortunately, like an unruly teen, I had managed to find myself in trouble.

So here I was, planning to start a business and now pregnant.

Telling Georgia was one thing but letting Sugardaddy know I was pregnant was a bigger problem – especially because it couldn't be his. By now our relationship had truly drifted into just a friendship. We were worlds away from each other. He still loved glamour models, fake eyelashes, big boobs, leopard print throws and anything chavvy. On the other hand, rehab had changed me. I was no longer interested in modelling, as it fed my addiction to surgery. I was searching for something else, and the business seemed to be the answer. I felt I had changed as a person, I cared about the environment passionately, I wanted to give back. Material things, shopping, clothes and shoes didn't matter to me anymore; I was ready to move on to the next phase of my life.

Being pregnant meant I was forced to transition to the next version of myself, not only as a businesswoman but as a person. There was no way I could have any surgery now. I decided to embrace it: I would use the time I was pregnant to grow my business. I knew that meant Sugardaddy and I might have to part ways. I doubted he would take on another one of my children and start the whole process again for the next 18 years. Like me, he was nearly at the finishing line. Besides, no matter how much make-up I put on, or my best dress, his interest in me was long gone, and of course, as he himself had pointed out, the implants had completely ruined the doll-like face he once loved. Sugardaddy was no longer excited by my surgery, which once upon a time would have re-ignited his desire for me. Even the next pair of bigger boobs no longer had the same effect. I felt like a doll that a child had painted all over, pulled the legs off and then thrown away because the toy was ruined.

I went to Sugardaddy's place to deliver this latest blow to our relationship, fully prepared to be shot down. It seemed like the longest journey of my life. Sugardaddy had become my family, my rock; in spite of everything, I adored him with all my heart. I loved that he gave me stability and was always there through all my mistakes, even when I married a total stranger. No matter how much I self-destructed, Sugardaddy had been there for me and I cared dearly for him because of that. He had cheated on me, which later became no secret; I had to accept it, but as the relationship turned into a friendship I still adored him just as much. I never gave up hoping he would see the error of his ways, realise we were meant for each other and give up the girls for good to live a quiet, happy life with me. I knew, though, that this latest news may be too much for him to take; I also knew, deep down, he just didn't fancy me anymore. The harsh reality was he got excited by 22 year-olds, which was the one thing I could never be.

Driving my beloved Audi Q7, which had been gifted to me by Sugardaddy, I arrived at his mansion in Surrey. This had a swimming pool, tennis courts, paddocks, gymnasium and a lap-dancing room, for his 'entertainment needs'. I was ready for our encounter, complete with my Christian Louboutin heels, Versace handbag, perfectly manicured nails and blow-dried hair. He was there to greet me at the door with his usual beaming smile. That smile always made me feel so warm, happy and wanted.

We sat together and chatted. I said, 'I have something to tell you. I'm pregnant and, as you must realise, it's not yours.'

Sugardaddy's face looked shocked. He stood up and started pacing, but then smiled, and went to light up a cigar.

'Congratulations! Wow, I'm going to be a dad again! Whose is it?'

I looked even more surprised than Sugardaddy had done. I could not believe how accepting he seemed to be. Since I found out I was pregnant I had been bracing myself for a storm but it seemed like the bad weather wasn't coming! Better still, I had found a great father for my unborn child, who I knew would never let me go without. This was unbelievably great! It wasn't a conventional relationship but it was looking like I had my dream, a bigger family.

We talked some more before he phoned his friends, like an excited father-to-be. It felt amazing to experience that: I had never had a man actually feel and act happy when I announced I was pregnant. I loved tasting the joy and happiness of that moment that other, 'normal' couples must go through.

Driving home I was so happy. I thought about how lucky this child was going to be as I sang lyrics from Paul Young's 'Love of the Common People' to the baby.

It was Georgia's birthday the next day. I thought it would be a lovely surprise if I were to tell her she was going to have a baby sister. She was just about to go to sleep when I said, 'By the way, I'm pregnant.'

Georgia thought I was joking and said, 'Ha ha, not funny.'

'No, really I really am,' I insisted.

Georgia sat up in bed. She looked worried. 'Not again?! Were you not using contraception?'

She seemed angry, but also sounded disappointed in me for being so irresponsible. 'How will you look after a baby? You have no money.' Georgia always put a dampener on things with her practical thinking.

However, it wasn't long before it looked like my pregnancy wasn't going to be a problem anymore.

That night I woke up and felt my bed was wet, so I got up and went to the bathroom. My nightie was soaked with blood. I collapsed on the floor, crying.

The next day I was still bleeding when, sullen and deflated, I phoned the hospital to tell them I had had a miscarriage and I needed a check up. They booked me in for a scan that morning. The blood continued to flow as I turned up for the scan. The nurses were very sympathetic and asked if I wanted counselling; like me, they seemed sure I had yet again lost my baby.

I just wanted them to confirm the end of this sorry tale and to walk away. A nurse put gel on her scanner and searched for the remains of the baby. Her face changed. She double-checked the screen and smiled at me as she turned to say, 'There's your baby and there's the heartbeat.' She moved the screen around to show me a white dot.

I was totally shocked. I really didn't expect that. The hospital explained it might have been twins and I lost one – it was too early to tell as previous scans hadn't picked up much – or I may just be one of those unlucky ladies who bleed heavily during pregnancy.

I realised again how precious life was and that it can be taken away from any one of us at any time. Life was to be treasured and we women, who are lucky enough to be blessed with children, should never take it for granted. My journey had been so rocky, both with men and miscarriages; I was not going to let this baby go easily. I decided then and there to basically not leave the bed, and avoid flying in aeroplanes or having sex. The doctors put me on Cyclogest, a tablet to support the uterus lining and reduce the risk of the baby miscarrying.

It was a scary thought that I was going into this without the biological father around, but at the same time I was excited: I had Sugardaddy, so I knew life was going to be great. I started dreaming about cute baby clothes and a designer pram. I was going to look like a normal, happily married woman, pushing my pram along the road; no one need know I went home alone. Georgia and I were going to be a proper family.

I carried on bleeding with one threatened miscarriage after another, spending the next three months in and out of hospital. In fact, I spent most of my pregnancy in bed, with pillows under my butt, determined not to lose my baby.

Of course, I still had my Avatar-Alien nose, long implanted chin and the weird implant under my lip, but I tried to just focus on the pregnancy and be grateful for my baby. Like a kid with metal braces, I didn't want to look in the mirror. I also banned my family from taking any pictures of me and even stopped going into the hairdressers, so I wouldn't be faced with a mirror. I didn't go out because if I did I would have to look into a mirror and see my reflection in order to put my make-up on. I was a pregnant Frankenstein's monster.

In the past my dad and even some boyfriends called me ugly, which had infuriated me. I found myself saying 'DON'T CALL ME UGLY' as a child; now as an adult, comments from the public would be littered with how 'ugly' I was. The funny thing was, those comments had pushed me towards this point: deformed and finally unmistakably ugly. The more I hated hearing the word used against me, the more a certain unpleasant section of society used it to hurt me; they searched for my weakness and preyed on it to stab me in the heart with their cruel words. Now that I was pregnant I was even more sensitive to this. The press were also often outside my house, eager to get pictures: they were particularly keen to follow my pregnancy because there was controversy over who the father was. I wanted to cocoon myself at home, deformed, pregnant but happy, only to appear again once I had transformed myself into a beautiful butterfly. I wouldn't even go to Tesco if I could help it; I became a recluse, only venturing out when I really had to. I never looked the person at the till in the eye, in case they caught sight of my face and commented on it.

It was too heartbreaking for me to have any pictures taken, which is why you will see so few pictures of me pregnant in the press – apart from paparazzi shots, of course. The papers went on printing them, though for a change their descriptions of me were very kind – they seemed to have stopped pointing out the obvious and calling me ugly. On the other hand, the readers' comments below the articles were horrific. Some people would call me all sorts of names, saying I had made them bring up their breakfast with my horrendous looks, that their 60 year-old mother looked better than me, that I looked like a car accident victim or a burns victim. These comments would make my heart sink. I tried to ignore them, thinking these people were probably no Naomi Campbell or Kate Moss themselves, but I couldn't pretend that their words didn't matter: they hurt and affected me.

One advantage of being stuck at home was that I was able to completely turn my attention to my skincare. Having sunk my last £20,000 into starting my business I had to make it succeed, to build a future for my baby and myself. I worked every day including weekends, staying up until the early hours. The effort paid off: Douvall's Ltd, a luxury organic natural skincare company, was launched in Harrods.

When building my company I had to learn how to be a businesswoman very quickly. I learnt along the way from the mistakes I made. Everyone kept telling me how hard it was, that over 300 skincare companies get launched every week and most fail within the first three years. I didn't care, I knew with sheer determination and with a great Argan brand I could build a successful company that would be around for a very long time and something I could pass onto my children, as I had no house or savings to pass onto them.

The business gave me something to focus on rather than surgery. I loved creating something that I knew helped others, that there was nothing else out there like it. I enjoyed pushing the boundaries with the lab, getting them to make skincare that was natural yet new and innovative.

Although I still had a face like a baboon's arse, I made sure I didn't let my mind think about the fact I had destroyed my looks. In interviews the press would often ask if I was happy with myself. I would say yes, as I really was: for the first time in my life I was happy. It was too distressing to even think, about let alone come to terms with, my ruined appearance, so I concentrated on the positives. I didn't let my ugly face let me down and carried on feeling beautiful inside, telling myself every morning I was beautiful from the inside out and that was what counted.

I had given up drinking completely since the day I found out I was pregnant, stopped going out to clubs and bars, cut off toxic friends; I concentrated on a positive mental attitude. I didn't even watch the news or listen to the radio, only Classic FM, as the news was depressing. Anything that could lower my mood I avoided. I put myself in a bubble, concentrating on work and my baby and nothing else. If you asked me who our country's prime minister was I couldn't have told you – not because I'm thick, but because I was cocooned. I had to heal myself before I could step back into the real world. I was very mindful what I ate, as food could affect my mood too. I stuck to only natural food, vegan, plant-based and green smoothies.

I decided to live a completely natural and organic, eco-conscious lifestyle, the opposite to my life so far, where everything fake must be good. In true Alicia style I did do it to the extreme, however: I decided I couldn't touch anything that was not natural and organic, including toothpaste, anything plastic, clothes, food, drink. I only bought ethically sourced clothes and food; I used lemons, vinegar and bicarbonate of soda for cleaning; I only shopped in Whole Foods or dined at raw vegan establishments. I refused to buy any food wrapped in plastic or touch a carrier bag. Even my shampoo had to be raw vegan.

I had also lost faith in surgery completely. Maybe I had had body dysmorphia, maybe I had been a surgery junkie, but whatever had been wrong with me, it wasn't wrong any more, I was sure of that. I had turned 360 degrees: the thought of having surgery now filled me with dread, I wanted nothing to do with the surgeon's knife again. It was as if I had been blind and could now see for the first time.

After years of seeking perfection through plastic surgery, it was ironic, in a way, that I had turned out so much uglier than I started. Which, I guess, is what fascinated the papers and their readers: they marvelled how messed up I had made myself. I dare say it was a reassuring fact to see there really isn't any cheating Mother Nature: having bucket-loads of surgery and money didn't necessarily make you more beautiful.

By now I think I was scared and put off men. I had become afraid of conventional relationships, I was too scared of becoming my mother and father, of bringing my children up the same way they did. My choice of men was still so shady, I wanted to take the good of my parents' parenting and change the bad; they say we become our parents, but in rehab they taught me we don't have to. We can change the circle. I was determined to do that: with Georgia I had done that – okay, Sugardaddy was a very distant father and boyfriend and I made some very bad mistakes along the way, sometimes slipping into what could have been the circle again and again. Luckily Sugardaddy stood by my messy life and acted as an anchor. Georgia had grown up to be a sensible, happy, level-headed, intelligent, studious young lady despite the odds against her; now I was about to do it all over again.

I think some people are not supposed to be a couple, some people are supposed to be alone and that's okay. It seemed to me I wasn't meant to have the mortgage, the conventional family and the man to hold my hand walking down the street: that life wasn't meant for me, maybe I wasn't 'normal' enough. I strived to be normal but it wasn't something I ever achieved. Maybe God or a higher being had other plans for me, and being a couple just wasn't part of it.

As the birth date for my child approached, I discovered I was going to have a girl. A household of women! How ironic – strong women, no men around to mess us up. I decided to call my new daughter Papaya, because when I was pregnant all I ate was fruit! The papaya is an exotic fruit but increasingly well-known internationally, reflecting the fact that in many ways the world is getting smaller. Conveniently, the word 'papaya' is said the same in most countries. Also, it's a love-it or hate-it type of fruit, which seemed to be the reaction my pregnancy was getting.

True, it was an unusual name, but the more people dismissed it the more I realised I called her exactly the right name. You see, the name Papaya sieves out the bad. Those that are controlling, prejudiced or self-righteous will immediately say, 'Papaya?! Is that a name?' Those that are good, non-judgemental and tolerant of people *and* all their differences will either accept the name as it is or say, 'That's a nice name'. Like Marmite, you love it or hate it, and in the same way Papaya herself, an innocent baby, was causing such a reaction with so many people.

Her name will give her a chance to see who the good people are very quickly. Imagine if, when someone says, 'My child is called Emily,' I were to reply, 'How very unoriginal!' I think it's great we are all different and we all want to call our children different names. Otherwise school would get very confusing!

I was having a planned caesarean section and was due around Christmas Day, so as the hospital was short-staffed that day I decided to make it an elective operation on 23 December. I walked to the hospital clutching my overnight bag with Georgia, both of us apprehensive and nervous as to how our lives would become different. It had been just me and her for so long; having a baby would change things forever, for better or for worse.

Baby Papaya was born on 23 December 2011. I spent Christmas Day alone in hospital: I wanted Georgia to have a good Christmas, so I sent her to stay with my mum and her new partner. Christmas dinner was cold hospital food, which I couldn't eat as I was vegetarian and they had no vegetarian options left; they did, to be fair, offer me a packet of biscuits, but I didn't think they would add anything to my breastfeeding nutrients so I politely declined. I was starving, with not a Christmas decoration in sight; all the other new mothers had a partner lovingly staring at their new-found family member – but I didn't care. I was happy, I had a beautiful baby. After everything I had been through I was amazed this had happened. It was bizarre and hardly the norm but here I was, having my second child.

I still couldn't smile at Papaya. I did wish I could have a picture with her to capture the moment. Life is all about moments, isn't it, so really the picture didn't matter. It made me savour the moment even more. I sat in my hospital bed, waiting to feel my legs again, hugging my delicate, perfectly formed baby, thinking life was perfect. I made a promise then and there to make sure I was successful in my business for her sake. I also made a promise to be that patient parent I had never had, and give her a safe home.

But there was another cloud on the horizon. Sugardaddy's joy over my pregnancy had turned sour. He didn't want to see me throughout it, and when I called him he would snap at me, becoming unbearably rude and dismissive. After all, I thought, I was pregnant with another man's child, so I put up with his comments and building resentment towards my unborn child.

I was sure that when he met my little princess his heart would melt.

CHAPTER TWENTY

Finding My Smile

THE DAY I got home from hospital I continued to work on the skincare company: as soon as Papaya went to sleep I would go into business-mode, exhausting myself. My determination to bring a future to my children drove me on: through lack of sleep and midnight feeds I balanced the needs of my new baby and of work like a professional juggler.

I exercised regularly, with my pushchair in the park: as a new mum, and a single mum at that, I didn't have the time or opportunity to get to the gym or yoga classes, so I found a way round it.

I soon secured a deal with a TV shopping channel, and in no time at all my company was making 100k a year; we were flying high. I had never felt so proud of myself: dyslexic, told I was thick and that I could never do it, I was actually making a living off my own merit.

There was one thing holding me back, though: with my business I still needed to do PR. Sometimes that required me to have my picture taken. I would try my best to get out of it. Georgia was the face of my company so did a lot of the modelling but as she was still in boarding school she wasn't around much. A lot of the photo calls I couldn't get out of. I would try and hide my face with my hair and smile with my eyes, as that was the only smile I could achieve.

Though I had been turned off surgery by my past experiences and my new healthy lifestyle and had been distracted by starting my business, I still retained my earlier desire to have one final operation, to fix the Boston Sadist's botched work. In particular, it really bothered me that I could not smile or laugh any more.

I decided it was best for Papaya that I took the matter into my own hands, that it was time to go under the knife again. I wasn't addicted to surgery any more, I wasn't craving to run away from Sarah Howes any more, or look like Barbie; I just wanted to look normal, and to smile again. So a new Google search began. This time I found a surgeon in Harley Street, well known for his work in facelifts: a top surgeon listed in *Tatler* and other high end magazines. (I soon learnt that *Tatler*'s list meant nothing.)

Let's call this surgeon 'Mr Con'. Mr Con was charismatic, warm and approachable; his waiting area was filled with yummy mummies waiting for facelifts and tummy tucks, fillers and Botox. I sat there feeling the stares of the yummy mummies. You may think at this point I am exaggerating, but I'm not. In my apartment in Chelsea I had a lift to get to the ground floor; whilst I was stuck in it a family with two kids entered, then one kid turned to her mum and said, 'Mummy, what's wrong with that lady's face? It's scaring me.' Her mother, highly embarrassed, tried to hurry her out and quiet her, but the brutal words from the uncensored tongue of a child told the truth: my face was scary. Luckily, Papaya was used to it as it was the first face she saw.

Sitting in that waiting room I was filled with hope. Maybe this would be the start of a new beginning, maybe I could finally look normal again, maybe I needed this lesson to lose everything, even the looks I started with, to make me realise what I had, so I could be grateful for what God gave me. (I use the word 'God' for whatever god or higher spiritual being you believe in.)

When my turn came I excitedly skipped in. I told him my problem; he examined my face. Nodding his head from side to side, saddened by what another surgeon had done to me for money, he said, 'Greed has done this to you.' I wasn't sure if he meant the greed of the surgeon or my greed for perfection and beauty.

Either way, I was delighted when he agreed to take out one of my implants, the implant below my nose that was stopping me from smiling. Even better, they had a cancellation and it would be possible to fit the operation the following week. I was still breast-feeding my baby who was only seven days old; I had to do this, though, so I could fully live in my next chapter.

It did cross my mind that I would become addicted again. I was spending the last of my savings; instead of investing in my business I gambled it on more surgery. It even crossed my mind that maybe this was still part of my addiction, but surely I wasn't expected to live like this forever? Being able to smile is a vital way we communicate.

The milky needle brought me back to a place I had been so many times. I still loved the feeling, and whilst drowsing off I must admit the thought crossed my mind: 'Must do this more often!'

When I awoke, my mouth was still stiff. The nurses and surgeon assured me it was because I had stitches in my mouth. The surgeon also said it was very hard for him to get the implant out: it had been screwed in with metal screws that were almost impossible to remove, so he spent longer than he wished on it.

I was just happy to start my new life and finally smile at my baby.

I went home the same evening. I couldn't wait to see my smile back. But as the hours turned into days and the days into weeks, I realised I still wasn't going to be able to smile: the operation had failed. My heart sank. I had been so excited to move on with my life, but it wasn't to be. I kept asking the surgeon why I couldn't smile, but all I got was the usual brush-offs that it takes time to heal and that I should leave it six months.

I wasn't about to leave it another week, let alone six months: plastic surgery had wasted fifteen years of my life, I wasn't prepared to waste another week on it.

I was still in contact with Rose who like me had had those bad implants from the Boston Sadist. She was on a long journey trying to fix the damage he had caused: her eyes had been pulled in different directions and he had convinced her to have temple implants which she also didn't like. She had a lopsided facelift which she hated. Rose was a very intelligent lady: she too had stopped her life because of the effects of her surgery. Her relationship with her partner had broken down and they had spilt up, she stopped buying clothes and getting her hair done due to her lack of self-confidence about her perceived ruined face, and even lost her job as she couldn't face clients any more.

Rose had put all her efforts into finding a surgeon to repair the complicated work the Boston Sadist had done: she found one called Jan Stanek who successfully repaired a lot of her surgery. Rose recommended I contact him too. To start with I was apprehensive, thinking I was setting myself up for a fall: I was going to get sold a whole lot more surgery, maybe I should just stop now and accept myself as I was, otherwise I might lose everything. Would I become one of those addicts who lived in a sleeping bag on the streets with nothing, because their addiction had taken everything from them? I didn't want surgery to rob me of everything; I was playing with the devil and I hated him now, but I had to gamble with him one last time, to see if I could break even and walk away from the table for good... hopefully.

So I went for a consultation with Jan Stanek. He asked for a woman surgeon called Caroline Mills, who specialised in facial plastic surgery, to join him. She reminded me of my older sister, who worked in a hospital: I instantly felt comfortable around her.

First, Jan and Caroline examined my upper lip below my nose. They could feel the implant that prevented my smile: though it had supposedly been removed by Mr Con, it was clearly still there. They also looked at the other implants, in my nose, chin, temple and cheeks.

After the examination Jan and Caroline told me that this would be a very risky operation: they needed time to think about if they wanted to take this on. I begged them, 'Please, I need to smile again for my baby, I just want to look normal again. I'm not even asking for pretty any more, just normal. Please can you give me back my life?'

I did not know what their answer would be until I got a letter in the post asking me to go for psychiatric assessment. Jan and Caroline needed me to do this before they would operate. At first I saw this as their way of saying no: the last time I had seen a psychiatrist I had been diagnosed with body dysmorphia and told to have counselling. I really wasn't keen to hear that I was still a broken human being and it was all in my head. In the end, though, I went: by now I had nothing left to lose.

The psychiatrist I met turned out to be very jolly and at the end of the assessment he said: 'Well, I don't think it's in your head. I can see you have a visible problem that would benefit you if it got fixed. You seem level-headed, I don't think you have body dysmorphia any more.' A huge wave of relief washed over me.

The healing of my mind I put down to my healthy lifestyle and the realisation that plastic surgeons often preyed on the weak and vulnerable, but mostly I thought it was because of my determination not to be broken.

I bounced out of his office: not only did I have the okay to have my operation, I was also officially no longer a sufferer of body dysmorphia, where there is supposed to be 'no cure'. Well, there was a cure, I was living proof of that; it was drastic and meant turning your life around, but there *was* a cure.

Not long afterwards I was excited to get a call from Jan and Caroline to come in. They told me they would work together to take out my implants and rebuild my face. Apparently I had a 40 percent chance of success.

By now I also had a problem with the left side of my lower lip not working. It flopped like I had had a stroke: one lovely surgeon had cut into a major nerve, destroying any movement on one side of my face. I also could not feel my lip at all: it was like what happens after you have been to the dentist and it's all numb. Caroline said she would try and repair this: she had treated kids in Africa for similar conditions. There was a metal clip that they could use to suspend the lip so it would at least look the same as the other side and stay up.

Jan and Caroline were planning to remove as many and as much of the implants as they could, but if they thought it would cause more damage they would have to abandon it. Even if they could remove the implants, I would need a facelift as I would be left with spare skin.

I could see the concern and disgust on their faces when they investigated the Boston Sadist's work, saying, 'Greedy, unscrupulous surgeon: he has destroyed a pretty face.' Their genuine efforts to help me get me back to looking normal made me feel safe with these guys, despite the fact that they were part of what I now thought of as the enemy. I had become scared and phobic of surgeons, scared of falling back into an addiction that had nearly killed me and scared to be a bad mother to Papaya, giving every last penny to a greedy industry. But Jan and Caroline's years of expertise made me think: 'I can do this, I can go under the knife one more time, I need to do this for Papaya's sake, I need to be able to smile again, and I need a face I can live with.'

So the date was booked. As per usual I checked in alone; this time Georgia knew about the operation as she would be looking after Papaya. I had paid for it with the last of my savings and the rest of my money that was to go into my business. I had even emptied Georgia's account and taken out a bank loan too. Sugardaddy was still paying me money every month so I knew I could pay the loan back quite fast.

Georgia was apprehensive about the operation; she too was worried I would slip into old ways. She was enjoying having her mother back, and for once eating homemade food, not breakfast, lunch and dinner in restaurants. It was a nice change for the two of us to go on a holiday that didn't include me lying in bed with bandages. It wasn't fun for her to watch Mummy playing Russian roulette with her life one more time.

Above all, Georgia wanted a mum she could finally imagine hanging around a while. There had been too many close calls which had ended up with me in A&E. Because of this, she and I often talked about who would have Papaya if the worst happened. After all, I had hardly ever been happy with any of the operations: what if one day I just couldn't live with the result, what if this operation made me look even worse? Georgia was always very worried of that – that one day I would stop fighting, that with my obsession about my looks one operation would go so badly wrong I would finally throw in the towel. So you can imagine, her mind worried for her and Papaya's sake.

I was still breast-feeding Papaya, but the feeding was not going well. As any new mother knows you want the best start for your child and I believed breast was best. Again, surgery stopped me from doing that – not, ironically, from my by now 21 breast operations, but from the previous and forthcoming surgeries, which meant that the milk would be polluted so I couldn't use it. It looked like surgery was still robbing me and my new child; I couldn't wait to wave goodbye and get off this roller coaster I had been on for almost 20 years.

I sat in my private room, apprehensive how this would turn out. Would the anaesthetic make me want more? Was I maybe addicted to that and surgery was just an excuse to get more? Would I get a good result and still keep chasing the dragon, or would I become even worse off? After all, this time the odds were against me: I was having my face completely taken off and reconstructed, as if I had been in a car crash. In a way I had, only it was the car crash of my life. This was my riskiest operation to date and my biggest gamble. Like a boxer coming out of retirement to have his last fight, I came back to surgery to fight for my face back.

My turn came around fast. I was the second one to go in and the rest of the day was dedicated to me. The milky needle went in; I savoured every moment, hoping it would be the last time I would feel its euphoria.

It was a long operation, perhaps nine hours. When I awoke the nurses reassured me the operation had 'gone great'. I felt my face and it already seemed smaller. Although I had just been given a facelift and had stitches inside my mouth and below my chin, I felt freer.

Then the ever so chirpy Caroline Mills walked into my room, explaining that all had gone well. She clutched a jar containing the implant from under my nose – the implant I had paid thousands to have taken out! The shocking fact was that surgeon put me under anaesthesia and did nothing. He lied and claimed it had been taken out, proving to me yet again just how unethical plastic surgeons can be.

Caroline said the implants were all screwed in using an unusual screwdriver that UK surgeons were not familiar with; luckily they had done their research beforehand and ordered the screwdriver in especially. They managed to unscrew most of the implants. I was excited when Caroline said: 'Chin implant is out.'

'Really? All of it out?' I asked, over-excited.

'Yes, all out. You really didn't need it, you have a good chin,' she told me.

'Really? The chin implant is all out?' I repeated to myself, several times. I just wanted to be sure that this time I really had one of the Boston Sadist's implants out. My face felt like it had been nailed to a wall and I was stuck on it, but it was like hearing I had won the lottery.

Caroline went on: 'The nose implants, temple and of course the implant under the nose are all out. We had to take quite a lot of skin in the facelift and give you a lip lift after taking the implant out. We also suspended the lip which I think you'll be very happy with. I think you'll have your smile back, but let's see.'

Covered in bandages and stitches I beamed with joy. This time my lip turned up: I felt the beginning of a smile I hadn't been able to use for years. Finally my new-born baby could see her mother smile!

I had to stay overnight in the hospital; the very next day I went home, eager to see my daughter and celebrate. I was bandaged and bruised, but looking in the mirror I saw the old Alicia Douvall back. My face shape was already becoming me again; my nose was nearly back to my usual button nose. 'Bulbous' is what a surgeon would call it – I call it a cute baby nose. I had missed my imperfections. The implant had given me a straight, narrow, bigger nose. The Boston Sadist said this was like Angelina Jolie, but I thought I looked like a bad drag queen. With this new operation I could see beyond the swelling and the bruises and for once in my life, I loved how I looked.

The day after the operation I felt much better and decided to take baby Papaya to the park (I was living opposite Hyde Park at this point). With my bruised face and two black eyes, I thought I looked the best I had for years. I was so happy to know I was on the road back to me again. In my own world, I didn't notice a papparazzo lurking near: his picture of me bruised and swollen went global – and I am not exaggerating: after going nationwide, it went to Germany, the USA and the rest of the world. I became the face of warning, the face of plastic surgery gone wrong.

I couldn't see what all the fuss was about. In my eyes I looked great; maybe bruised, but a lot better than I had for years.

And most of all, I had my smile back. Within a week I was smiling at my baby: watching her smile back at me was amazing. I was so grateful to Caroline Mills and Jan Stanek. I hadn't quite realised just how important it was to be able to smile, especially with a baby who learns from her mother's expressions.

It seemed I had to lose my looks completely to learn to be happy with what I had: now I was 'fixed' and I felt my face was back to being me, and most of all I could smile when a stranger smiled at me. I felt I could start living my life again. I planned to dye my hair blonde again; I had not bothered to colour it or even make any effort with it since the implants were put in. I had given up looking after myself, I stopped buying make-up, rarely wore it, and never bought clothes. I had felt that until my face was fixed it was, as they say, like 'polishing a turd'.

I felt like now I could finally get on with my life; I could concentrate on repairing my relationship with Sugardaddy. He was now in his late 40s and I was in my mid-30s; I thought surely like most men he would want to settle down, get more real, be a real family with me and Papaya. I missed the loving him and hoped he would come around, but it wasn't looking good. He referred to her as 'Mango' or 'Fruit Bowl' – supposedly a joke – and behaved as if he resented her very existence. The delighted father he seemed to be when he first heard I was pregnant had changed completely into a bitter man, tied up in hate and anger, and I was slowly getting the message that he didn't want to be in her life.

Things were going from bad to worse between the two of us as well. In spite of everything I still loved him with all my heart, but he was now acting very distant and not treating me well. Every Valentine's Day he had sent me a large bouquet of red roses; I had none this year. Whenever I tried to contact him he became more and more angry and told me to go away. He was pushing me away and we couldn't communicate amicably anymore.

When I asked him why he was acting so strangely, he angrily commented, 'You broke the rules.' Of course, the 'rules' were never outlined very clearly. I am guessing they meant that he had bought me, that he held the power and could two-time me whenever he wanted, while I would need to put up and shut up, happy with my gilded cage. When he said we had an 'open relationship' he meant it was open on his side, not on mine. I was not allowed to seek love as well; I should stay at home, unmarried, a kept woman in my rented penthouse with my fancy cars, preening and painting myself in a desperate attempt to hold on to my captor. That wasn't me and never would have been me: he caught the wrong bird, maybe. I was never going to be happy to be someone's captured bird, someone's lapdog; I wasn't the puppet on a string he hoped for.

Sugardaddy had often tried to exercise his control over me and my family. If he felt I wasn't toeing the line properly he would threaten to cut us off, or demand that we moved, which would happen every two or three years. He had certainly encouraged my breast surgeries and the kiss and tells and stopped my career from moving forward unless it was in the direction he wanted it. I didn't mind this, and I felt I was still the captain of my ship. It seemed to me that he gave me stability and of course an education for Georgia. Any mother would tell you, she would do anything for their children, even get run over for them if she had to.

Having Papaya proved to be the ultimate act of rebellion from me: it meant Sugardaddy had to face the fact that he wasn't in control of me any more. I was doing my own thing, I wasn't dyeing my hair the white blonde he liked or inflating or deflating my boobs every other week to his specifications.

Sugardaddy always told me he never wanted kids of his own. He said he would want to do it right and give it his all, so he would have to give up work. Sugardaddy, like me, was a perfectionist: just like Simon Cowell had said to me, being a perfectionist means we can never be fully happy, we are tormented by our thirst for more, never content with our lot. We had each other, our health and what a lot of people strive for – wealth – but somehow the old saying, money doesn't make you happy, was true. Don't get me wrong, shopping in Chanel is a great feeling; holidays in Sandy Lane, Barbados, rubbing shoulders with the rich and famous is good too, but actually they are no different to you or me, maybe just a little more guarded.

Sugardaddy had been fostered as a child and was also brought up in children's homes. I could tell he craved a family and love, but like me didn't know how to go about it. As I had learnt in rehab, I was like house built on quicksand with no foundations, and he was the same. Somehow we had found each other and loved each other in a way that felt safe for us both. Each of us gave the other the family we both craved; he gave me security and I gave him love. Both of us were misfits and possibly very hard to love, but we found a way to make it work for us. Both of us self-destructed endlessly in our relationship but due to the knots we had tied each other in, somehow we were as strongly connected as if we had that marriage certificate. We stayed together, unknowingly showing the other unconditional love, something neither of us had before, but didn't know how to handle it. I was in that relationship till the end, I was never going to leave. I wanted to work things out with Sugardaddy, to weather this storm we seemed to be in.

I certainly wasn't complete without him, but since he had distanced himself from me, I felt lonelier than ever. I craved his love again even though I knew it was elsewhere. I couldn't understand how a man I loved so much and had been with for 20 years could not even talk to me nicely for one moment. How had his love turned to hate towards me?

CHAPTER TWENTY-ONE

Homeless Overnight

SITTING IN THE living room of my four-bedroom flat overlooking Hyde Park, I got a phone call from Sugardaddy's PA. She said: 'I'm sorry, I didn't want to do this but I've been instructed to tell you my employer is no longer paying for anything, that's including your rent. He's giving you 48 hours to bring the car back. And you'll need to find somewhere else to live.'

'WHAT?' I screamed. I knew it was always a possibility but I thought loyalty meant something. Sugardaddy had said that as he had asked me to marry him once and I declined, I was like an ex-wife: he didn't mind keeping me for the rest of my life.

With a new baby, another child about to go to university and a new business that was just getting on its feet, I certainly could not afford the £4,500 a month rent for the 2,000 square foot flat in Lancaster Gate, or Georgia's university fees Sugardaddy had promised to pay, or even day-to-day food, nappies or utility bills for us all. The last of my savings I had sunk into surgery; I had pennies to my name. I was waiting for my allowance to come through before I went food shopping; I had noticed it was a few days late.

Sugardaddy wouldn't talk to me; he blocked my calls and e-mails. After the best part of 20 years together he showed himself in a not very manly manner. I had no idea why he had done this, or what was going on in his head. I only heard rumours that he had met a lap dancer: in other words, I had been ditched for a younger model. I had seen it coming and friends had warned me this 'type' of man would do that, but somehow the heart gets in the way of the head and you think love and loyalty, the connection we had, would be stronger than any young girl with perkier tits. Who was I kidding? Alpha males like Sugardaddy will always stray, only as faithful as opportunity allows.

I was distraught, especially when Sugardaddy sent heavies round to collect my car, my beloved Audi Q7. I was allowed to quickly take my baby seat out but I left my shoes and all sorts of personal goods in the car as they hurried me on to take it away.

To make matters worse, Sugardaddy's PA said: 'He said, he advises you to go back down south where you came from and go on benefits, where he had found you.' Maybe he had a selective memory, but when he 'found' me I was a successful model; I wasn't rich but I was happy. Now it felt like he had dumped me from a great height. I was worse off and this time I had further to fall.

When I first met him Sugardaddy was already a fairly wealthy man, earning hundreds of thousands of pounds. He had grown his wealth quite quickly and had become a billionaire. We enjoyed money and spent like we were in another world: my life was one of a multi-millionaire, but without the husband around. He would send private jets for long weekends away in one of the top luxury hotels of the world, there would be shopping trips where we would spend £40,000 at a time. We ate at the finest restaurants, Bond Street shop assistants knew me by my first name, we had a driver, we spent Sundays having lunch at Fortnum and Mason and shopping in Harrods for clothes for Georgia and me, and Gucci accessories for my dogs. Of course, this also meant that I could get all the surgery I (and he) wanted, with an unlimited expenditure. I treated my mum to many holidays, and my sisters to holidays too. They often complained I wasn't in the real world. I was; this world was very real to me.

But perhaps they had a point. I had never paid a bill in my life: his PA would do all that for me. My car was managed by his car maintenance man, even my mobile phone was in his name and managed by his PA. Any decisions that I needed to make I relied on him to help me make them; it felt as if he was the other half of me.

Not only did I feel lost without Sugardaddy, who I often called 'Daddy' on his request, I was panicked by how I was going to put food on the table for my children. I had been looked after and kept in his bubble for nearly 20 years. With a young baby, as a single parent and with no education or skills, what the hell was I to do next?

What made things so much worse was that at the same time Sugardaddy pulled the plug I found out the shopping channel which was helping my skincare company start to turn a profit had gone bankrupt, owing me £40,000. I was also owed another £20,000 from a company which was developing a perfume for me but that also went bankrupt before it provided me with any product. My only means of making money was gone; I had no money left in the business, only debts.

It wasn't long till the rent was due and the landlord was demanding their money. I gave them every last penny I could borrow in a vain attempt to keep my flat and not be homeless. What echoed in my mind were Sugardaddy's comments to 'go back south and get back on benefits'. I knew that is what he wanted: to let me fall, to control me and now that he was done with me to see me hit rock bottom, so he could bathe in the glory that he had picked me up, that without him I was nothing. Well, I wasn't one to sink easily. I might not be as young as I was before but I was a fighter, and I was determined to show him I could carry on just as well without his help. I was doing him a favour, not the other way round. I had been bullied and pushed around by men all my life: they might have determined my life's path, but they were not going to affect my children's future. I was staying put and I was ready to battle the next storm.

The problem was I had ridiculously big shoes to fill and the disadvantage of looking after a small baby full-time, with no childminding. At the time before he dumped me I was about to get an au pair, and a brace for my teeth; with no money and my priority to keep a roof over our heads it wasn't long before the au pair agency and orthodontist were coming after me with law suits because I had to pull out.

In fact they were coming from all angles: the landlord was on my case daily for the rent, the bills were piling up with final warnings. I had to think on my feet, so I quickly advertised my rooms. Georgia moved into my room, which meant that all three of us slept in the one room. I made the office into a bedroom and the living room into the office. I was then able to rent out the three other bedrooms to a Russian lawyer, a Greek girl (who it turns out was on benefits), and a businessman.

It kept the landlord at bay for a short time, but the bills were coming in thick and fast: electricity, council tax, water... None of these I had ever paid for in my life, it was shocking. I wondered how anyone survived with such a lot of financial demands on them.

I had run up every credit card to the max. It got to the point that we didn't have enough money to buy food; I had to put every penny on rent and bills to stop the electricity and gas getting cut off for the lodgers.

Things went from bad to worse. I couldn't keep up with the rent, and the landlord issued a notice to leave and evicted us. We had up until 23 December, Papaya's first birthday, to get out of our home. I had to ask the lodgers to leave. This was sad enough, but even worse, I had two kids and nowhere to go. I asked my mum if we could stay with her but she was now living with her new partner and there was no room. Old friends were nowhere to be seen.

I remembered my private doctor saying to me, 'Are you still with Sugardaddy?' When I said yes he said, 'Do you know what happened to his best friend?'

'No,' I replied, confused.

'He drove to a tall building and jumped from it, taking his own life. Sugardaddy bought him just like he bought you, then when he finished with him he dumped him like used garbage.

His friend looked after a wife, two kids and his elderly mother from what Sugardaddy gave him.'

I remember thinking as he told me that, why did the friend take it for granted? I never took kindness for granted and fully expected the lion to turn on me at any time, and of course I was right. What I didn't expect was the feeling of futility, and how fast you forget the real world and how to survive in it; also, how attached you get to material things.

Having my car wrenched from me felt like the end of the world. I never took tubes or buses and didn't even know how to.

I lay in bed in my Hyde Park apartment feeling utterly useless and uneducated and realising how hard it would be for me now to make money. I wasn't young enough to do what had made me money before and that was glamour modelling and dancing, and I had two kids, one a young baby, so I couldn't go back to school. I couldn't get a job working in a shop as I was a well-known face, and I couldn't afford the childminding anyway as it cost more than I could earn. Celebrity paid well for a lot of people, but I was no Katie Price. Being slightly famous certainly didn't bring much in for me.

In a bid to survive Georgia and I hatched a plan to sell my valuables. Georgia was in charge of putting all my designer gear on eBay: clothes, handbags, jewellery, anything that could earn us some money. This taught me a quick lesson in not holding onto material things. It was actually less painful than I thought it would be to see my handbags and shoes go; I felt I hadn't earned them so never really fully appreciated them. We would be really happy when something sold for a decent amount as it meant eating that week.

I was fast slipping into a depression, I felt like the walls were caving in on me and there was nothing I could do. I was trapped, sinking, trying desperately to swim. I searched for an answer and for the first time in my life I didn't have one.

On the 23rd of December we were evicted. I could not even afford a removal van and didn't have a car, so we packed up the suitcases that we had and as many black bags as we could carry and left. We had to leave behind all of our furniture, some clothes, shoes and even Papaya's toys.

It was a sorry sight when we checked into a two-star B&B on the Cromwell Road: a tiny room, dirty and dull, no better than the hostels I had stayed in as a teenager. I felt awful. Georgia by now could only remember a privileged life; Papaya was a baby still, but it wasn't nice that on her first birthday, instead of blowing out candles we were checking into a B&B as our new home. We had become homeless overnight.

On Christmas Day I sat in my hotel room and cried. I wanted to die; I prayed to God to take me. I thought about ending it. I felt so useless, I thought my children were better off without me – after all, I had led them to this. I didn't provide them stability or a family, I was dragging them down with me into my sorry life, a life that offered only tears, pain and moving from pillar to post with no home to go to. It was Christmas Day: there was no decorations, no room for a tree, no presents and no Christmas dinner.

At that moment I understood why Sugardaddy's best friend jumped: like me, he felt useless, embarrassed by his choices. His decision to allow another man to provide for his family had essentially led his family to this. I too felt that shame. I couldn't believe my decision to love Sugardaddy had got us here. How had I been so stupid? I always regarded myself as quite streetwise – not educated yes, naïve yes, but I had been brought up with the life of hard knocks so I felt I knew how to feel my way around the world.

Sugardaddy, it turned out, had a habit of pulling the plug suddenly: he preferred to cut you off unexpectedly, I'm guessing so you had less chance of getting back on your feet. Like a puppet-master he could stand in his high tower looking down, laughing at his sinking victims who only had themselves to blame. They ate from the hand and made a deal with the devil. In the same way I had allowed myself to relax; I had stopped fighting to survive, basking in the glory of being 'looked after' for once, enjoying not having to struggle. What a mistake. Did I forget who I was?

In a desperate moment I walked into a church, tears in my eyes, pushing my baby in her donated pram. Dropping to my knees, I prayed to God to keep me going and keep me strong for my children's sake: I had nothing, no one and I had two kids to provide for single-handed, and no means of doing so. Defeated, with my head down, I slowly walked out of the church. Who I was I kidding? No God would help a girl like me – not after how I had conducted my life. I couldn't turn to anyone, let alone Him. I had broken every rule He ever set.

Arriving back in my new home, this shabby B&B, I looked into the innocent eyes of my baby happily playing on the grotty, dirty floor. Crying, I said, 'Sorry, I'm so sorry. Mummy's not going to give up, I'm going to do everything I can to give you everything you need.'

In that hotel room, at my darkest moment when I hit rock bottom I was very near to ending it all. I had taken too many knocks in life; I was exhausted, I couldn't fight any more. Something inside me made me go on. Maybe God was on my side after all, maybe again I had more to give to this world; but most of all I had to give my children a mother. I kept remembering it wasn't about me or how I felt, it was about my children: they were the future and they needed a mother.

I had to swallow my pride, humble myself and take any job I could.

Georgia helped me get a CV together. It didn't read that great, as I'd never been employed as anything other than a model, actress and presenter!

I applied for dozens of jobs, from kitchen assistant to personal assistant. I got nothing – well, there was the one job where I applied to roll sushi from home: the woman phoned me up to ask if it was 'the' Alicia Douvall, and if this was a joke. She told me I was over-qualified for the job as she laughed and said her goodbyes.

It was soul-destroying, but to be honest at this point there wasn't much soul left to destroy.

When it got to the point that I couldn't pay the B&B the £30 a night, I had to resort to desperate measures. With my skincare still selling in Harrods, I had to risk it all and go back to glamour modelling. I never wanted to return to the very thing that fed my insecurities. Besides, I was in my 30s. Glamour modelling was a young girl's game. Going back was like a retired sportsman hanging onto his heyday, trying to relive his past. I never wanted to be that person; I wanted to retire from modelling gracefully, bowing out with dignity. But there was no room for dignity any more, it was do or die, sink or swim. Dignity, morals and self-respect had to be left at the door if we were to survive. I needed to feed my kids and keep a roof over our head.

So by day I did dodgy glamour modelling for international publications then at night worked on my skincare to try and rescue it and make it earn money again. With no money, however, it was very hard to make it work any more. I couldn't afford childminding so Papaya either came with me or I juggled childcare with work at home.

Life had never been harder; it was even harder than when I was young, because this time I had two kids. I knew what was out there, I had fallen from a higher height, and I didn't have youth and looks which I had relied on before to make me a dollar. My body wasn't fit any more; years of dancing had left me with a hip problem, so I could no longer do that.

I had no option but to apply for benefits. I really didn't want to but I knew it was the right thing to do for my kids. Walking into the place, being treated like cattle, took my last bit of dignity, especially when two girls spotted me and pointed, chatting to each other. I cried inside; I wanted to run away as fast as my legs would take me, but I stayed. I had to for my babies' sake. However, they didn't seem to believe my situation and it would take ten months before I could convince them.

We learnt to go without food for days on end, to only shop after 4 p.m. to get the reduced food from Tesco, and to walk for miles so we didn't have to spend a £1 on the bus. Plus it was free exercise anyway.

After surviving Christmas Day in the B&B with the children, I decided life couldn't get worse. I had to not let this get the better of me, I had to be strong for my children.

CHAPTER TWENTY-TWO

Rebuilding Alicia

WORKING TWENTY-FOUR SEVEN, I didn't let an hour go by without working on one thing or another. The moment Papaya slept I worked, never having a weekend off or a night watching TV, I carried on trying to build my crumpled world from scratch, desperately trying to piece the broken china of my shattered world together again. I felt sure that hard work would pay off eventually.

I was right. I was able to find a home for the family. When we moved in we didn't have enough money for furniture. Instead, we got some of it from the bins where rich locals had chucked out the odd chair or broken table; some of it was from charity shops or finds in skips. Funnily enough, though, I could not have felt prouder of our small home. It wasn't glamorous, I didn't have Versace cushions or throws like I had before, but it was mine, I had earned it, and provided my family with it completely, with no man helping at all. That felt great – a feeling I had not felt before, a sense of achievement that brought me happiness.

Then, out of nowhere, my agent called me. I was offered a chance to go on *Celebrity Big Brother*. I didn't want to leave

Papaya, but the fee would put me and my business back on track, so I knew I had to do it.

Luckily or unluckily for me I was part of one of the most explosive, most watched *Celebrity Big Brother* series ever on Channel 5, with the mix of that black-and-white thinker Katie Hopkins, the celebrity blogger Perez Hilton, and myself, portrayed as the token 'dumb blonde'. It also happened to be a house of arguments, tension and conflict, with three guests quitting or getting kicked off within the first few days. I was used to this type of house from my childhood so the drama that the viewer saw and was shocked by and the other housemates experienced was really nothing to me: home had been a battleground. I chose to ignore the dramas and not get involved, and because of this I was branded 'dumb'! I already knew what a real struggle was and the television studio set of the Big Brother house didn't measure up.

It was ironic when Katie Price walked into the *Celebrity Big Brother* house later in the series. She was short of a bed and asked the girls if she could share one of theirs. I was one of the few with a double bed to myself and I put my head down when the question arose. I thought, she managed to get in my bed once before, I'll be damned if she's getting into my bed this time. *Celebrity Big Brother* had been fun and I was enjoying my 'moment': sod's law that she had to walk in to piss on my parade like she did some 15 years before. Even worse, when I was up for eviction and she had a chance to save me, she didn't.

To start with, I felt gutted that the girl who I felt had ruined my world so many years ago, who had built an army of fans which made her untouchable, was here with me. I thought when I saw her that my *Celebrity BB* days were numbered, as I would have to give her some choice words: she stole my man, my daughter's potential father. I had hated her for many years, and the feelings were mutual. Then, when I started speaking to the woman who had inadvertently helped to launch my career, I realised she wasn't that dissimilar to me. She was, at the end of the day, a mother, a girl from Sussex, someone's daughter, who was insecure and searching for her bit of happiness in the world. Like me she was a girl of extremes; she obsessed over fame like I did surgery, living her life for the camera. Luckily for her she has five beautiful children to keep her grounded and save her from 'celebrity life' and the dreams it doesn't really fulfil.

My stint in the Big Brother House lasted only three weeks; I was happy to go home to my daughters but also unhappy that this big opportunity had been cut short. I knew the longer you stay on these programmes the more work you get out of them in the long run, and, God, I needed the money. But it wasn't meant to be.

Back in the real world I went straight back into hard work, determined to make my organic Argan skincare company a success and get it back on its feet again. We have gone into luxury retailers like Fortnum & Mason and launched on another TV channel called The Jewellery Channel, where we sell out every time we appear! We have built an army of loyal followers that love the naturalness of Douvall's skincare in exactly the same way that I do. Slowly I have started to repair and rebuild my world.

My house isn't a big four-bedroom flat, but it's mine, all mine. I have no puppet-master pulling the strings any more. It has made me realise the money meant nothing; I am happier now achieving my own money, looking after my family myself and feeling that sense of achievement than I ever was before with all the riches.

I had the expensive cars, jewellery holidays and designer clothes; it didn't mean a thing and didn't bring me happiness. I was poor inside; now I may be poor on the outside but I'm rich inside my soul.

When I lost everything I thought that it was the end of my life, that I would never be happy again, but the opposite happened. I found happiness, I found the real me, I found the strength inside me to fight on and through that I accomplished all my dreams. I felt a sense of achievement that I never felt before. Don't get me wrong, walking into Dolce & Gabbana buying clothes, shoes and bags gives you a buzz – but only for about ten minutes. Now I savour every day, I believe in myself, I acknowledge my achievements, however small or big. It makes me walk that bit taller and appreciate life that bit more. Plastic surgery could never have done that. No matter how many cuts of the knife I had, I still felt ugly. Beauty really does come from within. After all, we all have faults. Even Marilyn Monroe wasn't a surgeon's idea of perfect beauty. Sarah Jessica Parker is a great example of this: not aesthetically a perfect face, but her inner confidence shines through. Women love her, men adore her.

I get the same buzz shopping in high street shops as I did shopping in Armani; even now, when times aren't as bad as they were (thanks to my book deal) I still wouldn't shop in designer shops any more. I drive a Ford Fiesta, shop in Primark and Tesco (still can't resist the bargain bucket though) and holiday with Nelson. I had what seemed the dream – I was 'rich and famous' with a celebrity lifestyle – but really I had nothing. What I have now is living the real dream: waking up in the morning happy, healthy children, a job I love. I'm lucky enough to be able to give back, and I have plenty of friends, as everywhere I go I get recognised! As a single parent financing two children I work very hard, I get up at 6 a.m. every day and work till 10 p.m., but I wouldn't change a thing.

My daughter Georgia, now 20 years old, is also happy with herself; she would not even dye her hair. She is now in her last year at university doing an acting degree. She has 10 GCSEs, all As and Bs; she still doesn't drink, choosing instead to live a healthy lifestyle. She is the true face of our skincare company, organic and natural, everything Douvalls stands for and everything I have learnt – the hard way – is the best way.

Another source of joy is my relationship with my mum, who is well and truly in my life now. After finally splitting from my dad she slowly stopped being my distant mother and became my very best friend. I convinced her to join an online dating site: after several weirdos she met a great partner, maybe the man she should have been with in the beginning. She says now that her life began at 60 years old. Mum didn't go abroad as a child or as Dad's wife as Dad didn't like to leave the country, so now she travels around the world on as many holidays as she can fit in. I love who she has become. I don't recognise her from the terrified individual who was with my dad: she is a strong, powerful woman. I'm so proud of her. She was my anchor when I lost everything; she kept reminding me, 'If I can do it at 60 years old and start again, so can you.' You're never too old to start again, or find love; you're only too old when you're dead.

We speak to each other every day; she helps with my business and we holiday together as a family. Sometimes I see a glimpse of the old, afraid mum peeping through. If she spills something or doesn't get dinner on the table she will fret, apologising to her partner over and over again. He understands what she has been through; he'll put his hand on hers and say: 'It's okay.' He sees the scars of her past, he looks after her and appreciates her for her caring nature. Slowly she has become less afraid and has relaxed into a loving, caring and sharing relationship with her partner. The heart and head can heal, it seems; we all can heal, we can improve our lives, we can change, we just have to want to. Everything that we want is out there for us to take, it's about grabbing life by the balls and taking it, to hell with what people think or say.

As for Dad, he and I still talk now and then on the phone. I don't hold any grudges and know he did the best he possibly could for us and has always loved us. I still see him (in small doses). Dad is still searching for the right woman, but in the meantime is enjoying meeting lots of wrong women.

I'm glad to say, too, that Sugardaddy and I are friends again. I understand now why he had to cut me off; it was, in the long term, for the best. I will always love him and am grateful for the education and security he provided for Georgia and me, giving her a great start in life and an opportunity she may not have got. It is partly because of him she is doing so well and is the girl she is today. I still miss him to this day and wish him all the happiness in the world. How we brought her up wasn't conventional, but between us I think we did okay.

My craving for stability and a sense of family has led me to the Catholic church; I have realised the only one who can really provide those things is me, supported by a God that I believe in. Through believing in someone or something higher I can feel a sense of happiness; it is through faith that I find contentment, assurance and guidance. I don't think it matters who or what your god is. Over the years I got into Buddhism, Kabbalah, and spiritualism: they all lead you into realising that true happiness starts with serving others. Through the church I have met some lovely friends and regularly help with the homeless. I am reminded how lucky I really am, how beauty lies within, and how my beauty now shines through with my self-confidence – and a smile that now works!

I won't deny I still have a desire to run when life gets hard, but I run to the tennis court now, the gym, a yoga class.

Like my father, who I take after more than I care to admit, I can become obsessive with things. I have found it helpful to obsess over health, fitness, good food and my skincare. I've tried every diet going, searching for the anti-ageing answer with the same passion I searched for plastic surgeons. I found cutting out wheat, sugar and vegetable oil (so no fried food) or anything cooked in vegetable oil – basically, if you can dig it up then you can eat it – is the best diet out there. I have found better results through diet and exercise than I ever did with the plastic surgeons.

As I have mentioned, I tried raw vegan for a long time, but in the UK it's very hard, and long-term it's not sustainable. The best balance for me, I found, is about 70 percent raw. I also don't consume much dairy: I eat goat's cheese, and natural Greek yogurt now and then. I find you've got to listen to your body. I know plenty of women who are vegan or vegetarian and they are very unhealthy; their body isn't getting all they need. Starving yourself isn't good either, or over-exercising: these can both age you.

I also try to eat organic as much as possible: the fewer chemicals inside me the better. As a logical thinker I always look deeper, that is how my skincare was founded. The less we damage our cells – the more pure things we eat and the fewer chemicals and toxins we put on our skin – the better our cells will be when they are renewed as they have less work to do. (Most cells in the body are renewed every few weeks.) Perfect cells make for a perfect body, face and mind.

I no longer suffer from depression. I'm not sure why it went, but it went the same time as I stopped having surgery. Maybe it's a combination of giving up alcohol, a healthy diet, and exercise. I make sure that however dull it is outside I gaze towards the sun for ten seconds. This is supposed to boost the mood, and seems to work for me.

I suppose the old Alicia would have wanted to get a tummy tuck after I had Papaya, but not the new me. Although admittedly it was hard to get a flat stomach again it wasn't impossible. In fact, I loved the challenge of seeing whether a mother of two could actually get a flat stomach again. I was told by plastic surgeons that tummy tucks are the only way to get the muscles back; well, I can tell you that's not true. Obviously diet is 70 percent of the battle but I got there with a combination of diet, exercise and even some corset training wearing, especially when I was bigger. To be honest, I threw everything at it: I'm not sure if corset training actually helps but it did seem to play a part in my success.

I wrote this book myself. Granted, this was mainly due to the fact I couldn't afford a ghostwriter, but nevertheless I did it. That's from a girl who was branded 'thick' from schoolteachers, my father and, worse still, Katie Hopkins on *Celebrity Big Brother*. Great, let them think I'm thick, I say, while I silently overtake them. If this thick chick can do it, then so can you. Go after your dreams with total stubbornness and determination: you will surprise yourself. Don't underestimate anyone, most of all yourself.

Nothing has ever come easily to me. I haven't been one of those celebrities that gets offered book deals, presenting jobs, fitness DVDs and their own skincare line – they just have to turn up and see if they like the colour of the packaging. No, I have fought for everything and done it all myself.

Even this book deal didn't come easily. Georgia and I went to a book fair ourselves, looking for prospective book publishers. I wrote this book in the evenings and any spare moment I had. As I write this I am presently on a Greek island in the sunshine with the beach as my office. Georgia is playing tennis and Papaya is marching past in Kids' Club on her way to the pool: a holiday I paid for all myself. This, I think, is my proudest moment, this I think is what life is all about and how I want to live it; this is what gives me a feeling of power and confidence and a sense of self again, knowing I am capable of being a mother, friend and businesswoman, doing it all myself with a growing business and two beautiful children. I work hard and I don't expect anything to come without effort. I'm already working on my next book, a fitness DVD and expanding my organic Argan skincare range.

I have learnt beauty is wasted if the beholder doesn't know of their own beauty; it cannot be appreciated. I am older now, I practise yoga and running, I have never felt more beautiful than I do at this moment. It's been a rocky road, but like us all I'm still on the road, still on the journey, but most importantly I am now driving my own bus, with kids in tow. Teaching them along the way to be strong independent women, never to let a man tell them what to do, or run their life.

Thank you for reading my book, stay strong, live life to the fullest and remember, the answer is simpler than we thought...

EPILOGUE: BARBIE MELTS

I'M SURE YOU'LL be seeing much more of me on your TVs since, while I was writing this book, I was offered another TV job, to repair my encapsulated left breast on a show about botched plastic surgery. When the programme makers approached me they asked me if there was anything I was unhappy with. I could honestly say I was happy with myself. I knew I still had breast implants as well as my butt implants but they had grown to be part of me – and I had grown to love me, implants and all. I was finally settling into my body and face and for once in my life appreciating being just who I was.

However, my left breast was getting worse and worse as time went on. It was now so tight and hard I could no longer lie on my side in bed. I had to resort to occasionally taking painkillers again because of the pain I was in. The breast was visibly higher, rounder and tighter than the right one, which I thought looked really natural.

The TV show put me in front of a plastic surgeon who said the right breast was also not looking good and sent me for scans. I protested as I felt this was a waste of my time, but knew I had to go along with it for the show.

Whilst I lay there he scanned my breasts, looking more and more concerned. The nurse looked on as he talked in jargon, explaining to her what he was seeing. He asked if I felt pain or had redness.

'Well yes, but that's because my left breast is encapsulated,' I replied.

He then flipped me over to scan my butt. Again he asked questions about pain and redness.

'Well of course I have pain, I have two silicone implants in my butt! But it's fine, I'm used to it. Why, anyway?'

'Because your implants are split in your right breast, and both buttock implants are ripped completely in half. Silicone is leaking into your body.'

I was shocked. I didn't know what silicone in the body does to you. 'Ermm, am I going to die? Cos I feel fine!'

'No, but you need them taken out and you need to speak to your doctor tomorrow, please.'

Wow, what a bombshell: Barbie had melted. The girl I had spent almost 20 years building was breaking.

It was true that my body had been aching for some time and progressively getting worse. I had put this down to years of punishing my body through dancing, but I now understand it to be the silicone that has migrated into my body, causing the pain I have from my back to my butt, from my breast to my head… Shocking that implants break so easily, isn't it?

I didn't have any money to repair myself so I had to rely on the TV programme who were adamant that they were going to make me more 'natural' looking', so it looks like the butt implants will have to be removed as well as my breast implants.

I can't lie, a wave of panic rushed over me. I was slipping back into Sarah Howes, a place I had no plans to go back to. I had killed Sarah Howes long ago, but now it seemed as if it was actually Alicia Douvall who was cracking and falling to pieces. The implants were broken, my hair hadn't been dyed in ages, making me almost back to my natural brown; I was starting to see the natural Sarah Howes in my face again as it had been such a long time since I had last had surgery.

This was a turning point. Do I insist that the show put in new implants, or was I brave enough to be Sarah Howes again? Sarah Howes to me was a loser: I wanted no part of her in my life, so I decided Alicia Douvall was here to stay. I just had to repair her, make her a better version of the one I had built so many years ago.

I wasn't a quitter, and I wasn't one to look back at the past. This time I would do it on my terms, no Mr Fix-It or Sugardaddy telling me how to look... Alicia Douvall is a businesswoman, she still embraces the glamour model in her, she is still proud to be a sexy woman, but she isn't running away from Sarah Howes anymore and she certainly isn't trying to be Barbie anymore. She has been reborn; this time she's strong, self-confident and doing it for herself and of course her kids – happy, healthy and feeling beautiful inside and out.

USEFUL RESOURCES

Body Dysmorphic Disorder Foundation

A charity dedicated to the relief of suffering from body dysmorphic disorder

Address: 45b Stanford Road, London N11 3HY

Website: bddfoundation.org

Twitter: BDDFoundation

Douvalls Limited

Eco-friendly organic natural luxury skincare, working with a woman's co-operative

Address: Suite 181, 405 Kings Road, London SW10 0BB

Tel: 0330 0229202

Email: customer.services@douvalls.com

Website: www.douvalls.com

Twitter: Douvalls

Mills, Caroline

Consultant maxillofacial surgeon

Address: 60 Wimpole Street, London W1G 8AG

Tel: 08456 448337

Fax: 0207 487 4090

Email: info@thefacesurgeon.co.uk

Website: www.thefacesurgeon.co.uk

Passages Malibu

Offer a twelve step, holistic approach to helping with drug or alcohol addiction.

Address: 6428 Meadows Ct, Malibu, CA 90265 United States

Tel: 001 877 311 4506 / 001 866 257 5257 / 001 877 311 4506

Website: www.passagesmalibu.com

Twitter: passagesmalibu

Refuge

A UK national charity providing domestic violence help for women and children

Tel: 0808 2000 247

Email: info@refuge.org.uk

Website: www.refuge.org.uk

Twitter: RefugeCharity

Stanek, Jan

Leading cosmetic plastic surgeon

Address: 60 Wimpole Street, London W1G 8AG

Tel: 020 3468 8847

Website: www.janstanek.com

Twitter: surgeon_stanek